Involving People in Healthcare Policy and Practice

Susie Green PhD

Governor Member
South Staffordshire Healthcare NHS Foundation Trust

Foreword by
Shirley McIver

Senior Fellow
Health Services Management Centre
University of Birmingham

Radcliffe Publishing
Oxford • Seattle

D1385770

Radcliffe Publishing Ltd
18 Marcham Road
Abingdon
Oxon OX14 1AA
United Kingdom

www.radcliffe-oxford.com
Electronic catalogue and worldwide online ordering facility.

_____

© 2007 Susie Green

Susie Green has asserted her right under the Copyright, Designs and Patents Act 1998 to be identified as author of this work.

British Library Cataloguing in Publication Data

A catalogue record for this book is available from the British Library.

ISBN-10: 1 85775 773 4
ISBN-13: 978 185775 773 6

Typeset by Advance Typesetting Ltd, Oxford
Printed and bound by TJI Digital, Padstow, Cornwall

Contents

Foreword

Books about health policy can sometimes be rather impersonal and academic but this is not one of them. Yet it is not a purely descriptive case study either. This is a book which describes recent UK health policy relating to public and user involvement in some detail and presents a case study of how this has been applied in one particular NHS Trust in enough depth to satisfy both healthcare practitioners looking for help and health policy students looking for information.

The difference between this and many other texts on health policy is that the reader will find a warm authorial voice and continual movement between the lively emotion of personal experience and the more sedate realms of policy. In essence the book is that rather unusual combination of both policy and practice.

The early chapters in Part 1 describe policy relating to public and user involvement in the NHS since 1990 and one of the key messages of the book is introduced immediately:

> ... it is time the personal and individual aspects of our healthcare experiences were meaningfully integrated into the grand design.

The movement between personal experience and policy is also introduced quickly with the author describing an experience she had 25 years ago when her children were born. She comments:

> So, even that long ago, it was possible to experience an ideal situation in which I was a partner in the whole process, felt that I was receiving excellent services and was not exposed to unnecessary risk, but I'm pretty sure that others were less fortunate.

The reason for her good fortune was less to do with the general high standard of services provided across the UK in those days and more to do with the fact that she was married to a hospital consultant.

This example is typical of others provided in the book and they serve a useful purpose by rooting analysis of policy in personal experience, demonstrating what is achievable, and presenting a goal that lies at the heart of the NHS – to provide the same standard of care to everyone regardless of their socio-economic circumstances.

The example also introduces another theme that is present throughout the book: the continuity between healthcare staff and the patients they provide with services. Some analyses are careful to distinguish between patients, citizens and staff but in common with the thinking behind total quality management, the author emphasises the overlapping roles. Employees are internal customers in a provider–customer chain.

The lack of distance between the provider–customer roles is particularly noticeable in health services because here the provider is also likely to be a direct customer at some stage. This is made clear in several places in the book. For example she comments:

> There are constant attempts to 'seek users' views' but little recognition of the vast repository of knowledge and experience which must exist within the lives and families of those who are employed in health and associated services.

Somehow this knowledge becomes lost when health service employees go to work – perhaps because they need to put distance between themselves and the often sad and distressing circumstances of sickness and death that many face on a daily basis in hospitals and GP surgeries.

But what if the dual nature of health service employees as staff and users is acknowledged? This book raises some interesting implications. The author mentions one hospital trust where employees are given the benefit of fast-track opportunities when they need health services. Is this a legitimate way of rewarding employees and a route to raising awareness of their double role, or does it bring unfair advantages to certain sections of the population and so create a practice in conflict with the fundamental principle of providing the same standard of service to everyone regardless of circumstances?

Other examples of movement between the roles are provided and nowhere more starkly than in Chapter 12, where the Chief Executive of the Trust in the case study describes some of his experiences as a person suffering from depression. He comments:

> *Being a service user from my personal perspective is a much tougher place than being a chief executive.*

His account and those of the other contributors to this book add energy and colour to what in other publications can be a rather dry tale of how concepts of the relationship between the service user and provider are changing in healthcare.

The final section makes the book rather long but it is here that the translation of policy into practice really comes alive in the different voices of those who were part of the initiatives that developed user and public involvement in the NHS organisation that forms the case study. Other voices provide further insights into personal and organisational journeys on the road to developing greater public and user involvement.

This is a journey that many healthcare staff will be able to relate to. It describes the difficult context of organisational change following a merger between NHS trusts with different cultures and examines some of the tensions between clinicians and managers introduced by policy relating to public and user involvement.

The unusual mix of personal experience and policy also makes the book one that will be of interest to lay people working in one of the many new roles that have opened up in the UK health sector.

There are several 'how to do it' books on user and public involvement in health, a number examining different initiatives, and others that analyse health policy, but very few that combine elements of all three as is the case here. So this is a book that can be enjoyed by readers seeking different objectives. It can be read as an autobiographical story of a health service employee and her colleagues developing user and public involvement in an NHS organisation; it can be read as an example of how policy is translated into practice; and it can be read for its stimulating ideas and for the lessons learned from experience.

Dr Shirley McIver
Senior Fellow
Health Services Management Centre
University of Birmingham
November 2006

Preface

*I am constantly preoccupied with how to remove distance so that we can all come
closer together, so that we can all begin to sense that we are the same, we are one.*
David Hockney

My philosophy for service user and carer involvement in the National Health
Service (NHS) is very simple and depends on a key question: is what I am doing as a
healthcare worker good enough for me, my family and the people I care about?
With that in mind, it ought to be easy to ensure that what we do in the Health
Service for the people who need it never fails to meet this universal standard.

There are, of course, several difficulties. The first is that each of us, by virtue of our
different personal development, experiences and values, has different expectations
of what is 'good enough' and how the rest of the world should behave towards us.
We also have different tolerances to pain and emotional or physical discomfort
which influence whether we think we have been well treated or not. A further
difficulty, and this is a big one, is that no matter how well-intentioned we are, when
we try to do something within our own small area of influence, we become aware of
monolithic qualities in our Health Service and the policies that drive it. It trans-
mogrifies into one of those oceanic tankers that takes forever to execute a turn, is
relentlessly unstoppable and appears to proceed like a ghostly *Marie Celeste* with a
deserted bridge and helm.

Government policy over the past couple of decades has gone some way to
challenge this image on behalf of the recipients of our Health Service, that is, the
electorate. It started with Thatcher's consumerist drive and has continued with the
Labour government's NHS Plan of 2000, supported by considerable investment and
the conviction that 'the patient must be at the centre of everything the NHS does'.

Several National Patient Surveys later we find ourselves jumping to the tune that
is being called, implementing directives with impossible deadlines and ticking
boxes in order to survive. For some chief executives, this has meant the difference
between an almost intolerably pressured working life and 'gardening leave'. Under
these circumstances, it is hard to look beyond the demands of the next imperative
and give thoughtful consideration to how we can draw on this all-important
personal knowledge and experience of how we would expect our own healthcare
to be provided, to influence our organisational cultures.

This book aims to do precisely that. It describes how I came to be making this
particular journey and how I discovered why it can be so difficult for us to practise
what we preach about involving those who receive health services. In order to put
this in context, it looks at recent policy developments that have promoted the user
involvement concept and how these came about. It outlines what needs to be in
place at a local level to take this forward and presents the case for the 'do as you
would be done by' approach and how this can influence organisational culture.
Throughout, numerous practical examples are given. The final section contains
first-hand accounts from people who have experienced working and receiving
services delivered within this theoretical framework, and includes reference to a
new National Centre for Involvement supported by the Department of Health. All

of the contributors, both workers or recipients of services, freely acknowledge their own service use. The book aims to recognise the value of that personal experience and demonstrate how it can influence front-line staff and be meaningfully integrated into healthcare organisations.

As for my own experience, I have worn several hats during my NHS career. The first of these was as an occupational therapist working in the mental health field, and although I subsequently had a development role and launched both clinical audit and clinical effectiveness in a community trust, the hat that fitted me best was that of researcher – or as my family describe me in their less affectionate moments, super-snooper. Coupled with working on the implementation of mental health policy, I had the opportunity to explore the field in a research project; this to me felt like having my cake and eating it. Doing research whilst holding down a demanding full-time job was tricky, but it meant that I could keep my sleeves rolled up and remain in the real world of work and policy implementation: doing it whilst theorising about it. However, there was a price to pay. With little time to read academic papers, let alone to write them, little time to debate post-modern this or deconstructed that, or hold forth about Foucauldian discourses, I felt that such academic credibility as I had was being compromised by my determination to remain in the grubby and pressured world of practical service delivery where we seemed to be speaking a different language.

It took me a while to realise that I was, in fact, looking at the very nature of the chasm between the theoretical world which largely dominates, or one could say determines, professional practice and the messy world of process and experience where we muddle along as best we can. I became aware that my own difficulties in trying to bridge this gap seemed to mirror the experience of service users and carers in feeling that their needs, as they articulated them, had little credibility in the highly specialised world of professional practice.

By this time I was working in a 'new' organisation, South Staffordshire Healthcare NHS Trust, which had heaved itself into existence in 2001, following a reluctant merger. Inevitably at the time heads had rolled and those of us who survived to take the new organisation forward were unsure whether we were to be envied or pitied. The way ahead looked tough. My new responsibility as an associate director was to ensure that the Trust followed through all the policy requirements related to working with service users and carers, and this book reflects how my attempts to reconcile these two seemingly disparate worlds of policy requirement and reality experience influenced our interpretation of that policy, and the culture of our organisation.

South Staffs Healthcare is a large organisation employing over 2000 staff and providing Mental Health, Learning Disability and Children's services, mainly in the community. It spans a geographical area of around 720 square miles with a population of just under 600,000. Although much that is described relates to mental health service provision, the trust's varied portfolio of services and the systems we set up enabled us to generalise these examples, demonstrating that they could be adapted and applied to a range of different service areas. The principles underpinning the practices described in this book could be useful across a wide spectrum of services, including primary healthcare.

This is more than a cookery book. There are practical examples aplenty, but they are located within a theoretical framework that hopefully gives them coherence, consistency and a sense of direction. For me, practice that is not underpinned by theoretical knowledge is blind and mechanistic; it may enable one to tick the boxes, but it does not facilitate reflection or developmental thinking. Good grounding gives confidence, courage, flexibility and the ability to face and welcome change, but it takes time and thought, both of which may feel like obsolete luxuries in the present climate of instant communication, targets and 'do it by yesterday'. In spite of this, there is another reason why healthcare workers may find it hard to pause for reflection, and this is because all too often we see ourselves as doers rather than thinkers, when in truth we need to be both. Please share with me some of your precious thinking time...

Susie Green
November 2006

About this book

Who should read it?

- Anyone who uses the NHS and wants to work in partnership with people who provide services, e.g. governor members of foundation trusts, voluntary sector representatives and activists in service user and carer groups.
- Professionals who work in the NHS and want to join in partnership with people who, like themselves, use services, e.g. Patient and Public Involvement (PPI) leads, Patient Advice and Liaison Service representatives, managers, clinicians, board members, students.

Why?

- It gives a clear description of the origins and present progress with PPI policy.
- It describes an organisational model and many practical examples for involving people in their healthcare that could be utilised in both trusts and primary care trusts.
- It reminds us of our individual ownership of the experience of sickness and health, whether we are providers of services or recipients.

How?

As an author, I would like to think that every single word is a pearl to be cherished by every single reader, but I think I'm probably deluding myself. Although you may want to read the whole book from cover to cover (in which case, thank you), I would guess that it's much more likely you will want to pick and mix according to your needs – as service user, clinician, manager, student or simply someone who is interested in getting inside the NHS.

About the author

Susie Green has used the NHS throughout her life. She has also worked in it for 30 years, initially as a clinician but more recently undertaking research and development in community and mental health services. Her interest in 'real world' research has resulted in her keeping a foot in both academic and practical fields, a key area being the mismatch between policy requirements and the experience of people on the receiving end of services. This was the topic of her PhD thesis. As an Associate Director at South Staffs Healthcare NHS Trust, she pioneered innovative schemes to enable those people to have an influence on services – this is her passion. She now writes and undertakes freelance work to promote service user and carer involvement in the NHS.

List of contributors

Mike Cooke BSc(Hons), MHSM, Dip HSM
Chief Executive
South Staffs Healthcare NHS Foundation Trust

Lindsey Dyer BA, MPhil
Director, Service Users and Carers
Mersey Care NHS Trust

David Gilbert MSc
Director of Organisational Development
NHS Centre for Involvement
www.nhscentreforinvolvement.nhs.uk

Donna Wedgbury
Former Associate Director
South Staffs Healthcare NHS Trust

Acknowledgements

There are always a million and one people who deserve appreciation for their contribution when one is writing a book, whether the contribution is technical, practical or moral support. Much of the effort and thinking that went into this particular work took place as part of my paid employment and so I am eternally grateful to a multitude of lovely people from South Staffs Healthcare NHS Trust, both people who worked there and people who received its services, who were stimulating, supportive, patient and generous with their time and interest. Two stalwarts, Karen Hirons and Helen Klich, deserve a special mention for their administrative help and for their sense of proportion (and humour) when the going got tough. Technical help came particularly from the Trust's librarians, Lyn Pitt, the Manager of Library Services, and Liz Askew, who never failed to come up with the goods when they received my panicky demands for detailed information. Support from the Trust board, Lesley Francis, Director of Human Resources and Organisational Development and especially Mike Cooke, the Chief Executive, enabled me to do a job I cared passionately about and provided much of the material for this book. As for my associate director colleagues, to whom it is dedicated, all I can say is simply 'thank you – it was a joy to work with you'.

One person I am unable to thank is Dave Follows, who drew the cartoon for 'Telling It Like It Is' and was in the process of doing another one for our Heart of the Trust Scheme, when very sadly he died of cancer. Dave kept his delightful sense of humour right up to the end and it was a privilege to have worked with him. My thanks go to Audrey, his wife, for allowing us to reprint his work here.

Finally of course, I must thank my long-suffering but ever-supportive family who have seen less of me than they might have liked, but especially Tony who fed me coffee, tea and gin at appropriate times of the day and was a thoughtful and responsive sounding board whenever I needed one.

Thank you all.

For Will, Jo, Kathy, Linda, Jan and Donna, with thanks.

Part I

Theory and practice of policy implementation

Introduction

The priority for involving the public should be that their interests are embedded into all organisations and institutions concerned with quality of performance in the NHS: in other words, the public should be 'on the inside', rather than represented by some organisation 'on the outside'.

Kennedy Report, 2002

Getting inside the National Health Service (NHS) has proved much harder than we think. Whilst there has been an increasing emphasis on developing working partnerships between NHS providers and the public who are on the receiving end, surveys and feedback continue to demonstrate that progress is apparently slow. This can be frustrating both for service users who feel that their voices are not being heard, and for NHS staff who struggle to reconcile their clinical responsibilities with increasingly burdensome bureaucratic demands. For both, time is an issue. Whilst the general public may be dissatisfied at the rate of change, NHS employees are left breathless by the expectation that they will respond instantly to yet another reorganisation or policy instruction. Policy, in this sense, is the government's interpretation of what needs to be done to achieve a certain outcome, such as Professor Sir Ian Kennedy's recommendation quoted above.

In this first part of the book, we look at the nature and origin of those demands and what they require of NHS organisations and the workers within them. These are the official Patient and Public Involvement directives, as they have emerged from the Department of Health. In Chapter 1, the policy expectations are defined. It looks at these policy expectations and how they have evolved, why they have evolved the way they have and some key factors influencing their development. This includes a detailed look at the NHS Plan of 2000, the Health and Social Care Act (2001) and the Kennedy Report which emerged in 2002.

Chapter 2 looks more closely at some of these influential factors, including a series of tough inquiries when things went badly wrong, the consumerist ethos of the 1990s and the technological revolution which makes us expect instant information, instant responses and instant cures. There is reference to clinical governance, introduced in 1999, and its requirement for healthcare workers to think more deeply about the quality of the services they are providing, not just in relation to outcomes but also as experienced by those of us who use services. This raises questions about the effectiveness of clinical practice and whether the right systems and resources are in place to support the involvement of patients and the public. Most importantly, are our attitudes and values compatible with the user involvement ethos? Do we understand the challenges sufficiently to know how to respond positively to them?

The final chapter in Part 1 moves us to the 'coal face' and establishes the 'must dos', service user and carer policy obligations for healthcare organisations and the workers within them, as they exist at the present time. This includes the Patients' Advice and Liaison Services, Patient and Public Involvement Forums, the Independent Complaints and Advisory Service, Overview and Scrutiny Committees, patient surveys and patient prospectuses. If all this is in place in an NHS organisation and the agencies it engages with, we then have to ask ourselves, are we 'doing' patient and public involvement?

If the answer to this question is in any doubt, it is worth reading on. Part 2 of this book describes what happened in one organisation when it attempted to redress the balance between providers and recipients of its services. It describes the developmental process and contains many examples of how specific issues were tackled. This is not a 'PPI and how to do it' manual. Organisations are infinitely variable and one size simply won't fit all. The idea is to stimulate thinking around the different issues and challenges and find possible routes through the difficulty. As with most good sandwiches, the 'filling' is more substantial than the bread on either side, i.e. this part is much longer than the other two because it contains a considerable amount of detail.

Part 3 has been written by service users who have worked within the NHS and have first-hand experience from both sides of the fence. Listen to their voices. As people who have managed to get 'inside' the NHS, they have some uniquely important things to say.

Service user and carer policy: its origins and aims

Introduction

'Policy' and 'service user' are not words that sit comfortably beside each other. The one speaks of government action, political expediency and the conduct of public affairs with a sub-text of diplomacy, prudence and skill, even craftiness. The other takes us to the world of the individual, their family and their needs in sickness and in health: a world of physical and emotional pain and suffering, an intensely personal world of hope, joy, resignation and compromise. No wonder there has been such difficulty in making a connection between the two. Healthcare policy speaks of 'us' and 'them', the attempts the government makes to establish goals, and systems for achieving them that ensure that the health of the nation is maintained and if possible improved within the economic resources available. For a number of reasons that we shall explore in this first chapter, there has been recognition that the distance between 'us', the recipients, and 'them', the policy makers, has to be reduced. Instead of regarding each other from afar, as if looking down the wrong end of a telescope, it is time the personal and individual aspects of our healthcare experiences were meaningfully integrated into the grand design.

Policy is definitely moving that way, as we shall discover in Part 1, but there is still a long way to go and the need for a significant shift in our thinking. We shall look at this in Part 2 but first we need to know what is already in place and where it has come from, as well as the requirements and responsibilities defined within it. The NHS Plan (2000),[1] the Health and Social Care Act (2001)[2] and the Kennedy Report[3] are all presented here in some detail as they are the key policy responses to the social developments that are described, but how successful are they in putting the public 'inside' the NHS, as was Professor Sir Ian Kennedy's urgent recommendation? And do they really tell us whether our thinking is service-user and carer sensitive?

A word about terminology

Before diving in to the apparent complexities of policy development, there is something we must get straight and that is the matter of what to call people who use health services. In any service-user and carer-focused activity, it has become inevitable, almost traditional, that precious time is spent deliberating over this particular question. The difficulty is that it doesn't have an answer; one can only state a personal preference and respect the right of others to have a different one. I don't actually mind whether we call ourselves patients or clients or customers or service users, although I guess for me a 'patient' is somebody who receives 'treatment' from a doctor, nurse or therapist and 'client' or 'customer' has a transactional ring to it that makes me think of cash registers and credit cards. I do know that some people take violent exception to being called 'service users' because it reminds them of those who use or rather misuse illicit substances and they object to the association. Wherever possible my preference is to simply talk about 'people' or 'individuals', but sometimes there is a need to be specific.

However, maybe it isn't such a small matter after all. If we are seeking to diminish the gap in thinking between ourselves as professionals and ourselves as service users (and hands up anyone who isn't or hasn't been or doesn't know someone who has been? – exactly), then shouldn't we be dropping the differentiation between ourselves and 'others' as it is embodied in a name? Shouldn't we be thinking much more inclusively in terms of 'we' instead of 'you' or, even worse, 'they'? We can look at the policy and see what it requires of us but we should also be considering how we can interpret it within the framework of our own experience. This also means that the differentiation between 'patients' and 'the public' is actually specious. There are people who are patients at a particular point in time or those who suffer from long-term conditions requiring continuing contact with services, but the majority of us will have been patients at some point in our lives and will retain the memory of that experience, to contribute to the debate. The more recent the experience, the better it will reflect current practice, but differentiating between patients and the public as though we are two separate and finite entities, for me reinforces an unhelpful sense of 'otherness' when we should be recognising the totality of ourselves and our experience.

Nevertheless, as Anna Coote, Head of Engaging Patients and Public at the Healthcare Commission, has pointed out in a recent policy briefing (2005),[4] those of us who become patients with immediate and urgent healthcare needs will need to be involved in different ways from the general public whose interests are likely to be wider and related more to their future needs and those of their families. 'Patients cannot be a proxy for the public, or vice versa', she says, but I'm not so sure. Certainly there is the potential for conflicts of interest where questions of resource allocation and priority setting arise and different methods may be necessary to engage them, but I'm happy to settle for the general practitioners' (GPs') view that their 'list' or 'panel' of patients will comprise everyone in their patch be they young or old, sick or healthy.

The language of policy

Policy itself has moved considerably in terms of the language it uses as well as its content. In the dim and distant past, health policy contained firm statements of requirements and how they were to be met in a language that brooked no opposition. Barbara Castle's report when she was Health Minister for a Labour government, 'Better Services for the Mentally Ill' (1975),[5] with its caring, first person plural approach, marked a distinct if patronising change. It was couched in terms of 'we, as representatives of this humanitarian state, would like to share with you our plans for your future care'. Once the Conservative party had taken over in 1979, the language of consumerism and self-reliance emerged. Policy was set out in broad terms, but detail was often lacking, possibly because of the speed and haste with which it had been conceived. This was the sharp and snappy language of self-determination based on 'you and what you should expect as your rights'.

Recently, the change has been even more marked. A few examples demonstrate the point:

> *The rationale for this reorganisation is the empowerment of users and carers. Instead of them being subordinate to the wishes of service providers, the roles will be progressively adjusted.*
>
> NHS and Community Care Act, 1990[6]

> *The drive to place quality at the heart of the NHS is not about ticking checklists – it's about changing thinking.*
>
> 'A First Class Service: quality in the new NHS', 1999[7]

> *Patients are the most important people in the health service. It doesn't always appear that way. Too many patients feel talked at, rather than listened to. This has to change.*
>
> 'The NHS Plan', 2000[1]

> *The balance of power must be shifted towards front-line staff who understand patients' needs and concerns.*
>
> 'Shifting the Balance of Power', July 2001[8]

> *... the patient must be at the centre of everything the NHS does.*
>
> 'Involving Patients and the Public in Healthcare', September 2001[9]

Of course it is easy to pluck appropriate quotations out of dense and detailed policy documents which, when taken in their entirety, embody more questionable intentions. For example, the NHS and Community Care Act (1990) was seen by many as the thin end of a wedge that 'empowered' people to care for their elderly dependent relatives at home or else contribute a major chunk of their lifetimes' savings to residential care. Health became a marketable commodity.

Nevertheless, there has been a definite shift in recognition of the need to engage with the experience of receiving healthcare. The Department of Health has produced a useful policy timeline that summarises these developments (see below).

Patient and public involvement in the NHS: policy timeline

2003: The national choice consultation, 'Building on the Best: choice, responsiveness and equity in the NHS',[10] emphasises the links between individual patient choices, service responsiveness and equity of provision.

Patient and Public Involvement (PPI) Forums are established in all NHS trusts. The Commission for Patient and Public Involvement in Health begins work. Community Health Councils are abolished.

'Strengthening Accountability',[11] policy and practice guidance for implementation of Section 11 of the Health and Social Care Act, is published.

The Department of Health's Planning and Priorities Framework 2003–2006[12] includes the national priority of improving the overall experience of patients. The document stresses the role of primary care trusts in creating local plans that take account of patient and public knowledge as well as professional knowledge.

2002: Primary care trusts take full responsibility for the health of their local populations. Patients' Advice and Liaison Services (PALS) go live. Separate

Independent Complaints Advocacy Services (ICAS) are also established.

2001: Section 11 of the Health and Social Care Act places a new duty on NHS institutions to make active arrangements to involve and consult patients and the public in (a) planning services, (b) developing and considering proposals for changes in the way those services are provided, and (c) decisions that affect how those services operate.

The Bristol Royal Infirmary Inquiry report emphasises the role of patient and public involvement in building a more open, responsive and safe health service. The government accepts the report including the principles that 'patients and the public are entitled to be involved wherever decisions are taken about care in the NHS' and 'the involvement of patients and the public must be embedded in the structures of the NHS and permeate all aspects of healthcare'.

'Shifting the Balance of Power' defines a restructuring of the NHS that aims 'to foster a new culture in the NHS at all levels which puts the patient first'.

'Improving Health in Wales',[13] the health strategy of the Welsh Assembly, seeks to 'enter into a partnership with the people of Wales so that each citizen and each community is helped to play a role, directly or through bodies representing them, in the development of health policy, the setting of aims for the NHS, the improvement of health and well-being and the narrowing of health and social inequalities'.

2000: The NHS Plan defines a 10-year programme of modernisation for the NHS. At the heart of the NHS Plan is a vision of a service 'designed around the patient'. Chapter 10 'Changes for Patients' describes a range of initiatives to improve patient information, patient choice and patient and public involvement in the NHS. These include:

- expansion of the Expert Patient Programme
- a requirement for letters between clinicians about the care of individual patients to be copied to their patients
- better information about local services to inform patient choice
- new patient advocacy and liaison services
- a requirement for NHS trusts to seek patient views on their services and publish an annual prospectus
- the creation of a Patients' Forum in every NHS trust to provide input into how services are run
- a new local authority duty to scrutinise the local NHS.

The Scottish Executive publishes 'Our National Health: a plan for action, a plan for change'[14] which aims to build a service 'designed for and involving users' where 'people are respected, treated as individuals and involved in their own care; where individuals, groups and communities are involved in improving the quality of care, in influencing priorities and in planning services'.

1999: 'A First Class Service' introduces a new approach to improving the quality of patient care in the NHS – clinical governance – that requires a shift towards a culture that is 'truly patient-centred'.

1998: The voluntary sector 'Compact'[15] aims to strengthen partnerships between public services and the voluntary sector.

1997: 'The New NHS: modern, dependable'[16] seeks to 'rebuild confidence in the NHS as a public service, accountable to patients, open to the public and shaped by their views'.

1992: 'Local Voices'[17] recommends community involvement to help the NHS 'establish priorities, develop service specifications and monitor services'.

1991: 'The Patients' Charter'[18] establishes a clear framework for patient entitlements.

1990: The Community Care Act[6] requires local authorities to consult with users and carers.

© Department of Health: The Evidence for Policy Implementation, 2005

This timeline demonstrates that momentum for increasing the participation and therefore the influence of people using services has been growing steadily, regardless of which party was in government. Key elements are the NHS Plan which aimed to redesign services around the needs of patients, and Section 11 of the Health and Social Care Act 2001 which placed a duty on all strategic health authorities and NHS trusts to involve and consult patients and the public in relation to service planning, changes and operational issues. Notice that at this point the policy started to include the wider public and is thereafter known as the Patient and Public Involvement policy.

The NHS Plan

There was no messing with the NHS Plan as the following forthright quotation demonstrates:

> *This is a package of radical reform. It will enhance and encourage the involvement of citizens in redesigning the health service from the patient's point of view.*

Although several public reports and inquiries into health service malpractice were yet to appear, particularly the influential Kennedy Report, it could be that ministers within the dim recesses of the Department of Health were already aware that unless a firm grip of accountability issues within the NHS was seen to be taken, there could be trouble from the general public, i.e. the electorate.

So how was it to change? In general terms, the NHS Plan was a direction statement for the next 10 years of NHS provision. It required the following:

- More information. Information is one of those ragbag words that need opening up to see what's inside. For a start, in this context there are two categories: information to patients and information from patients. In the first category, the Plan included the following:
  - patient-friendly versions of clinical guidelines
  - NHS Direct (the health advice and help phone line) going online
  - information about treatment planned
  - the right to see medical records
  - letters between clinicians about individual care copied to the patient, as of right.

- Information from patients included:
  - patients leaving hospital recording their views on the standards of care
  - development of the Expert Patient Programme
  - consent issues, e.g. local resuscitation policy, sound consent practice (and for a scary example of why this should be necessary, in 2003 I heard on the radio, medical students describing how they felt unable to refuse to undertake unnecessary 'practice' intimate examinations of patients under general anaesthetic for which consent had not been given, because of jeopardising their future career prospects with the consultants overseeing their tuition)
  - annual patients' survey contributing to a patients' prospectus (linking to performance indicators giving star ratings)
  - smart cards, allowing easier access to health records, connecting with the development of the electronic health record.
- Greater patient choice:
  - the right to choose a GP with information to be available about each practice – list size, accessibility, performance against National Service Framework (NSF) standards etc.
  - by 2005, hospital appointments/elective admissions to be by patient choice, not hospital dictat
  - patients to have a choice in the hospital they are referred to.
- Patient advocates and advisors in every hospital:
  - a new Patient Advocacy and Liaison Service (PALS) to be developed (this was subsequently changed to the Patients' Advice and Liaison Service following strong representation from various advocacy groups who feared confusion with their role).
- Redress over cancelled operations:
  - cancellation on the day for non-clinical reasons – an alternative opportunity to be offered within 28 days or alternative treatment elsewhere at the patient's convenience.
- Patients' Forums and Citizens' Panels in every area:
  - direct input from local people in to how their services are run and to monitor the quality of those services from a patient's perspective, with administrative and secretarial support and also training
  - Overview and Scrutiny Committees (OSCs) – to broaden representation with local councillors, i.e. elected by the community, having a say in the quality of services, leading to an increase in representation of citizens
  - lay membership of local scrutiny and national regulatory bodies.
- A new national panel to advise on major reorganisation in hospitals:
  - this was to be an Independent Reconfiguration Panel to deal with contested major service reconfigurations, for example when flagged up by an OSC.
- Stronger regulation of professional standards:
  - quality assurance of standards of care, e.g. as described in the various NSFs
  - risks to be minimised – with a mandatory reporting scheme for adverse healthcare events
  - annual appraisal for doctors plus rapid objective assessment. This was to avoid the costly situation where a consultant might be suspended on full pay for a year whilst under investigation, requiring the costs of locum cover to be met
  - mandatory participation in clinical audit

- regulatory bodies (e.g. the General Medical Council, UKCC) to be smaller with more patient and public representation
- common approaches across professions to deal with complaints against practitioners (to limit the opportunities for one profession to scapegoat another in the event of an inquiry).

The Health and Social Care Act 2001

Hard on the heels of the NHS Plan came the Health and Social Care Act, which was in effect the government saying it had not been joking about its earlier intentions. The Act placed a duty on strategic health authorities and NHS trusts to involve and consult patients and the public wherever decisions were being made to plan, develop, change or operate services. Specifically identified were:

- the Independent Complaints Advocacy Service which was to link with Patient Forums
- Overview and Scrutiny Committees, already identified in the NHS Plan as the link with local democratic processes
- Section 11 which firmly placed a duty on all NHS bodies to involve and consult with patients and the public.

Policy triggers

The Department of Health's timeline suggests that policy evolves and is formulated through a process of ordered and incremental development. Not so. 'Events, dear boy, events' is what Sir Harold Macmillan, Britain's Conservative Prime Minister from 1957 to 1963, is reputed to have enigmatically replied when asked what determined the direction of policy and government action. This of course is a typical politician's response suggesting that it could be proactive, but then again it might be reactive, or perhaps something between the two, depending on how you look at it. Be that as it may, events during the evolution of this policy timeline tell an interesting but sobering tale.

It's a tale of shameful things that should never have happened – of children who died needlessly, such as the four who were murdered by Nurse Beverley Allitt and nine others who became seriously ill as a result of her attention, resulting in the Clothier Report in 1994.[19] It's a tale of more babies dying in Bristol at the Royal Infirmary where they had been taken for heart surgery to improve their life chances, not reduce them. An anaesthetist, who questioned the length of time surgery was taking, set up an internal audit process, the first audit being completed in 1994; but a full inquiry was not launched until 1998, and it was only in 2002 that the full scale of the tragic malpractice was revealed in the Kennedy Report. Although the Kennedy Report appeared some time after the NHS Plan of 2000, it is hard not to believe that policy writers of the time were only too aware of the implications of what Professor Sir Ian Kennedy had to say and were hurriedly covering the government's back.

Then there was Alder Hey, where children's organs were kept for years for research with neither the knowledge nor permission of their parents, resulting in the Royal Liverpool Children's Inquiry of 2001.[20]

Meanwhile, the Manchester GP Dr Harold Shipman had been quietly killing off his elderly women patients and was only found out in June 1998 when he foolishly tried to forge a will. Three months prior to this, a police inquiry into his actions had been dropped due to 'lack of evidence'. He was convicted of 15 murders in January 2000 (although it is likely to have been in the region of 300) and the Department of Health commissioned a report, published in December 2000, which drew attention to the problem of poorly performing doctors. A full inquiry was subsequently set up under Dame Janet Smith which delivered further reports between 2002 and 2005.[21]

Poor little Victoria Climbié died in February 2000 aged nine, after she had been brought from the Ivory Coast to live with her aunt, first in Paris and then north London. Her death, as a result of the neglect and maltreatment of those who were supposed to be caring for her, triggered an extensive review of child protection arrangements that identified 12 possible turning points at which her life might have been saved.[22]

This awful series of tragedies forced the government to think about how it was possible for people in the 'caring' professions to get away with poor practice, neglect or, at worst, murder, and not to be called to account until it was too late. Accountability was indeed the issue and it was the Kennedy Report, dealing with the events at the Bristol Royal Infirmary, that attempted to grasp this particular nettle.

The Kennedy Report

It is useful to quote some of the opening statements in this report, which sensitively reflect the realities for many who work in the NHS.

> *The story of the paediatric cardiac surgical service in Bristol is not an account of bad people, nor is it an account of people who did not care, nor of people who wilfully harmed patients.*
>
> *It is an account of people who cared greatly about human suffering, and were dedicated and well-motivated. Sadly, some lacked insight and their behaviour was flawed. Many failed to communicate with each other, and to work together effectively for the interests of their patients. There was a lack of leadership, and of teamwork.*
>
> *It is an account of healthcare professionals working in Bristol who were victims of a combination of circumstances which owed as much to general failings within the NHS at the time than to any individual failing. Despite their manifest good intentions and long hours of dedicated work, there were failures on occasion in the care provided to very sick children.*

What Professor Sir Ian Kennedy then attempted to do in his report's recommendations was to identify these failings and promote solutions. His list of principles to inform future policy about involving the public and patients in the NHS can seem axiomatic; the first, for example, is that 'Patients and the public are *entitled* to be involved wherever decisions are taken about care in the NHS'.

Well of course we are, or should be, everybody knows that. But how easy it is when we are wearing our professional hats, anxious to get on with the job, meet a target or deadline, to make those decisions regardless of that entitlement. We know best anyway what patients need – or do we? That entitlement speaks of an inclusive and participative approach which may be a far cry from the distancing that professionalism has created.

Similarly, 'The involvement of patients and the public *must be embedded in the structures of the NHS* and permeate *all* aspects of healthcare'. How on earth do we do that, and won't they get in the way of the real work, especially when we are so short of time and have so much to do? Will foundation trusts with their members and boards of governors manage to bridge the gap between the organisational structure and the function it is there to perform?

Then there is 'The public and patients should have access to *relevant* information'. A recent trip to the local library told me a great deal about hospital bed occupancy rates in an unappetising format that had clearly been lifted from an internal reporting system, but I had much greater difficulty in establishing on the internet the likelihood of my succumbing to an infection or the comparative success rates of different surgeons at the same hospital. It could rightly be argued that over-simplification of outcomes, for example eliminating confounding variables, can render information both meaningless and misleading. It is hard, really hard, to make available relevant information for every individual who seeks it, simply because their needs are individual. The present response relies on the blunderbuss, or the popcorn machine, firing out as much of the stuff as possible in the hope that some of it will make sense to some people – but it's a very hit-and-miss affair. It doesn't need to be, and perhaps it should be more dependent on the response of individual clinicians taking time to ensure that what is available suits the needs of the person seeking it.

Here's a nice example: an e-mail I received from my sister about our 94-year-old father who for years had suffered from a disabling tremor. Old he might have been, and anxious, but he was as entitled as anyone to receive accurate information about his condition in a way that made sense to him.

Hi Susie

The specialist that father and I went to see last week was brilliant. She listened very carefully to his story, which he embellished with little anecdotes, and got him to say where the main problem areas were. She asked him to copy various shapes and then confirmed and carefully explained that it was indeed benign essential tremor and that his present medication regime, although sensible in that larger doses had side-effects, could be timed to better effect. She said that a little tipple would do him no harm and might even help, that he was managing very well and that his tremor needn't prevent him from joining in social events, especially those for older folks, all of whom were likely to have some sort of disability. In fact Sue it was just what father (and I) wanted, someone who would listen to his explanation of what it is like to have a tremor, to clear up his queries about whether the drugs were right or whether there was anything else more effective and to encourage him to be a bit more sociable. The NHS did us proud!

Love Catherine

This links with Professor Kennedy's next point, that 'Healthcare professionals must be *partners* in the process of involving the public', something that is easier said than done. As with marriage, as individuals we all need different sorts of partners, maybe even different partners at different times. Understanding this and being able to relate to an individual in a way that accommodates mutual understanding is a very subtle process indeed. Once we start talking pluralities – 'healthcare professionals', 'the public' – the concept, though easy to articulate, becomes incredibly difficult to realise. Where public involvement is concerned, attempts to engage its interest can result in bland indifference unless there is a particular issue that fuels its involvement, such as local hospital closure.

The report then goes on to recommend that 'There must be honesty about the scope of the public's involvement, *since some decisions cannot be made by the public*', and this can be linked to the next point which is that 'There must be *transparency and openness* in the procedures for involving the public and patients'. Both are concerned with issues of trust, both between individual clinicians and patients but also between the NHS and the general public. There is a difference. As patients we need to be involved in knowing what is to happen to us and why, and if there are risks in relation to our specific health problem, how they are to be managed and, if possible, minimised. As members of the public our interests are probably broader – none of this supposed 'consultation' about decisions that have already been made, but open dialogue and opportunities for debate. There are decisions that cannot be made in public, for example where details of an impending sale of property could prove prejudicial or where employment issues in relation to a senior member of staff have to be discussed at board level, but these are few and far between.

The following two recommendations are both indicators of the integrity of the intention to engage patient and public interest. Firstly that 'The *mechanisms* for involvement should be evaluated for their effectiveness', in other words that the methods of involving people should be clearly defined and their effectiveness demonstrated, and secondly that 'The public and patients should have access to training and funding to allow them to *fully participate*'. This is where the all-important resource contribution comes in which will be discussed in more detail later. Is there funding available, and is it recurrent or is it part of invisible costs that never actually get acknowledged? Both of these recommendations, when not met, signal tokenism.

Finally, 'The public should be represented by a wide range of individuals and groups and not by particular "patients" groups'. This recognises the point made earlier about differentiating between the public at large, the wider community and those with specific healthcare needs. It represents an argument against undue attention to 'drum-bangers' and lobbyists who have every right to champion their particular cause but have the potential for destabilising a local health economy. Guaranteeing 'representativeness' is an impossible task. Perhaps it is more about a way of thinking that is able to progress beyond personal experience and apply such knowledge to broader healthcare issues.

A final comment from the Kennedy Report reflects an earlier Department of Health discussion document and reminds us of our move towards an 'insider' view of service user and carer involvement. 'Involving Patients and the Public in Healthcare: a discussion document' (2001)[9] says:

> *We want to move away from a system of patients being on the outside, to one where the voices of patients, their carers and the public generally are heard and*

listened to through every level of the service, acting as a lever for change and improvement.

Professor Sir Ian Kennedy's response is:

The priority for involving the public should be that their interests are embedded into all organisations and institutions concerned with quality of performance in the NHS: in other words, the public should be 'on the inside', rather than represented by some organisation 'on the outside'.

Kennedy Report, 2002

This takes us straight back to an earlier policy statement which introduced health-care workers to the notion of clinical governance ('A First Class Service', 1999) with its emphasis on clear lines of responsibility and accountability, progress on assuring and improving the quality of clinical services, progress on all sorts of risk assessment and procedures for all professionals and groups to identify and remedy poor performance. These were the guarantees of quality performance and they had to be demonstrable, hence the Commission for Health Improvement inspections and the increasingly sophisticated surveys undertaken with different service user groups.

Summary

In this chapter, we considered initially whether there is a difference between the contributions that patients, the general public and healthcare workers can make to the healthcare involvement agenda, the value of having an integrated view but the importance of their various and complementary standpoints. We also identified the difficulty in humanising government healthcare policy and making it feel as though it relates to our own needs, whether we work in the NHS and/or use it. A good example of this difficulty is what we call ourselves, whether we are patients, service users, clients or customers.

We have looked at the significance of changes in policy language and some of the major accountability issues that surfaced at the end of the twentieth century. These contributed to an increase in momentum and the formulation of new policy for increasing the participation and therefore the influence of people using services. However, in spite of the Kennedy Report and a whole raft of social policy designed to improve the engagement between patients and service providers, progress seems to have been limited. Key elements were the NHS Plan which aimed to redesign services around the needs of patients, and Section 11 of the Health and Social Care Act 2001 which placed a duty on all strategic health authorities and NHS trusts to involve and consult patients and the public in service planning, changes to services and operational issues.

Some background information is given about how service user and carer policy has evolved as well as some dramatic events that triggered urgent recognition of the need for change. The Kennedy Report is described and explained in some detail as a particularly significant and influential example of what the government was expecting of healthcare organisations and the workers within them.

Chapter 2 will continue this theme, first of all by recognising the significance of the introduction of clinical governance in 1999. This drew attention to the responsibility that healthcare workers have for ensuring the quality of the services they provide. It will take a broader look at some of the social issues influencing the direction that policy development has taken as well as reviewing evidence of progress. Consideration will be given to an alternative way of thinking about what is going on in healthcare organisations and how we make sense of this activity.

References

1 Department of Health. *The NHS Plan*. Cm. 4818.1. London: DoH; 2000.
2 Department of Health. Health and Social Care Act. London: DoH; 2001.
3 Department of Health. Learning from Bristol: the report of the public inquiry into children's heart surgery at the Bristol Royal Infirmary. 1984–1995. London: DoH; 2001.
4 Coote A. Policy briefs. Think tank. *Guardian Society*, 20 April 2005.
5 Department of Health and Social Security. *Better Services for the Mentally Ill*. Cmnd. 6233. London: HMSO; 1975.
6 Department of Health. The National Health Service and Community Care Act. London: DoH; 1990.
7 Department of Health. *A First Class Service: quality in the new NHS*. London: DoH; 1999.
8 Department of Health. *Shifting the Balance of Power*. London: DoH; 2001.
9 Department of Health. *Involving Patients and the Public in Healthcare*. London: DoH; 2001.
10 Department of Health. *Building on the Best: choice, responsiveness and equity*. London: DoH; 2003.
11 Department of Health. *Strengthening Accountability*. London: DoH; 2003.
12 Department of Health. *Improvement, Expansion and Reform: the next three years' planning and priorities framework, 2003–2006*. London: DoH; 2002.
13 Welsh Assembly. *Improving Health in Wales*. London: HMSO; 2001.
14 Scottish Executive. *Our National Health: a plan for action, a plan for change*. Edinburgh: Scottish Executive; 2000.
15 Department of Health. *Compact: a dynamic mechanism for an evolving relationship with the voluntary and community sector*. London: DoH; 2002.
16 Department of Health. *The New NHS: modern, dependable*. London: DoH; 1997.
17 Department of Health. *Local Voices*. London: DoH; 1992.
18 Department of Health. *The Patients' Charter and You: a charter for England*. London: DoH; 1996.
19 Department of Health. The Allitt Inquiry: the independent inquiry relating to deaths and injuries on the children's ward at Grantham and Kesteven General Hospital during the period February to April 1991. Clothier Report. London: DoH; 1994.
20 Department of Health. Royal Liverpool Children's Inquiry – Report. London: DoH; 2001.
21 Department of Health. The Shipman Inquiry [Dame Janet Smith]. London: DoH; 2002–2005.
22 Department of Health. The Victoria Climbié Inquiry: report of an inquiry by Lord Laming. London: DoH; 2003.

2

A further look at factors influencing policy development

Clinical governance

At the end of the last chapter a reference was made to clinical governance. This policy was introduced in 1999 in a document entitled 'A First Class Service'[1] and warrants more than just a passing reference. Although in policy terms it preceded the main Patient and Public Involvement developments, it nevertheless made the connection between the quality of services and accountability issues. You may have noticed, for example, that in the Department of Health's timeline in Chapter 1 it is billed as a 'shift towards a culture that is truly patient-centred' – so the intention was already beginning to emerge. In effect it recognised how any of us as patients might describe our experiences of healthcare as being dependent on the quality of care that staff were able to give, and that it was their responsibility to provide the best possible services they could. It had four defined aims:

- clear lines of responsibility and accountability for the overall quality of clinical care
- a comprehensive programme of quality improvement activities
- clear policies aimed at managing risk
- procedures for all professional groups to identify and remedy poor performance.

It also involved patients and the public in the monitoring process by including them in the visiting teams set up by the Commission for Healthcare Improvement (CHI; now the Healthcare Commission) to provide 'independent scrutiny of local efforts to improve quality and investigate serious problems'.

But what should this mean in practice and what should it feel like to patients? Here's an example. I've got three lovely children of whom I am very proud. They are all grown up now but about 25 years ago when they were being born, this is what happened to me as an NHS patient:

- My appointments with the obstetric service were always made at my convenience, sometimes in the evening, sometimes in the daytime – whatever suited me.
- I never had to wait or queue or sit in a line of women on cold benches, wearing flimsy theatre gowns, waiting to be weighed or have urine samples checked, as was the custom at the time.
- I held my own case file and could read whatever was written in it.
- I saw the same doctor throughout, in fact I saw the same doctor for all three pregnancies over a period of nearly five years.

- I was never seen in a curtained-off cubicle, sharing intimate details of my obstetric progress with the people on either side of me, but always in a fresh, well-appointed consulting room.
- I was given any information as I needed it and the opportunity to discuss anxieties or concerns.
- I trusted the clinicians who looked after me and was confident that I and my babies were safe and receiving quality care from people who knew what they were doing.

So, even that long ago, it was possible to experience an ideal situation in which I was a partner in the whole process, felt that I was receiving excellent services and was not exposed to unnecessary risk, but I'm pretty sure that others were less fortunate.

The reason I was so well treated during my pregnancies was that I happened to be married to a hospital consultant at the time and this was how doctors treated each other and their families. I'm not particularly proud to have received such partial treatment but if we *can* manage to do it for ourselves and each other, we really ought to be striving to do it for everyone else too. This is where a do-as-you-would-be-done-by approach should come in that should be the clinical governance yardstick for every professional. If we are health service workers, there are questions we should be asking ourselves. For example, if I were a patient rather than a professional, would I want to be receiving treatment in this way, from this person? Is it the best they can manage and how do I know it is the best? Would I want my relatives, my nearest and dearest, to receive this sort of care? Would I be satisfied with the evidence and explanations I have been given around clinical decisions that have been made on my behalf? Have I had appropriate choices and do I feel vulnerable? Being treated as a valued human being should be a right, not a privilege. That is the connection we should be making between clinical governance, which is a rather tedious sounding bit of policy, and the experience of those on the receiving end.

Other factors influencing policy development

The Kennedy Report,[2] which followed a ghastly series of disasters, has been a highly significant influence on Patient and Public Involvement policy, but other factors had also contributed to a seachange in thinking. Earlier, for example, the accrued influence of Thatcher's consumerist and individualist policies would appear to have contributed to undermining our sense of social responsibility. Who can forget that chilling quote, 'There's no such thing as society'? What we have forgotten is that she then went on to say, '... there are individual men and women, and there are families. And no government can do anything except through people, and people must look to themselves first.' There were many implications to this and one of them was to make people much more conscious of their right as individuals to challenge authority, particularly the authority of social institutions and the professionals who supported them.

What had started during the Conservative years with the promotion of market forces, trade unions rendered toothless, solicitors competing through advertising their services, architects losing their professional grip through deregulation and the like has more recently been continued under the Labour government. In both teaching and healthcare, professional functions have been parcelled out to the less skilled with the long-term effect of diminishing the power and authority of professional groups. This may be no bad thing. In a way, those earlier inquiries into health disasters demonstrated that the unprecedented attack on professionals, which was part of the Thatcher ethos, was probably justifiable, certainly in relation to the Health Service. What we saw in these particular cases was that the authority figures in whom we had put our trust were invested with that authority through a myth that they were beyond reproach, the myth of professionalism.

All of this was enhanced by the technological revolution which, through the provision of information, particularly via the internet, has enabled us to take responsibility for finding things out for ourselves. We no longer need to rely on professionals to do things for us; many of us will have undertaken our own house conveyancing and some may have tackled legal issues via the small claims court process. We may also have booked our holidays and done our shopping and banking via the internet. We live in a do-it-yourself society where easy access to information gives us power to challenge those who previously held sway through their exclusive knowledge. It is estimated that more than one-third of people accessing the web are looking for medical or health information[3] with 77% of that number seeking answers to specific health questions. In terms of its convenience, its accessibility and the range and diversity of information, it could be seen as a wonderfully empowering tool. Nevertheless a quick cruise around the websites would suggest that it is a double-edged sword, especially for those who are unable to discriminate between sound, evidence-based information and sheer quackery. Fortunately, healthcare professionals are becoming increasingly aware of the need to provide help with these new challenges and the changes in practice that they stimulate.[4–6]

A consequence of this very immediate access to information is that we have become a very impatient society. Karen Armstrong[7] has suggested that 'the culture of the sound bite and the instant opinion' deprives us of the opportunity to reflect on complex issues and 'truths that are not immediately accessible'. Certainly the current trend is for instant gratification and instant decision making with everything in immediately digestible forms, whether it is fast food that we can eat as we walk along or sound-bite information via the internet. We want miracles and perfection – now. We want perfect breasts, wrinkle-free faces, perfect relationships, all of which amounts to a loss of fatalism, possibly putting up with things as they were, which was once an accepted part of the human condition. As a young student of occupational therapy, I was told by our psychiatry lecturer that 'maturity was the ability to defer pleasure'. At the time we all giggled as the pleasure that we were struggling to defer was related to not losing our virginity. But not any more. Our world and our lives seem to have accelerated[8] and this has contributed to exaggerated expectations of science and indeed medicine, with a massive increase in litigation when things have not worked out. It is right that accountability issues should have come to the fore in the wake of the various inquiries, but we cannot on the one hand expect to be empowered and take more responsibility and control of our lives and then on the other want somebody else to be accountable when things have gone wrong.

Policy development as a two-way process

In 2003, a national consultation was undertaken to give NHS staff, patients and the public the opportunity to tell the government about the choices they would like to be able to make about their healthcare. The idea was to make public services more customer focused, by listening to what people said they wanted rather than expecting them to fit pre-established systems. It was anticipated that this more personal approach to the wishes and choices of different groups of patients would improve access to services and reduce health inequalities. The aim was to improve the patient and service user experience and build new partnerships between users and providers. The resulting report, 'Building on the Best',[9] identified the following priorities:

- for everyone to have a bigger say in how they were treated
- to increase the choice of access to a wider range of services in primary care
- to increase the choice of where, when and how to get medicines
- for people to be able to book appointments when they wanted them from a choice of hospitals
- to widen the choice of treatment and care, especially in maternity services and care at the end of life
- for people to have the right information when they wanted it.

It was recognised that change on this scale would require:

- a clear vision and values shared by local and national leaders
- continued investment, capacity and growth
- empowered, well-supported staff
- high-quality information systems
- a stronger patient voice
- coherent systems of incentives, regulation and inspection.

The centrality of the patient's experience was clearly here to stay and this was demonstrated in a follow-up document to the NHS Plan of 2000. The 'NHS Improvement Plan: putting people at the heart of public services'[10] was launched in June 2004 and contained priorities for the NHS up to 2008.

- The NHS was to ensure the drive for responsive, convenient and personalised services was embedded throughout all services and for all patients.
- Local communities were to have local services and greater influence over the way local resources were spent and local services run.
- There would be a new spirit ensuring the improvement of the personal experiences of patients as individuals.
- By meeting the needs of patients and the public, the NHS would thrive.

Key targets of another report, also published in 2004,[11] were to improve the patient experience and the choices that they have, resulting in more positive health benefits. Public involvement meanwhile would influence planning and development of services and increase confidence and understanding.

This report defines a 'patient-centred' consultation as:

> ... *shared control of the consultation, decisions about interventions or the management of health problems [made] with the patient and/or a focus in the*

consultation on the patient as a whole person who has individual preferences within social contexts.

It then goes on to say:

The experience of this kind of approach makes patients feel that they matter, that professionals are being honest with them, and that meaningful discussion is possible. In contrast, staff who are impatient, patronising or disrespectful, or who appear to be too busy, inhibit opportunities for involvement.

'Patient and Public Involvement in Health: the evidence for policy implementation', 2004[11]

The impact of the policies: evidence of progress

Meanwhile, the Commission for Healthcare Improvement (CHI) had been quietly accumulating evidence from up and down the country of the impact of the Patient and Public Involvement (PPI) policy. Following more than 300 inspections of NHS organisations, it produced a report in 2004, 'Involvement to Improvement',[12] that demonstrated that progress had been slow.

Whilst organisations *were* getting better at providing people with information and obtaining feedback, there was little to suggest that anyone, whether patient or public, was having any influence on decision making. Pockets of good practice were not being shared or picked up at a strategic level and PPI was neither integrated, nor a core part of thinking and everyday activity. There seemed to be many useful initiatives, but at that point in time these had failed to have a widespread impact so involvement was not leading to improvement.

The CHI's view was that there was a brick wall between PPI activities and any changes being made to health services. In order to overcome this, some best practice guidance was hurriedly produced by the Department of Health entitled 'Getting over the Wall: how the NHS is improving the patient's experience'.[13] This was an illustrative document that included many examples of how outputs from PPI activity had positively influenced service planning and development in the NHS. It made the following suggestions for NHS organisations (p.11):

- Be clear about what Section 11 of the Health and Social Care Act 2001 is requiring.
- Be clear about the role non-executive directors have about the PPI agenda. (They are not PPI 'champions' and do not lead on the agenda. At board meetings they must make sure that there are structures in place, and that the board is getting all the information it needs to monitor progress. Non-executive directors do not 'represent' the public. They are there to govern the organisation, by using their experiences in other fields and as residents in the areas they serve.)
- Understand that PPI is *everyone's* responsibility.
- Always consider the outputs from PPI activities when making decisions about planning and improving services.
- Make sure that PPI is not considered an 'add on' or as a separate agenda.
- Demonstrate how PPI makes a difference to the organisation's decision-making processes.

- Understand that small changes made as a result of what patients and the public have said are as important to improving the patient's experience as major service redesigns.
- Build on and celebrate small successes.
- Be aware of the language used.

It emphasised the importance of making choices real for patients and suggested that without involving patients and setting up and delivering choice locally, the NHS would simply swap one NHS-focused system for another.

Hang on a minute...

The massive change agenda of recent years, which has included a radically different way of defining the relationship between patients and clinicians, is something most healthcare workers have learned to tolerate. It could even be said to have generated its own responsive culture, with the more enthusiastic leaping to attention at the next government directive or inspection. This enthusiasm might just be tempered by fear for those nearer the top of the tree. Mostly, it seems to have been a question of juggling, keeping as many balls as possible in the air and hoping that if one or two of them get dropped, they will roll out of sight and nobody will miss them. Policy statements are fine but for those of us with our noses to the organisational grindstone, i.e. doing the juggling, we need to ask ourselves a few searching questions:

1 Have we got systems in place or is user involvement seen as a bolt-on extra to the main task of providing services?
2 Can we meet the deadlines of policy requirements, or are we simply scuttling to get it done for the sake of it, setting up a PALS office here, doing a survey there, but paying scant attention to the outcomes and how they should be influencing service development?
3 Have we ensured that the *real resources* needed by our staff and service users – the cash, the support networks, the training time and skills – have been embedded in the business planning processes?
4 What about *attitudes and values*? Do people really believe in developing mean-ingful partnerships or are they happy with traditional values and belief systems – the 'us and them' approach?

In other words are we motoring, entering into real partnerships with patients and the public, which means sharing power, or are we tinkering under the bonnet in order to tick the boxes, rather than changing thinking?

Understanding the challenge

Beneath this final question lies an uncomfortable challenge for healthcare pro-fessionals. Clearly if entering into partnerships involves sharing power, empower-ment for one group could mean that somebody else has to relinquish it; and I can imagine some clinicians saying, 'What about the years we have spent acquiring our professional skills, knowledge and expertise? Should patients really have a finger in every pie, influencing everything? Is our carefully and painstakingly acquired knowledge no longer to be respected?'

The straight answer to this is no, professional competence is not being questioned or undermined. On the contrary, people need to be affirmed in professional aspects of their roles; as knowledge increases and becomes ever more specialised, so does the need for experts who can make sense of its complexities. Where the confusion has arisen is in differentiating between areas of clinical knowledge and areas of partnership that recognise and value the wisdom of the service users' and carers' experience. Professional knowledge may feel as though it is under siege but this is far from the case.

However, there are many difficult issues to be negotiated and the question remains as to how much these have been recognised within healthcare professionals' training and acculturation processes when there is a tension between political correctness and addressing challenges. All too often we have been happy to play the service user involvement game until such time as our professional authority is challenged.[14] For example, spending time on giving people information or involving them in decision making may appear to create time pressures, although research has demonstrated that this is not necessarily the case. Professionals may lack knowledge and both they and patients may have limited interpersonal skills with which to communicate, and finally patients may express preferences that contradict those of the clinician or guidelines.[5] Are those of us who are working in the NHS able to face these difficult and demanding situations and respond to them in a way that enables us to meet the policy requirements by developing real partnerships?

A report published by the Picker Institute,[15] drawing together key findings from 15 national patient surveys carried out between 1998 and 2005, says that generally the quality of NHS care has improved during this period and that levels of satisfaction in relation to eight areas that patients consider most important are good. However, it cautions that although 'the quality of patients' experience in the NHS in England is improving, there is still a long way to go before the service can be said to be truly patient-centred'.

Anna Coote of the Healthcare Commission,[16] which assesses the performance of healthcare organisations, is more forthright: 'The NHS has still not got the hang of listening to patients.' Her view is that in spite of the policy-related structures and requirements, 'confusion, fragmentation and a lack of any common framework for developing theory and practice' inhibit cultural development, learning and change. Among the challenges she identifies are the lack of a 'mutually respectful collaboration' between the health system and the people it is for; the need for open-ended dialogue and time to work through and consolidate good ideas before being faced with yet another policy initiative; and the need for a coordinated approach that recognises the value of engaging patients and the public, knows how to do it and uses the knowledge that emerges to good effect.

These problems aren't just the result of poor policy implementation but could be in part because the familiar ways of interpreting it and measuring success are through traditional organisational models that collect, analyse and understand evidence that is based on scientific methodologies. There are frequent demands for evidence of progress, hard facts that demonstrate that requirements are being met. Equally frequent is the 'but it's only a box-ticking exercise' response, suggesting that the essence of what is to be measured is somehow escaping the measuring tool.

Nobody is suggesting condoning excuses that justify inertia. What is important is to recognise that involving patients and the public in their healthcare is indeed complex and standardised measurement tools may leave much of what is happening untouched and therefore invisible.

If we use a different and more subtle conceptual model such as complexity theory,[17] it enables us to 'view the world as a network of interacting systems where change in any one element can alter the context for all other elements'. This is a much more flexible and dynamic approach anticipating change as having open-ended and possibly unpredictable, even chaotic, consequences. Modern science sets a defined target output for a system. Outcomes are compared with predefined standards against which progress is assessed. Using complexity theory, we move away from this kind of prediction and control to a world where different and possibly unexpected patterns of order are established within the existing social systems. This sits much more comfortably with the need to establish new connections and different ways of thinking about PPI policy.

Be this as it may, policy 'must-dos' remain and it is these that we shall be considering in Chapter 3 before taking the plunge into the murky waters of organisational cultural change.

Summary

We started the chapter by considering clinical governance, a policy requirement of the late 1990s, and how it should link with the personal experience of patients. In other words, what should clinical governance actually feel like to those on the receiving end?

This was followed by a look at other social factors influencing health policy development, such as the curtailed power of some professionals counterbalanced by the interpretation of health services as a marketable commodity with patients as 'consumers' with the right to choose what they want. Reference was also made to the influence of the technological revolution and the ever-accelerating haste and demand for instant responses which typify today's culture. Other linked factors influencing policy development and our response to it, such as our do-it-yourself culture and the immediacy and availability of information, were also considered.

The policy developments appear to have resolved some of the accountability issues by making the NHS more risk-aware with structures for dealing with concerns and complaints, but arguably have done little to influence the thinking within organisations to promote cultures that demonstrate democratic partnerships.

Following national consultation, the NHS Improvement Plan[10] was published. This document signalled an attempt to put people at the heart of public services, the aim being to improve the patient experience and their choices, resulting in more positive health benefits. The idea was that patients should feel that they mattered.

However, evidence of positive progress is sparse and as a result further guidance has been produced. A number of challenges have been identified. Do healthcare organisations have the systems and resources to cope with patient and public involvement? Can they meet the policy deadlines and how do staff feel about the apparent challenge to their professional competence if they are to enter into partnership with service users and carers? The challenge is not what it seems as we need to differentiate between clinical knowledge and knowledge gained through experience of being a patient.

Complexity theory is proposed as a more realistic and action-orientated way of understanding outcomes to the policy.

Chapter 3 moves us closer to the coalface as it describes the policy 'must-dos', the things that healthcare organisations should have been doing on which service user and carer-related performance has been monitored. Chapter 10 of the NHS Plan 2000[18] spelt out the detail, a comprehensive package of reform that included notions of citizenship and community engagement. This was further reinforced with the introduction of specific structures identified in the Health and Social Care Act of 2001.[19] Some recommendations such as PALS and patient surveys were not legally required but provided useful clues about progress with the PPI agenda, and star ratings have certainly improved performance – but cultural change? Well, that's another story that we shall consider in Part 2 'The reality of policy implementation'.

References

1 Department of Health. *A First Class Service: quality in the new NHS*. London: DoH; 1999.
2 Department of Health. Learning from Bristol: the report of the public inquiry into children's heart surgery at the Bristol Royal Infirmary. 1984–1995. London: DoH; 1999.
3 Taylor H, Leitman R. New data show internet, website and e-mail usage by physicians all increasing. *Healthcare News*. 1(8): 1–3.
4 Chambers R, Drinkwater C, Boath E. *Involving Patients and the Public: how to do it better*. Oxford: Radcliffe Publishing; 2003.
5 Say R, Thomson R. The importance of patient preferences in treatment decisions: challenges for doctors. *BMJ*. 2003; **327**: 542–5.
6 Greenwood J. Employing a range of methods to meet patient information needs. *Prof Nurse*. 2002; **18**(4): 233–6.
7 Armstrong K. Creativity cannot be hurried. *The Guardian*, 24 April 2004.
8 Hutton W. When do we want it? Now. *The Observer*, 13 July 2003.
9 Department of Health. *Building on the Best: choice, responsiveness and equity*. London: DoH; 2003.
10 Department of Health. *NHS Improvement Plan: putting people at the heart of public services*. London: DoH; 2004.
11 Department of Health. *Patient and Public Involvement in Health: the evidence for policy implementation*. London: DoH; 2004.
12 Department of Health. *Involvement to Improvement*. London: DoH; 2004.
13 Department of Health. *Getting over the Wall: how the NHS is improving the patient experience*. London: DoH; 2004.
14 Rhodes P, Nocon A. User involvement in the NHS reforms. *Health Expectations*. 1998; **1**: 73–81. Blackwell Science Ltd.
15 Picker Institute Europe. Is the NHS Getting Better or Worse? An in-depth look at the views of nearly a million patients between 1998 and 2004. Oxford: Picker Institute;18 April 2005.
16 Coote A. Policy briefs. Think tank. *Guardian Society*, 20 April 2005.
17 Kernick D. Organisational culture and complexity. In: Kernick D (ed.) *Complexity and Healthcare Organization*. Oxford: Radcliffe Publishing; 2004.
18 Department of Health. The NHS Plan. Cm. 4818.1. London: DoH; 2000.
19 Department of Health. Health and Social Care Act. London: DoH; 2001.

3

'You *will* reach for the stars': policy requirements

The missing link

For readers who don't work in the Health Service, it might sound as though you could give this chapter a miss. These are the things that 'they' have to be seen to do in the Health Service, rather than anything that might affect you – but think again. Last Christmas I found myself cornered on three separate occasions by relatives anxious to sound me out because of my health service connection. To me, the solution was obvious. 'Have you come across PALS?' I would ask, only to be met by blank stares of incomprehension. Was this some new brand of dog food, and what on earth had it got to do with their various tales of difficulty and frustration in getting the help they needed from the NHS? In response, a further question arises. What is the point in setting up a service to 'deal with people's issues and concerns before they get to the stage of complaints' if they don't know it is there or are too anxious to use it for fear of contaminating future healthcare needs because of being seen as a 'nuisance'? No doubt all of the NHS organisations they were in contact with could comfortably tick the box that said, yes, they had a Patent Advice and Liaison Service (PALS). The real questions are: do people know about it and how much is it used? Staff may well feel they have done everything they can to respond to a policy directive. If that response fails to result in uptake of a support opportunity created by new policy, even though a new structure has been put in place, then it has clearly failed. It's like having a state-of-the-art plasma screen television with no electricity supply to connect it to. This is a neat example of exactly the sort of situation that complexity theory, mentioned at the end of Chapter 2, recognises. It is the work that is being done to ensure that the service is known about and used, not the existence of the service, that is most important.

My grandson Ben is of an age when he delights in all things wheeled, especially tractors and diggers. For his second birthday treat, we took him to a theme park called Diggerland near Taunton, absolutely stuffed with real working diggers. Ben's joy knew no bounds when he set eyes on the first one. When he turned round, pointing, to tell us about it, he saw another. And then there was another and another. He simply couldn't believe his eyes. Policy is a bit like that for those of us in the business except that instead of joy, it gives one a heartsink feeling. No sooner have you got your head round one bit then there's more – and more, and more. All of this creates so many obligations at so many different levels that we never have a chance to see if it is really working or to benefit from learning that takes place as part of the implementation process. Anna Coote[1] likens this situation to that of abandoned villages with all sorts of useful objects and artefacts simply left behind because people have been forced to move on. Her answer is, if possible, to protect people from 'politicians with short attention spans and serial enthusiasms'. Ministers need to make their mark but we can certainly spare a thought for healthcare workers whose heads are spinning with the pressures and demands that are generated as a result. Unfortunately, there is little we can do about a political process more concerned with expediency and a five-year electoral cycle than consolidated and longer-term social benefits.

Returning to our theme of 'must-dos' for this chapter, we need to revisit the NHS Plan of 2000.[2] This contained recommendations that were not enshrined in law, therefore not technically 'must-dos', but nevertheless created definite obligations for provider organisations.

This was all part of what was seen as a new system of Patient and Public Involvement aimed at putting the patient at the centre of everything the NHS was doing. Two aspects not requiring legislation were the introduction of the PALS, already mentioned, and the requirement for regular trust surveys to monitor patient and carer experiences and satisfaction levels. More of these surveys anon.

Patient Advice and Liaison Service (PALS)

I have been in the Health Service most of my working life and know its language. You would think I'd be reasonably confident when visiting my local GP, that I could voice the things that were concerning me without coming away feeling that I'd not been able to get it out right or ask about what I wanted to know. Not a bit of it. All too often I've come home only half reassured and without the answer to something that may have seemed trivial but was really bugging me. This feeling is common and is why PALS seemed such a good idea.

The original intention was that by April 2002, every NHS trust and primary care trust (PCT) should have a PALS service available to deal effectively with patients' issues and concerns before they became problems. They were to network across organisational boundaries and to send anonymous reports to the local Patients' Forum to act as an early warning system, detecting, reporting and where possible resolving problems before they escalated. Outcomes to their work were to be reported in each trust's Patients' Prospectus. You will notice, of course, that this is the first real mention of both Patients' Forums and Patients' Prospectuses, both of which had yet to take shape. This is one of the difficulties when a whole raft of new legislation is introduced; it takes time for the different components of the whole system to be developed and put in place. If you are working on one of the initial aspects such as PALS, it's a bit like the famous Pont d'Avignon – you set off to walk across it and find that it ends in mid-air because the last bit doesn't exist. This inevitably results in insecurity as those who are attempting to develop the new system have to take bits of it on trust, not a propitious way to launch a scheme. PALS had four key functions:

1 to answer questions about care and to give information
2 to advise and support patients and their families
3 to respond to concerns if people were unhappy about aspects of their care
4 to listen to suggestions for improving services, and to pass them on.

For acute trusts, often with a single hospital base, the NHS Plan suggestion was that there should be an office in the front foyer, peopled with friendly hospital 'Red-coats', who would be available to listen and respond via a drop-in service. For ambulance trusts and community-located services with anything up to 70 or 80 different geographical bases, this arrangement was simply not workable. It was just as difficult for the developing PCTs, some of which also covered huge areas. In the absence of any guidance, a popular solution has been to recognise that if staff are doing their job properly, then patients should feel able to mention to them the things that are worrying them directly, without the need for an external advocate. The fact that this wasn't happening suggested the need for an extensive/intensive staff training programme. Many trusts have responded by giving all of their staff PALS training and responsibilities, with a small designated PALS team to help with the more complicated, time-consuming or perplexing issues. The idea was to heighten everyone's awareness, not just clinicians', that they could and should take responsibility for people's issues and concerns.

PALS is not the same as a complaints service, which has formal processes and time-related standards so that people who have dissatisfactions know that they are being taken seriously and, wherever possible, resolved. Opinions vary as to how closely linked PALS and a complaints service should be. Some trusts have put them within the same management structure. Others have kept them at arms length to emphasise the informal and supportive nature of the one and the statutory obligations of the other. Nevertheless, the NHS Plan gave PALS considerable authority. If necessary, the PALS worker had direct access to the chief executive and the power to negotiate immediate solutions, so PALS was no pushover. Many PALS workers would say even so that the going has been tough. Those who worked in isolation had to resist becoming the local dumping place for issues brought to them by patients that should have been dealt with by clinicians or ward managers. Below is an example.

Patients detained under a section of the Mental Health Act in forensic units are generally there for many months. During this time they may not be able to leave the compound. One of these patients complained that the windows were dirty and he couldn't see outside. This complaint had been made to staff but when nothing was done about it he contacted the PALS person. She could see that the windows were indeed dirty and discovered that there was a monthly contract arrangement with a local window cleaner who was being paid regularly but not doing the job. No member of staff appeared to have specific responsibility for following this up, nor was there a system for checking that it had been done. This meant that not only was the patient dissatisfied but the trust was spending money on a service that it wasn't getting.

One can understand nurses feeling that in this example the state of the windows is not a clinical role, but if it isn't then whose is it? Staff may resent being reminded of things they have missed which, like this one, may not appear to have profound clinical implications or is not part of their high-powered clinical toolkit. Nevertheless, it is all part of that patient's experience of the service and therefore matters. It also provides useful clues about an organisation's culture. Are the people who work behind the scenes to make sure that the environment is safe, comfortable, fresh and clean doing it because 'it's a job'? Or are they doing it because that's how they would like it to be for themselves? Facilities, estates and finance directors who have overall responsibility for these areas should be just as concerned as clinicians about the quality of service provided. This is why monitoring of PALS issues, complaints and feedback mechanisms has been of considerable interest to healthcare commissioners, as an indicator of organisational responsiveness and culture.

> *The last three people I talked to who had made a formal complaint said that if only there had been someone to listen to them and help them sort things out, they'd never have needed to complain.*
>
> NHS Trust Service Relations Manager

And so to surveys and the Patients' Prospectus

Another 'informal' requirement of the NHS Plan of 2000 was that trusts should undertake systematic and rigorous monitoring of patient and carer experience and satisfaction. This information was to be published, with details of actions taken to remedy any shortcomings, in an annual Patients' Prospectus, to be distributed to all households within each PCT area.

It took a while for the survey programme to get established although it was first announced in a policy document, 'The New NHS: modern, dependable', in 1997.[3] Fifteen surveys have been undertaken since then in England, starting in 1998. More recently, the Healthcare Commission has taken to overseeing a comprehensive patient survey programme. This has been done in conjunction with the Picker Institute Europe where an NHS Surveys Advice Centre has designed, developed and coordinated the surveys. It has the advantage of ensuring national consistency and the creation of a UK survey dataset facilitating comparative monitoring between trusts and different parts of the country. A national health service should be equally good, wherever we live. Survey datasets are publicly available through the UK Data Archive held at Essex University.

Undertaking the surveys has been made a great deal easier through the provision of detailed advice for every stage (available on the Department of Health's survey website). This too must have improved the consistency and generalisability of the results. At a national level, the streamlining of the survey process and the external analysis of results has made it easier to make comparisons. Locally, results can easily be misinterpreted if staff are not wise to the subtleties of data analysis. For example, a response to the question 'Were the activities provided by the day centre helpful?' that put a trust in the top performing 20% of all trusts could suggest that its day centre was flourishing with no more questions asked. Supposing there were a low number of respondents to this question, there could be a range of reasons for this apparently good performance. Had the sample of people completing the survey simply bypassed the day centre population? Or, if the sample was representative, were the few people who attended genuinely enthusiastic and, if so, should more people be benefiting from this helpful service? What was it about the day centre programme that was appreciated and should this be introduced elsewhere? This is an example of box-ticking par excellence. Yes, the survey has been done, but the tool may be insufficiently sensitive to capture all-important detail reflecting local need to inform and influence future service development.

The Picker Institute Europe has published a useful compilation of results[4] that relates to eight aspects of healthcare that patients consider most important. These are:

1 fast access to health advice
2 effective treatment delivered by staff you can trust
3 involvement in decisions and respect for patients' preferences
4 clear, comprehensible information and support for self-care
5 physical comfort and a clean, safe environment
6 emotional support and alleviation of anxiety
7 involvement of family and friends and support for carers
8 continuity of care and smooth transitions.

In summarising its findings, the report says:

> *Priority areas which have been the focus of coordinated action and investment, such as waiting times, cancer care and coronary heart disease, have seen major improvements. Levels of satisfaction with NHS care are high and improving, but these overall ratings mask some key problem areas.*
>
> *...patients still want more information, more involvement in decisions about their care, more help when transferring from hospital to home, and easier access to their GP with appointments at more convenient times.*
>
> *Hospital cleanliness is of increasing concern to many patients.*
>
> *Many patients need better help with pain relief and more information about medication side-effects.*
>
> *The quality of patients' experience of the NHS in England is improving, but there's still a long way to go before the service can be said to be truly patient-centred.*

So although we seem to know exactly what it is that people consider important about their healthcare, we are still missing the mark. And we are missing it by quite a long way, as may be demonstrated by the response to the Patients' Prospectus. In an attempt to give everybody information about their local services and show them how money was being spent, the Department of Health required all PCTs to publish a leaflet entitled 'Your Guide to Local Health Services'. This was to be delivered to all homes in their area to provide local information about services and to demonstrate responsiveness to the patients' feedback, and accountability. As with the surveys, clear instructions were given as to how they were to be set out, produced and distributed. An initial survey by MORI, the independent market research company, found the guides to be informative and useful. There was evidence to suggest that they may be changing behaviour with people making more use of NHS Direct and local support groups, in other words taking more responsibility for their own state of health.

However, the MORI survey[5] established that only 12% of their sample population said they had received a guide. This was higher in the Humber region (22%), lower in Essex (5%). Of these, 16% had read it all or nearly so, 21% had read most of it, 12% a few sections, 30% had just glanced at it and the remaining 21% hadn't bothered although 50% had kept it for 'future reference'. This means that for every 1000 people who had received a copy, around 19 actually read it. So, although the surveying process itself may have become more rigorous and comprehensive, circulation of information may be inadequate and it would appear that the general public is, on the whole, indifferent to what is provided, at least in this format.

Perhaps like telephone cold-calling, for many people it is just another leaflet dropping through the door to be binned. Or we may be confused and just want things to get better in a straightforward way without all the detail, the sort of way we would all like to remain in perfect health, never grow old, and not succumb to illness and uncertainty or fearful accidents or ultimate death. Is the Health Service bombarding us with information about how much better it can always do in an attempt to insulate us from our immature inability to reconcile ourselves to our mortality? We want the NHS how we want it when we need it, otherwise perhaps we simply don't want to know.

Star ratings

Star ratings picked up on the key areas identified in the NHS Plan, although they varied according to the type of trust and the services it provided. The system monitored NHS trusts' performance on an annual basis in relation to government targets. This meant that it was no longer possible for organisations to snatch at the bits of policy they thought they could manage or that some senior executive had a particular enthusiasm for or that were attached to the next most urgent deadline. For mental health, acute and ambulance trusts, there was a cluster of targets relating to clinical and patient focus, capacity and capability (i.e. staffing issues) and performance in clinical governance reviews conducted by the Healthcare Commission. These reviews were important as they focused on the quality of clinical care: Is it safe? Is it effective? Is it up to date? Is it an efficient use of resources?

For primary care trusts the targets were to demonstrate health improvement activity, i.e. what they were doing to keep people healthy, how easy they were making it for people to see a doctor if they needed to, and what sort of services were provided when they got there. There was also consideration of clinical governance reviews to look at the quality of those services. Within all these target areas there were a number of indicators that demonstrated levels of achievement contributing to a zero, one, two or three-star rating. All of this information is publicly available via the Healthcare Commission's website which means that comparisons could be made and benchmarking undertaken. A zero rating is not good news for any trust but those who have achieved the dizzy heights of three stars have been able to apply for foundation trust status. This gives them greater autonomy with freedom to innovate and improve care for patients, and local accountability, all within a framework of clear national standards and inspection.

Technically, star ratings have been 'a good thing', although they are now being replaced by a more comprehensive 'annual health check' which is said to be less target driven. Even so, they have addressed many of the issues that concern us, such as how long we have to wait for different services or to be attended to if we arrive in the Accident and Emergency department. They have considered whether we get enough information and whether we are seen in a clean, comfortable environment. They have considered the choices we are offered, whether trusts manage their budgets effectively, whether the services they provide actually work or not and how much at risk we are when we are receiving them. All of these issues and many more have been monitored by a whole battery of inspectors from different organisations such as the Audit Commission, the Healthcare Commission, the Mental Health Act Commission, the Commission for Social Care Inspection, the National Audit Office, the NHS Litigation Authority and more. Recognising that their combined demands of trusts might leave the trusts little time for the real work of seeing patients, they signed a concordat. This committed each inspecting organisation to a set of principles to support improvement in the quality and performance of health services whilst minimising disruption and duplication. The focus was on the patients' experience and that of other service users and carers. As well as inspection, they monitored existing datasets and used remote information (for example, consulting with voluntary sector groups) and organisational self-assessment to formulate recommendations, linked to a template for effective action planning. Poorly performing trusts have found themselves subject to enforcement powers to ensure action and improvement.

This is all grand stuff and has contributed to well-recognised improvements in waiting times, standards of care and some outcomes. However, we may be left wondering how much it has to do with the aspects of care that patients consider most important, mentioned earlier from the Picker Institute Report, while Professor Sir Ian Kennedy's strong but compassionate and patient-orientated recommendations (*see* Chapter 2) hardly get a look in. This might be surprising were it not for the fact that as Chairman of the Healthcare Commission he has overseen the revision of the role of the now defunct Commission for Healthcare Improvement. It is now a much more tightly defined inspectorate, an iron fist inside a velvet glove, requiring specific and detailed evidence of progress. It is as though he is saying enough is enough, we need to demonstrate that the money we are pouring into the Health Service is making a difference. This has come through star ratings which have understandably consumed the attention and energy of chief executives, board members and senior managers. Those near the top of the tree may have aspired to foundation trust status and those at the bottom simply wanted to keep their jobs. But the declared focus on the patients' experience still retains an outsider feeling, as though all this frantic activity is being done *to* us as service users, rather than done *with* us. How can this change?

How can we think about it differently, in order to do it differently? This is the theme for Part 2. Before moving on, however, we need to avoid a particular trap, and that is the danger of only considering the things that should be done *within* healthcare organisations, rather than looking at collaborative aspects of the PPI requirements. It would be easy at this stage to suggest that having identified the main requirements placed on NHS trusts, we can retreat to our healthcare ghetto and ignore or at least pay less attention to other interagency policy arrangements. This might seem very obvious; numerous joint working partnerships and committees regularly thrash out the detail of how they should be working together in response to policy demands. It is only when inquiry reports land on the table that we realise how superficial some of our work has been and how very difficult it is to even recognise, let alone reconcile, our cultural differences.

Working together on PPI

Recognising that no single agency can possibly accommodate the whole gamut of health and social care needs, there is much talk among strategists and managers about 'seamless' services as though the boundaries between different agencies should be invisible. As far as those of us who need and use services are concerned, it is a well-known fact that we tend not to care who it is who provides the service, as long as we get it. From this perspective, perhaps, it should be seamless. However, given the number of inquiries that have criticised the nature of interagency collaboration, we should pay much more attention to the very real differences that exist between us, both in what we do and how we do it. In order that the services should be strongly connected, we should be aware of the nature of the joins and how we can strengthen them so that they are 'seamed' and not 'seamless'. Here's an actual example which shows how easily we can trip over our under-standing of where we are each coming from:

> Social worker (about a nursing report of a particular patient): 'I can't make head nor tail of this report – it doesn't give an opinion about the patient or tell me what decisions were reached.'
>
> Nurse: 'We always work as a multidisciplinary team and discuss what should happen next together. What I've written is about my nursing contact with the patient. If anyone has to write a report it's usually the consultant – after all, s/he's the legal can-carrier if things go wrong.'

The difference here is that it is part of the social worker's job to write their own reports and, if necessary, to present them in court, possibly leading to significant decisions. Healthcare decisions are usually made following discussion with a multi-disciplinary team. No one person has identified individual responsibility for a particular decision, except the consultant who holds ultimate legal responsibility, or in some cases the team leader. Under these circumstances, a nurse might feel very exposed if required to write a report and might well sit on the fence rather than give a specific opinion. This is a difference in practice and culture, not an example of inadequacy in report writing, but it is unlikely in the example given that the nurse and the social worker felt they understood each other or had confidence in their respective skills.

The usual response to healthcare policy that requires a collaborative approach is for the lead agency to set up a training programme to which all are invited, often including service users and carers. This is done on the assumption that learning 'together', with everyone being exposed to the same information, will result in everyone coming away with a common understanding of what it is about. Not so. Different experiences, different ways of thinking about what we do, different legal responsibilities and different ways of monitoring activity will all contribute to differences in understanding. Give everyone the same recipe for a cake and they will all produce something different because there will be qualitative differences between the ingredients. The answer to this is not to retreat to professional ghettos but to anticipate the difficulty and allow time and a safe environment in which to explore issues, doubts and concerns together. It also suggests more careful consideration on the part of policy makers.

There is no doubt that working together is much harder than it seems, and this can apply to different disciplines working together within teams as well as links between healthcare and other agencies. One detail of the NHS Plan which was required to happen by 2004, but which has been causing problems, was the 'clinician to clinician' letter being routinely copied to patients. There are constant exchanges of referral letters and reports passing from one clinician to another. These may use highly technical language or refer to sensitive interpersonal situations and highly confidential material or occasionally contain forthright opinions irrelevant to the person's health condition. The attempt to minimise anxiety and 'protect' patients (and, it must be said, sometimes clinicians themselves) by not sharing what has been written about them with them has been well intentioned. However, it suggests an inappropriate element of control and is a far cry from the notions of partnership that are currently being championed.

PPI Forums

An important link for anyone concerned with making the connection between patients and the public should be their trust's PPI Forum. Legislated for via the NHS Reform and Healthcare Professions Act 2002,[6] which also dictated the demise of community health councils (CHCs) and their supporting association, PPI Forums got off to a belated start in December 2003. The idea was that they should comprise local volunteers who would play an active role in health-related decision making in their own communities. Every NHS trust and every PCT in England was to have one and they were to be supported by a Forum Support Organisation and a regional centre for the Commission for Patient and Public Involvement in Health (CPPIH). That was the theory.

In practice, they have struggled. There was delay in their initiation and an over-hasty recruitment process in order to meet the CPPIH deadline. In addition, poor preparation for the daunting task of finding your way into the complexity of NHS organisations and systems has meant for some, a slow and hesitant start. This wasn't helped by a strong emphasis on their 'independence', resulting in considerable reluctance by some Forum members to have anything other than arms-length contact with the organisation they were supposed to be monitoring.

Many people regret the passing of the CHCs that had much the same function. Some of these were very active, well established and respected by local communities, others less so. As well as obtaining views from local people, members of PPI Forums have rights of inspection of trust facilities but their opportunities for doing this vary enormously. A Forum for a PCT may cover 20 or 30 general practices scattered across a large area whereas a Forum for an acute trust may only support a single hospital, and yet each may have a similar number of members, anything from seven to 20. The suggested time input is two to three hours per week per member but enthusiasm varies and some Forum members sometimes feel they are carrying the burden of involvement for their less active colleagues. More recent guidance has clarified some of these issues, for example roles of PCT Forum members have been differentiated from those of other trusts, and this is likely to enhance the efficiency and profile of Forums in the future.

Strengthening accountability to the local community

Healthcare organisations don't exist in isolation, they are there to serve a local community to whom they are accountable. This can only be demonstrated if there are ways for them to do it, structures and processes to support engagement between them. PALS enables an organisation to monitor and respond to issues and concerns experienced by people receiving its services before anything gets complicated. Feedback should come directly from someone in the organisation who has taken action where necessary, and reported on the outcome to the individual concerned. Next comes a more formal internal complaints process. This can be supported by an Independent Complaints Advocacy Service (ICAS), the key word here being 'independent'. Although the Department of Health has lead responsibility for ICAS, sets the quality standards and supports development, the actual service is delivered via four voluntary sector organisations. The task of their trained advocates is to support patients and their carers, provide them with information and guidance so that they can articulate their concerns and, if they wish, help them to find their way through the complaints system. With Patient and Public Involvement Forums having access (on an anonymous basis) to both PALS data and ICAS complaints, they should clearly be able to identify areas of concern within their particular trust. What is more, they have the opportunity to feed this information through to the trust board as they are represented at non-executive director level through co-option of one of their members onto the board. The top three areas for complaint over a single year of monitoring (September 2003 to August 2004) of ICAS activity were aspects of clinical treatment, staff attitudes and communication and information to patients.

In order to broaden the accountability network, a further structure was developed to undertake the role of health scrutiny: local authority Overview and Scrutiny Committees (OSCs). These comprised non-executive councillors who were to hold the executive to account about the economic, social and environmental well-being of an area. External scrutiny of the NHS was to complement and enhance the work being undertaken within the service by stimulating a sense of community responsibility and hence a local community voice. The value of this in broadening the responsibility for good health by linking it to education, housing and social care may have been implicit, rather than overt. Nevertheless, the signal was there and the opportunity for a joined-up local approach. The Committees have the authority to call NHS managers to provide information not only about major changes but also about ongoing planning and operational issues. They also have to be consulted by the NHS where major changes are to take place and they can refer contested changes to the Secretary of State. Their recommendations can be locally reported. All of this was seen as a means of creating a patient-centred NHS, promoting citizenship and being more open about accountability to the immediate community.

One final statutory duty defined within the Health and Social Care Act for NHS trusts, PCTs and strategic health authorities was to ensure that consultation was not a hollow gesture. As with the OSCs, they were to involve and consult with patients and the public, not just when major changes were afoot but also over ongoing service planning and development. Ideally, this was to happen when proposals were still on the drawing board, rather than presenting them for 'consultation' as a fait accompli. Overseeing all of this, PALS, the PPI Forums, ICAS, the OSCs and the statutory duty to consult and involve people was a new independent body, the

Commission for Patient and Public Involvement in Health. This reported to the Secretary of State and other national bodies on progress, but in 2004 it was subsumed within the Healthcare Commission.

Summary

This seemingly complicated network was how the government translated its vision of a patient-centred NHS into mechanisms for involving patients and the public. The grand plan was to improve the quality of services by listening and responding to what people had to say about their experience of them (PALS, ICAS), and by giving them more choices and ensuring rigorous standards of treatment and care which were both internally and externally monitored (PPI Forums, surveys etc.). Modernisation Agency funding (originally made available to support the NHS Plan) also meant that there was a massive cash injection to support this. Information was also a priority so that people were in a position to take more responsibility for decisions that previously had been made on their behalf, and therefore more responsibility for their health. Providing information was also to lead to greater participation in design, planning and development issues and more transparent decision-making processes in turn contributing to more actively involved citizens. A neat package – but a complex one.

So, if we are part of a healthcare organisation or are using one that has PALS, is in productive contact with its PPI Forum, that is surveying, writing its Patients' Prospectus, has got all three stars (or nearly), and has access to the various policy-defined structures and processes to ensure engagement between healthcare providers, patients and the public, is that it? Is it 'doing' patient and public involvement? On the one hand, yes. There has to be the will and an enormous amount of hard work to follow through these requirements in order to tick the boxes. On the other hand, as we have seen, having the required components in place doesn't necessarily mean that they are working as they should, and I would suggest that the problem lies in too much 'doing', not enough 'thinking'.

The interpretation, described in this chapter, of the policy-determined and patient-centred vision has been introduced with amazing speed. The statutory structures are in place and for the most part are starting to be effective, but what is going on within organisations? The evidence is that the balance of power still isn't right as people using our services still feel themselves to be 'outsiders' to the healthcare system in spite of the Kennedy Report exhortations. This is what Part 2 is about. It begins by describing a piece of research that drew attention to this difficulty and how it has affected policy implementation. It then goes on to tell the story of one particular trust where gradually the balance started to shift and then identifies some of the areas where the seeds of cultural change are more likely to find fertile soil.

References

1 Coote A. Policy briefs. Think tank. *Guardian Society*, 20 April 2005.
2 Department of Health. *The NHS Plan.* Cm. 4818.1. London: DoH; 2000.
3 Department of Health. *The New NHS: modern, dependable.* London: DoH; 1997.
4 Picker Institute Europe. Is the NHS getting better or worse? An in-depth look at the views of nearly a million patients between 1998 and 2004. Oxford: Picker Institute; 18 April 2005.
5 Market and Opinion Research International. *Winter Tracking Survey: public perception of the NHS.* London: MORI; 2003. http://www.mori.com/polls/2004nhs-tracker.shtml [Accessed 12 April 2006.]
6 Department of Health. NHS Reform and Healthcare Professions Act. London: DoH; 2002.

Part 2

The reality of policy implementation

Introduction

> *Out of the strong came forth sweetness.*
> *Tate & Lyle syrup tin (Old Testament, Judges 14, v.14)*

This part of the book is essentially practical and contains many ideas that could stimulate changes in how we as individuals approach the Patient and Public Involvement agenda. However, changing practice blindly, without understanding the whys and wherefores, is a recipe for limited, short-term success and longer-term failure: 'Oh, we've tried that before and it didn't work.' Changing ideas and ways of thinking is what is required. This is the reason for including Chapter 4 which describes a research project that stimulated some of the thinking in the organisation where much of the work was undertaken. It is in effect grounding, creating the opportunity for the seeds of change to be sown. It includes detailed research findings in order to demonstrate that sensitivity to underlying issues can contribute useful insights and a confident sense of direction.

The next chapter sets the scene by describing a newly merged organisation where the examples described were developed, and how the service which supported the involvement of patients and carers took shape (a 'trust timeline', showing progress, is included in the Appendix). It is not presented as a particular 'model' of how to do it, more as an individual case study reflecting organisational growth and change. There are some personal observations about being 'professional' and how this can distance those of us providing healthcare from patients in an unhelpful way.

Chapter 6 describes the early stages of an emerging new approach to involving people in their healthcare. Patients, carers and professional health carers worked together in a way that enabled them all to recognise their shared expectations of a good service from the point of view of someone who is on the receiving end. Staff attitudes, time-related issues, information and partnerships that really worked emerge as priority areas with attention to detail being an important way of demonstrating that staff were actually noticing and thinking about what it must feel like to be the person receiving healthcare. The introduction of an action planning group was the first step in attempting to share all of this knowledge throughout the organisation, and to stimulate awareness of how it might be able to better involve its service users and carers.

The 'Telling It Like It Is' process described in Chapter 6 triggered a series of important developments. The first of these was a courageous announcement by the trust's chief executive that led to real consideration of what the organisation was doing to demonstrate its commitment to its users' and carers' needs. This is described in Chapter 7. Creating employment opportunities for them was how it chose to interpret this commitment and this included detailed exploration of how other trusts had tackled the issue. The implications of the Disability Discrimination Act and the Positive about Disability Two Ticks Symbol are considered and the Heart of the Trust Scheme takes shape. Little by little, the 'tanker' changes direction...

Chapter 8 describes how one trust took a major step in promoting the involvement of people who had experience of its services as either users or carers by giving them jobs, not any old jobs but seats at the boardroom table. After researching how it might be achieved, six associate directors were appointed, had a thorough induction to introduce them to key people and enable them to move freely around the organisation, and then joined with the trust board in helping to run it. To do this they established networks and feedback cycles and set objectives both for themselves and their team. To support them, they had team development opportunities and individual supervision and mentoring. Most importantly, they were paid at the same rate as non-executive directors. The chapter includes examples of recruitment materials used.

So far we have largely been considering actions that resulted from a particular interpretation of Patient and Public Involvement policy. Chapter 9 describes the strategy that accompanied this approach and discusses some general points about developing strategies. It also considers how we can establish structures and systems which are sufficiently integrated to ensure that implementation of a strategy is not dependent on haphazard individual enthusiasms, but is part of a whole organisation culture. Checks and balances need to be identified and included to ensure that important aspects do not disappear into black holes, never to be seen again.

Chapter 10 takes a look at policies, protocols and procedures relating to service user and carer involvement, and why we need them. Straightforward definitions are given but it also considers where they fit with the integrated approach to policy and professional and personal experience of healthcare, which has been our recurrent theme. With this in mind, several examples are described. They demonstrate how a shift in the balance of power between service users, carers and healthcare workers can be threaded through an organisation. They also recognise that the going is not always easy in achieving this.

Part 2 of this book has looked at the development of an organisational culture that embodies the principles of real engagement identified in Part 1. In doing so we are reminded that organisations comprise individuals, who themselves will need to be supported by the organisation if they are to be effective. Chapter 11 takes a general look at some of the individual needs of those who are involved, whether they are staff, service users or carers. It also provides some final examples of what may be done to encourage a real partnership orientation. Further different examples can be found in contributors' chapters in Part 3. We are looking at individual actions now which show that 'partnership' thinking is well and truly integrated into people's everyday activity.

4

Rethinking how we interpret service user and carer policy

Introduction

In 1995, driving along between Bridgnorth and Wolverhampton, just past a pub called the Royal Oak, I had a 'eureka' experience, one which made me realise that I'd found the right question even if I didn't know the answer. Why is it, I thought, that there is such a gulf between what mental health policy makers say should be happening and what service users say they experience? Are those old chestnuts trotted out by the professionals – under-resourcing, power issues, poor communications and limited interagency collaboration – the real reasons why we can never seem to get it right, or is there something else going on? Or, rather, what *more* is going on which makes it so hard?

Fortunately for me, various planets were in conjunction. I had just got a job as a Care Programme Approach Coordinator, linked to a research opportunity. Whilst ensuring that the Care Programme Approach (CPA) was being properly implemented in my employing organisation, I was to evaluate progress across what was then a district health authority with two main providers of mental health services: my own trust and an adjacent one. I also embarked on a further piece of research to explore why there seemed to be a discontinuity between policy requirements and the experience of people on the receiving end of that policy. At this stage, I was unaware that although my research field was mental health, my findings could have much broader applicability.

Taking the Care Programme Approach as a specific example of mental health policy, I followed its progression from Whitehall to local healthcare organisations, past trust boards and their hierarchies of managers and clinical staff, until I reached those the policy was designed to benefit: the service users and carers. Exploring their thinking and that of the providers of the services they were receiving gave me valuable insights into their inter-relationship. I found that the principles that emerged related not only to mental health services and their users but were generalisable across healthcare services and specialisms.

So why describe details of the journey when it is the destination that matters? One reason is because if I didn't, you might wonder what evidence there was for the insights I shall be describing. Another is that it is the attention to apparently insignificant detail which gives us clues about how meaningful change can be accomplished. Too much of what we are now expected to do in the Health Service feels as though it is imposed on a 'do it' basis, without consideration of the complexity of how it will be achieved. I want to draw attention to this complexity. It provides important indicators of how change can be brought about and should not be ignored. It is on this foundation that much of the material in this book was built.

A policy model: the Care Programme Approach

A key component of community-orientated mental health services was the requirement for collaboration between several different agencies, and it has been the limitations of integrated working that has been highlighted when things have gone wrong. This was demonstrated in inquiries as long ago as the Spokes Report in 1988.[1] The Care Programme Approach[2] was introduced as a response to these limitations and became a requirement in April 1991. It was heralded as the cornerstone of the government's mental health policy and was initially a response to major concerns that had been brewing for some time in the UK over the care and aftercare of those who might previously have been admitted to hospital, but who were increasingly being supported by services based in the community. There was also concern that the newly developing community mental health teams were drifting away from treating the most severely mentally ill in favour of those with more tractable problems.

The policy had stipulated that the CPA should be health led and was to comprise a systematic arrangement for assessing and reviewing the health and social care needs of people who might be about to be discharged from hospital but who could also be treated in the community. The details of how it was to be implemented were left to practitioners but the key components were the need for regular assessment and review, the importance of interprofessional working and keeping in touch with patients, the need for involvement of users and carers, and coordination of the process by a named individual, the key worker or care coordinator. These key components have not changed but there continues to be difficulties with their interpretation. The policy also had a strong collaborative focus, providing a model of engagement for whichever disciplines or agencies might be called upon to contribute to an individual's care plan. As a sound, common-sense approach to care management, the model is one which resonates as much for district nurses and health visitors as it does for those in the mental health field.

Looking for clues: the start of the journey

Before focusing on the particular policy, I thought I had better check the accuracy of those chestnuts: the poor resourcing, power issues, poor communication and interagency working. Various reports on the CPA[3,4] had implicated them, but how much were they a smokescreen behind which lurked other issues? And yes, my exploration of these documents and associated reports on progress clearly demonstrated that mental health policy implementation had suffered for decades, indeed nearly two centuries, because of all the traditionally identified problems. The question in my mind was: if we've known about this for so long, why are we still wading through treacle, apparently unable to change things for the better?

Inevitably, it was complex. For example, as a new piece of policy, CPA had not had any resources attached to it, the justification being that it wasn't new, it was simply a case of doing things differently. Innovation *can* of course be revenue neutral, but the immediate requirement to train large numbers of staff in a new procedure, not to mention administrative costs, made it obvious that there were indeed hidden costs that had either been ignored or not anticipated, but that nevertheless had to be met. Shepherd[5] has identified the myth of 'free' staff time, for example senior ward staff being able to take time out to attend a training or development session while their juniors, the least experienced staff, keep an eye on things back at base. Free time it certainly isn't and it could be argued that if wards are to be deprived of staff, it should be those who are confident about what they are doing who should hold the fort, not the least secure. Failure to recognise the cost implications of adequate training and support, failure to clarify areas of responsibility in relation to this training and also lack of thought as to its content all contributed to poor uptake of the model.

However, the fact remains that some trusts did manage to find internal resources to pay for a worker to support the initiative on a day-to-day basis and these trusts reported much better progress than the rest. This, of course, weakened the claim that there should have been an external resource allocation and demonstrated that it was indeed possible to improve policy implementation at a local level *without* extra funding. This suggested that 'resource limitations', in this instance at least, were being used as a mantra, obscuring the need for more precise analysis.

All of this was evidenced in relation to the implementation of the Care Programme Approach, as a number of studies had demonstrated. Progress since 1991 had been so slow and ineffective that in 1995 the then Secretary of State for Health Gerald Malone, seeing the results of a national audit, issued a stern directive that what we hadn't managed to get sorted in four years had better be sorted within the next four months, or else.

The importance of informal relationships in interpreting policy

Lipsky[6] has suggested that informal relationships within the working situation are just as important as those which are structurally defined. He called it 'street-level bureaucracy', his idea being that people will find their own personal and unauthorised solutions to organisational problems and uncertainties posed by a particular policy, especially where it may conflict with their professional values and culture. When aggregated, these solutions amount to a street-level interpretation and in effect *become* that policy. It is not a deliberate attempt to sabotage policy intentions but a product of numerous decisions requiring individual discretion.[7] This is very significant in relation to the tradition of professionals' clinical autonomy, not to mention the isolation of community practice leading to unsanctioned decision making.

So, it becomes clear that although policy may appear to determine the grand scheme of things, it is subject to the differing ways people think about it and interpret it. Where a lot of people are involved, for example in a large organisation, what emerges will be the result of their collective thinking, not necessarily the policy as it was originally designed. This opens up the possibility that 'reinterpretation' of the CPA was not in accord with the original policy design.

Unravelling the policy process and perceptions of progress

From the various national reports, it was already clear that this particular policy didn't appear to be working very well. At a local level, two audits seven months apart demonstrated that although progress *was* being made, the all-important community links that were supposed to provide the 'net of community care' were extremely limited. However, this account, based on the audit findings rather than being evidence of actions, was in fact *what was recorded* as evidence – clearly not necessarily the same thing.

The local perception of progress might also be different for both individual providers and recipients of the services, and if there was a discrepancy in their views, what was going on within the organisation and between key participants to influence this process?

Everybody will have a different view of what is progress, which will have been filtered through their different perceptions, values and beliefs. However, what people actually do to make policy changes happen isn't an individual thing because we don't work in isolation – we are constantly interacting and negotiating with colleagues.[8] If we are going to find out more about policy implementation, we need to put together all the different understandings that we have as individuals and find out what the experiences are that are common to them all. The more we find out from individuals, the more accurate a picture will emerge of their common experiences, what has worked and what has not.

Uncovering the 'private perspectives'

Staff interviews and patient discussion groups created opportunities to get under the skin of the more private worlds of people's experience, the objective being to go beyond organisational views and obtain qualitative insights. What I wanted to know about were the practical difficulties associated with policy implementation, but also people's view of their involvement, how it had become part of their thinking and how this influenced their actions. Specific examples demonstrated that things were not what they seemed.

1. Information proved to be a significant area

I looked at what people – both staff and service users – received and what they passed on, the importance that they attached to it and how they prioritised it, what they wanted and didn't get, and what they got but didn't need. Information is power so I was able to use it to explore how important different staff groups were to each other and how this influenced their priorities. For example, there was a huge number of complaints from staff about 'information overload' – too much paper-work, difficulties with the computer system and dislike of bureaucratic form-filling – but clinicians were prepared to spend time unsuccessfully attempting to engage GPs and bemoaned their lack of success. Clinical staff were, however, very aware of the need to provide evidence of their activity in order to protect themselves in the event of litigation. Although this was seen as a priority, it was also viewed as a tiresome necessity, rather than a useful aid to the review of working practice or as a means of negotiating a patient's care plan.

Meanwhile, service users and carers were desperate for *exchanges* of information, knowing more about their illnesses and their medication but also wanting to *tell* staff about their experiences:

> *... people want more information but there's a gulf between feeling that what you have experienced is important enough to be communicated to other people. You know the difficulties that you've lived with but that doesn't seem to count somehow. People seem to want all these highly technical things when the real experience is what you've had at home, day after day.*
>
> Service User

In addition, carers experienced unfavourable discrimination because staff expected them to provide information whilst being reluctant themselves to divulge anything. This was done in the interests of patient 'confidentiality'. This looked very much like the trappings of authority with information retention being used as a device to sustain that position.

People's relationship with information, information exchanges, the value they attached to it and how they prioritised it was clearly a significant indicator of skewed power relations within the organisation, contributing to a very limited sense of reciprocal trust between users and those delivering services.

2. *Key working was another productive area*

Key workers are usually clinicians, acting as the reference point for each individual service user. There had been an assumption by policy makers that clinical and administrative responsibilities could be conveniently combined in the role, but it was deeply unpopular with staff, partly because it created additional work, and also because it was unaccompanied by any authority:

> *It makes an attempt to bring adequate awareness to all concerned, of someone who may be in difficulties, but it doesn't give you any adequate powers to manage that situation.'*
>
> Operational Manager

According to Lipsky,[6] front-line practitioners do not see themselves as working within a particular ideology and they can therefore deliberately evade or dispense with associated values and beliefs and the manipulation of them by their superiors. So, data collection and administrative tasks, both required of key workers, could be dismissed as of lesser importance than their professional role. Certainly they were reluctant to combine the two, even though for service users this was exactly what they wanted: their own benign and practical 'fixer' with professional knowledge.

Many of the users' dissatisfactions with their experience of CPA were to do with this coordinating role being poorly carried out. The model of care within the policy made sense to them, especially the importance of the key individual who was their point of contact with services. They wanted involvement at all stages and to be considered as equals in the therapeutic process. They communicated a strong sense of the importance of the *individual* as their means of accessing help, rather than the team, which was the professionals' preferred model.

Ambivalence on the part of staff was further reinforced by organisational signals such as the resourcing of clinical support in preference to administrative back-up, possibly because senior managers, responsible for the choice, themselves all had a clinical background and strong professional identification. Directors and executives were also not immune to the professional influence; when resources were limited (and they are never anything else), a virtue was made of putting money into patient services rather than organisational supports which might have ensured more efficient service delivery. All of this suggested that although professionals were *seen* to be subsumed within a bureaucratic framework,[7] it was an uneasy alliance and one which it was possible for them to subvert to their advantage.

3. A final example: the difference between words and deeds

The majority of staff said that being told what to do was *not* a good motivator and, predictably, when asked about leadership style, their apparent preference was for a democratic approach. Wanting to benefit patients was seen as a positive motivator and even executives and directors saw themselves as working with users and carers on a person-focused approach in which patients were knowledgeable participants. However, a different account emerged suggesting that hierarchical organisational obligations actually demanded the opposite:

> *The only way to get things done is with an authoritative leader.*
>
> *Operational Manager*

> *Clinicians are having to come to terms more and more with who gets a service and who doesn't or actually providing less of a service than they used to. If I don't nag the ones who are overspent, I'm prejudicing the ones who are handling their money properly, so although I'd like to be democratic, I'm having to be authoritarian.*
>
> *Senior Manager*

> *Sometimes it simply has to be 'do it'.*
>
> *Senior Manager*

These examples suggest a culture of telling people what to do that is likely to be extended to the service users, reflected in this comment:

> *They should ask us what we need, not tell us what they want us to do.*
>
> *Service User*

In other words, at a personal and individual level, people espoused choice, shared responsibility and negotiated decision making. When filtered through the requirements of professional obligations within a hierarchical organisational framework, these egalitarian values were subverted and lost. The overall outcome was a marked disparity between what staff *said* was happening in terms of policy implementation and the users' experience.

Overlapping roles: healthcare professional as administrator

Chris Argyris[9] has commented upon the contrast in behaviour of people who in their social and family lives are self-motivating, honest about their emotions and values, and take responsibility for themselves as individuals in society, and then become dependent, passive to their superiors and avoid taking individual responsibility when their actions are framed by a professional or organisational structure.

Clinicians were disaffected by the administrative aspects of their key working role and this diluted their interest in implementing policy, but there is another aspect to this. Community nurses – no matter what sort of service they are providing – visiting individuals in their own homes spend many hours away from their institutional base. Not only does this detach them from support afforded by their colleagues back at their base,[10] but it can also create both actual and perceived distance between themselves and the executives of the organisations with responsibility for determining their working conditions and monitoring outcomes, i.e. knowing what is going on. Out there in the community, not only were the opportunities for professional scrutiny reduced, but with more agencies involved it also increased the number of variables influencing the outcome. Thus, the clinical role was further reinforced at the expense of organisational accountability.

Although this particular policy intention was to create a 'net' of community care, it was targeted at a single component of that net – the mental health services – which were at the time of its initiation seen to have the greater responsibility for resettling people in the community. Systems were devised for healthcare workers to routinely collect information on the CPA, on the assumption that it was their responsibility. Directors and executives of trusts providing mental health services, who were accountable for policy implementation, were confident that the messages they were receiving about progress with the CPA policy were accurate and they appeared to demonstrate little interest in extending their influence beyond their own organisation to promote the interagency aspects emphasised in the policy, for example to find means of joint performance monitoring. There appeared to be an assumption that existing networks should suffice.

The account of CPA activity according to the 'official' evidence gleaned from case files which were audited demonstrated little or no input from agencies other than health. The fact that this did not seem to be a particular cause for concern for directors was puzzling. Like other staff, they appeared to attach limited significance to the information they received, viewing it with an indifference possibly based on mistrust but perhaps also a realistic sense of the impossibility of gaining anything accurate; they certainly didn't see themselves as having responsibilities beyond the boundaries of their own organisations in spite of the collaborative requirement of this particular policy. Clinical staff found the requirement to produce evidence of their activity tedious and indeed it could be suggested that failure to do so was an effective means of sabotaging managerial control. There was greater concern to demonstrate clinical and professional competence in the face of litigation than to be seen to be conforming to policy requirements or to be providing service users with information. So, yet again the clinical role was reinforced at the expense of administrative accountability.

Clinicians in the driving seat

There was no doubt that data collection to monitor activity had a lower priority than clinical practice and there was only limited belief in the organisation as 'seeing' and 'understanding' what it was being told. All this served to undermine attempts at making it accurate. Staff saw themselves as providing an account of what they were doing in order to be seen as 'accountable', but in fact there was no sense of owning this account or of being responsible for outcomes. What is more, with only limited commitment to the monitoring of performance, the incompetent practitioner could be concealed from view, both in terms of the quality and the quantity of what was being delivered.

It was clear that in the field of mental health, at least, the professional role over-rode that of administrator so clinical concerns would have primacy. Indeed staff rated the involvement of clinical colleagues highly, especially psychiatrists and GPs, the gatekeepers to the service. This was in contrast to service users who rarely referred to either. Even when users discussed their experience of the CPA, it was as though the things which mattered to *them* as indicators of a quality service, such as coping with the ordinary aspects of their lives or having help available when they needed it, were detached from the medicalised gaze of the professionals. Their needs were personal and individualised, pointing to a fundamental difference in the social construction of their role from that of the providers of services. They saw doctors as those who defined client problems by diagnosing them as efficiently, effectively and economically as possible, thereby demonstrating a 'quality' service.

However, professionals would know that whether individuals were satisfied with the nature and outcome of their efforts or not, they were monopoly providers and there would always be someone else waiting for their help. It therefore did not appear to matter if the quality of what they were able to provide within all the limitations identified was compromised. In addition, their detachment from an institutional base, because they were working in the community, rendered much of their activity invisible. Whilst depriving them of helpful support, it also deprived users of the opportunity to make comparisons with other users or take responsibility for prioritising their need.

> *From what I saw of Malcolm last week, if he had the same key worker as me, I'd have said leave me, he needs you more.*
>
> *Service User*

Healthcare professional as service user

What happens when the issue is located within the experience of the individual, who as administrator or professional may themselves become ill? What happens when they or a member of their family crosses the divide between these roles, as so many of us are likely to do? For example, three out of every 10 of us will have time off work during the coming year because of mental distress, one in three GP consultations are associated with a mental health problem and, at a conservative estimate, one in 34 of those people will be ill enough to require admission to a mental hospital.[11,12] Then there are the other visits to GPs, the need for obstetric services or surgery, our personal need for healthcare and those of our families. This means that within all families there *must* be experience and knowledge of health-care provided by the NHS, and yet somehow that personal experience is denied credibility or even existence and the demand for 'official' information continues insatiably.

As we have demonstrated, knowledge can confer power and control; this may explain the huge demand for it in the face of situations which are often typified by loss of control, but if what is provided as a result of the demand fails to satisfy, then perhaps it is inappropriate knowledge or presented in a way which does not relate to the difficulty. This particularly applies to mental health problems, but simply saying that 'more information should be available' is like offering people a haystack and telling them to find the needle.

Acknowledgement of the validity of personal experience of illness only seems to occur once people have been labelled as 'other' by virtue of being recipients of services. There are constant attempts to 'seek users' views' but little recognition of the vast repository of knowledge and experience which *must* exist *within* the lives and families of those who are employed in health and associated services. It could be argued that an 'insider' knowledge of health services for those who work in them gives a different perspective from those who are totally uninformed, but as part of the largest service organisation in the country with not far short of a million people employed in hospital and community services, not to mention social service workers, there must be a considerable number of us who know of this 'other' experience. And yet this knowledge appears to have limited currency.

Is there such a gap between what ought to be possible and people's *actual* experience, as well as what the country can afford, that nobody dares to say we're really not very good at this and sometimes can't even agree on how we should define it? Is our reluctance to admit to these difficulties perpetuating the gulf between the world of the professionals and the experience of the service users and creating a sense of 'otherness'?

So far, these arguments have greater relevance to mental health services, but waiting lists, apparently unavoidable delays and lack of information all reinforce the state of dependency regardless of the service. This dependency is an inevitable component of ill health as interpreted using the medical model.[13] What is more, when Health Service employees and sometimes their families become service users, all too often they do not have to tolerate the same inconvenience because of what has been, until recently, an invisible two-tier system which generates fast-track opportunities. I once asked a group of doctors and senior NHS staff if this had been their experience. Some looked at their laps in embarrassment and shuffled in their seats, a few raised their hands, smiling wryly; they clearly knew what I was talking about and yet it has remained a tacit aspect of healthcare delivery for far too long. Dartford and Gravesham NHS Trust in Kent is among the first to openly acknowledge this by including among its staff benefits fast-track access opportunities to its own services. In other words, the service is looking after its own. This can be seen as a justly deserved reward with the added advantage that the sooner healthcare workers are restored to health, the sooner they can return to restoring the health of others. Alternatively, it may appear to be unfair discrimination in favour of NHS staff.

Doing their best for each other also occurs because staff have a better idea of what that best should be. This means that the experiences they have as recipients of services may indeed be different from those of people who are external to this working world. We should not be surprised to hear of workers being stereotyped as out of touch with the real world in user group discussions and of the existence of an inverted form of stigmatisation identified by Rogers and Pilgrim.[14] This research supported their view that '... if professionals were to approximate to the conception preferred by users, they would shed most or all of their pretensions to specialised knowledge' (p.178). Service users, as evidenced by this research, were indeed desperate to have their *ordinary* needs recognised and to have a valued social role.

This all suggests a real difficulty in reconciling professional and user roles, with the balance in favour of the group whose knowledge is associated with their professional status rather than being gained by experience.

An overview of the issues

During the two years that I was gathering data for this research, it was apparent, in South Staffordshire at least, that the policy under scrutiny simply wasn't doing what it was supposed to do. Some progress was being made but the 'net of community care' which was supposed to be in place for people with complex and enduring mental health problems at that time largely comprised health services with a dash of social services.

There were clearly major differences about the kind of help that was needed with mental health workers using professional knowledge to distance themselves from the immediacy of service users' needs. Users' interpretation of the CPA and what it could most usefully do for them was located in the real world of their experience.

For healthcare staff, accountability to an organisation was of lesser significance than professional autonomy and individual responsibility, and this undermined management function, organisational effectiveness and policy implementation. Questioning how an individual might relate a professional role with the possibility of their own personal experience of illness led to consideration of how internalised roles are reconciled. The conclusion here was that prioritisation takes place, with professional knowledge and its associated rewards such as status and power being more important than personal experience. This is exacerbated by the long-standing tensions between professionals and political power brokers. It follows, therefore, that if policy implementation is directed through organisational channels, as was CPA, and that ambivalence is rooted within both organisational structures and internalised by individuals, then the chances of 'successful' implementation are slim indeed.

Service user and carer involvement: doing it better?

Close examination of a single piece of policy and how it was implemented has drawn attention to organisational roles and boundaries as well as consideration of the social constructions made by individuals in undertaking these roles. The state administrator has responsibility for devising, administering and managing policy implementation. The specialist professional's activities, in this case clinicians, should be framed by it, as should the activities of other specialist professionals with an extended role in the community. The fourth group of individuals is those who are recipients of services defined within that policy framework. The key issue is that these roles do not necessarily exist as discrete entities. Individuals may have to reconcile competing requirements, for example with roles that have been amalgamated by policy definitions (notably the key worker role combining a clinical and administrative function) or organisational management models (where a clinician is also a manager) or else combined as a result of an internalised integration process (patient and professional). Difficulty in role reconciliation is exemplified in the value and thus the distinctive priorities which individuals attach to information, knowledge and experience, which contributes to perpetuating the problems we have in responding fully and appropriately to the needs of service users and carers.

With all of these, it is the professional role in terms of its status and power (and the accompanying rewards) which rises to the top, which means that individuals in this position have greater authority, and are possibly accorded it, by those the organisations are there to serve.

Somehow, something needs to be done to redress this balance and help us to reconcile the knowledge that is necessary for us to practise as healthcare professionals and that knowledge that any of us may acquire through our experience of ill health and health services. The technological explosion that has many of us scouring the internet for information about conditions or treatments may mean that we are better informed (or unfortunately sometimes misinformed), but it does not necessarily give us knowledge. Of course we need to understand and share as much as possible in decisions that are made about our own bodies and minds, decisions that are made about services and the allocation of healthcare resources, and decisions that affect the communities we live in. However, there is a danger that we are in effect attempting to professionalise service users and carers and perhaps patronising them too by wanting to 'bring them up to our level' or tell them about our world without sufficient heed for the worlds that they come from. I would suggest that we should be in a different place, looking at *their* knowledge, acquired through experience, which we, as service users ourselves, also have. We need to recognise its essential value and find ways of ensuring that it is central to the task of meeting healthcare needs.

Summary

Consideration of the Care Programme Approach, as an example of mental health policy implementation, led to an exploration of the strategies which individuals adopt to reconcile role discontinuities which are inherent within the policy. These are typified by an imbalance in the values, attained through various socialisation processes, we attach to knowledge, experience and information. It is possible that further understanding of the interaction of these roles could contribute to a fresh look at how the process of policy implementation might be changed, leading to a reduction in the gap between the rhetoric of policy frameworks and the reality experience. A past response to poor policy implementation has been to produce a 'better' policy, but perhaps more could be achieved through a more considered approach to how we make sense of policy requirements and the influence this has on our actions.

How this way of thinking can influence service delivery is the subject of the rest of this book. The following chapters describe in practical detail how one organisation developed its approach to involving people in the services it was delivering. Each of these practical chapters includes a checklist of aspects that needed to be considered in introducing the changes described.

References

1 Spokes J. Report of the Committee of Inquiry into the Care and Aftercare of Miss Sharon Campbell. London: HMSO; 1988.
2 Department of Health. *The Care Programme Approach for People with a Mental Illness Referred to the Specialist Psychiatric Services*. HC(90)23/LASSL(90)11. London: DoH; 1990.
3 North C, Ritchie J. *Factors Influencing the Implementation of the Care Programme Approach*. London: HMSO; 1993.
4 Carpenter J, Sbaraini S. *Choice, Information and Dignity: involving users and carers in care management in mental health*. Bristol: Policy Press; 1997.
5 Shepherd G. *Creating Effective Multi-disciplinary Teams*. London: Sainsbury Centre for Mental Health; 1995.
6 Lipsky M. *Street-level Bureaucracy: dilemmas of the individual in public service*. New York: Russell Sage Foundation; 1980.
7 Hill M. *The Policy Process and the Modern State*. London: Prentice Hall/Harvester Wheatsheaf; 1997.
8 Whitmore R. Modelling the policy/implementation distinction: the case of child abuse. *Policy and Politics*. 1984; **12**(3): 241–67.
9 Hill M (ed.). *New Agendas in the Study of the Policy Process*. London: Harvester Wheatsheaf; 1993.
10 Green S. Nurses cry freedom. *Health Service J*. 1992; **102**(5311): 21.
11 Brindle D. Opinion. *Guardian Society*, 11 May 2005.
12 Goldberg D, Huxley P. *Mental Illness in the Community: the pathway to psychiatric care*. London: Tavistock; 1980.
13 Stanton-Rogers W. *Explaining Health and Illness: the exploration of diversity*. London: Harvester Wheatsheaf; 1991.
14 Rogers A, Pilgrim D. 'Pulling down churches': accounting for the British Mental Health Users' Movement. *Sociol Health Illness*. 1991; **13**(2): 129–48.

5

Making policy happen

Getting personal and declaring an interest

Some years ago I undertook some qualitative research looking at the relationship between occupational therapists (OTs) and their trained, but at that time unqualified, assistants.[1,2] I learned a lot about professionalism and also about what I called the 'spiral of academic incrementalism', which in plain language is the tendency of some healthcare professions, especially the insecure ones, to try and improve their status. They do this by becoming more and more specialised in what they know in the hope that one day they will be like doctors, at the top of the tree with lots of knowledge, lots of money and lots of power. This was what OTs seemed to be doing, whilst in the meantime being supported by a whole army of 'assistants' getting on with the more ordinary job of keeping the ship afloat.

I was stopped in my tracks one day when my very perceptive supervisor asked me, 'But whose side are you on?' As a researcher I didn't think I should be on anybody's side as I was supposed to be objective and impartial, but I was wrong. What I needed to recognise was that it is impossible to deny the existence of a personal reaction to the research field and those who occupy it. This should be part of the qualitative researcher's toolkit. Recognising this response and being open about it enables one to use it as a yardstick against which findings can be analysed and measured. Pretending it isn't there will *increase* the likelihood of biased interpretations, rather than reducing it.

I realised that I felt angry with OTs for not doing more to recognise their assistants, who at that time were known as OT (mother's little) helpers. It seemed that they were dependent on this poorly paid but invaluable source of support, which they had rendered invisible by failing to provide them with the career development opportunities that they were eagerly seeking themselves. They appeared to be more concerned with improving their status in order to compensate for professional insecurity than they were with the main task of helping people to get on with their lives. It was as though the profession was anxiously but determinedly facing inwards and looking at itself and its insecurities, paying more attention to its own future than that of the people it was there to help. Neglecting the profession's primary purpose is like taking one's eye off the ball, the ball being patient needs. Keeping these in focus means that one has a sure and confident sense of direction. Fortunately, times and career structures have changed, but it is interesting that recent policy documents are still reflecting that healthcare professionals have a tendency to be inward-looking and exclusive, leaving service users and carers on the 'outside'. What is more, exhortations to bring them 'inside' the NHS seem to result in attempts to 'professionalise' people by giving them professional knowledge and skills, rather than recognising and valuing their particular knowledge of the experience of both illness and the services they receive to mitigate it.

Processes of professionalisation have a lot to answer for. When I trained as an OT, we were told that on no account should we divulge any personal details about ourselves to patients because this was seen as 'unprofessional'. We were therefore expected to gain their trust and confidence, which might well have included them confiding intimate details of their lives, whilst we remained insulated by our own cloak of professionalism. I can see the necessity for this. It is not a bartering situation where personal information is exchanged tit for tat. There need not be any reason for patients to know anything other than that we are suitably qualified for the job we have to do, and our name, and there could be situations where we might put ourselves at risk by getting too closely involved. In addition, healthcare can be a tough and distressing area in which to work, so maintaining professional distance can be an important survival mechanism. However, the downside to this kind of personal disengagement is that we can become remote from the real experience of people who are using the services that we provide. We may need to avoid sharing their suffering, but their frustrations and the nature of their experience may well be something we should recognise and listen to, rather than holding them at arm's length.

Being 'professional' can also cause problems for the back-up squad, those people who provide secondary supports such as accountants, clinical auditors, the whole army of domestic and kitchen staff, and the estates staff, from the managers to the man who cleans the drains. They may not see themselves as directly contributing to patient care but the whole Health Service edifice would collapse without them. I once worked in a very hierarchical mental health unit where the professor of psychiatry would sweep around with his retinue, terrifying the wits out of everyone. There, patients used to say that they talked more to the cleaners about their problems than they could ever say to these remote individuals who seemed detached from their reality. So we need to think how we can attach value to that particular contact.

In another hospital where patient and public involvement had a much higher priority, I had sent the finance director copies of our payment policy on the understanding that the process for reimbursing patients when they had incurred expenses would be passed down the line to the clerks who actually made the payments. Some months later, a patient complained at the delay in receiving money she was owed; she was living on benefits and didn't have a lot of leeway with her finances. The excuse of the particular clerk when we finally tracked it down was that because of pressure of work, she had been 'too busy' to attend to this payment. If an organisation puts its patients first, then they are the priority and every single department needs to question itself to see whether that is the guiding principle for all of its actions. We shall be referring to this example again when we look at policy development in Chapter 10.

It has taken me some time to recognise why I have responded so passionately to this particular political agenda and what the particular interest is that I need to be aware of. The research described in Chapter 4 was significant but there is another reason why I am on the side of the disempowered, those without a voice, those without representation. There was a time when I was one of them, when I was up against the might of a professional institution that deprived me of the right to bring up my three lovely children. We survived, in fact we did better than that, we learned that surviving such a challenge gives courage, confidence and also humility, and this is the voice with which I tell this story. It isn't about how anything 'should' be done but describes how recognising the value of experiences such as illness and loss can influence the balance of power within an organisation.

Are you sitting comfortably?

The recent history of healthcare in England has been one of constant change. Indeed, as I write, my newspaper announces yet again, 'A huge shake-up in NHS care ... many of the 303 primary care trusts responsible for commissioning or providing services face a merger.'

So change is nothing new; it's a familiar experience for NHS staff up and down the country, many of whom can ruefully describe a whole series of unwanted shifts and accompanying uncertainty throughout their careers. It is a common experience. Describing some outcomes to one particular merger is not therefore to draw attention to something unique or special, but to recognise aspects of this familiarity and see what we can learn from them.

This story begins in 2001 when a new organisation, South Staffordshire Healthcare NHS Trust, heaved itself unsteadily into existence. In fact it wasn't a new organisation at all but resulted from an amalgamation of three pre-existing trusts which between them had provided mental health, community nursing, forensic, learning disability, children's and several other community services such as sexual health, dentistry and therapies: all this to a large area of South Staffordshire with a population of just under 600,000. There had already been several acrimonious and unsuccessful attempts to merge the three trusts. These had resulted in one of them sticking its head in the ground, hoping it would all go away, and the other two confronting each other like small whacky David, innovative and ahead of the pack but weak at promoting its good ideas, and cumbersome but steady Goliath, lacking inspiration but big, confident and powerful. At this stage, those of us with responsibility for patient involvement in both 'David' and 'Goliath' (the other trust was nowhere to be seen) realised that what had seemed like a threat, i.e. our loss of individual identity, could indeed be an opportunity for promoting the service user and carer agenda.

We agreed on two key priorities that we would promote as the new organisation took shape: firstly that we expected the new trust to have a ring-fenced budget for the purpose and secondly that the appointment of the new chief executive should involve active participation of people who used the trust's services. With the first we were successful. Our budget provided for a team of eight, thereafter known as Centrepoint, and resources to support it, with the sole aim of ensuring that patients and carers came first in the organisation.

However, service user involvement in the chief executive's appointment was a sorrier story. Yes, service users were present at the traditional 'trial by sherry' but they had received no briefing and candidates were surrounded by an impenetrable barrier of senior staff like bees round a honey-pot. No arrangements had been made for candidates to be identified to the service users and carers, let alone introduced, and they were given no opportunity to feed back their views. Inevitably they hung around on the fringes of the group, uncertain of what they should do. The box could be ticked, they were there, but to all intents and purposes they were treated as though they were invisible. Was this a sign of things to come?

Post merger, the fusion process, three into one, started with a vengeance. Each trust had well-established but differing traditions, creating an uncomfortable climate for the constructive development of a corporate identity. Within a very short space of time our new chief executive had made it clear that he was a force to be reckoned with and, like it or not, we were to change. He and the board chairman moved around the organisation with speed and steady determination, identifying and reinforcing areas of good practice, establishing standards and dismantling that which served no useful purpose. It was strenuous and stressful. At that point we were unsure as to whether his avowed intention to put service users at the centre of the organisation was sincere or 'CE speak' to match the policy requirements; we all had to learn to trust each other.

With no established routes or communication networks, finding one's way around this new organisation, with its 73 geographical bases across 700 square miles and about 4000 staff, was particularly difficult for those of us providing a trust-wide service. Each organisation had had different systems and processes for doing things and different priorities that somehow had to be united. This applied as much to pre-existing service user and carer groups and priorities as it did to internal processes, generating considerable anxiety and mistrust. Once board members had been appointed, however, leadership was strong (some would say forceful) and focused. Inevitably faces that didn't fit vanished and new, enthusiastic ones appeared or familiar ones reappeared in different guises. Occasionally jobs and people simply evaporated. Had there been time to consider all the changes, issues and difficulties, it might have provided a valuable organisational learning opportunity, but once a decision had been made there was no looking back, no time to reflect on underlying dynamics. This avoidance of problem areas is typical of the present NHS target-driven culture which is unable to tolerate failure as a creative part of the process of growth. It leads us to distort performance in order to demonstrate degrees of success, never to review uncertainty.

During this period, service provision became more streamlined with community nursing services, therapies, community dentistry and sexual health being transferred to PCTs. This left around 2500 staff to provide children's (including child and adolescent mental health), mental health, forensic and learning disability services, each located in a clinical directorate. In addition there were six other support directorates: Human Resources, Finance and Information, Health Informatics, Nursing and Operations, Clinical Development, and Development and Partnerships. This last became the home for the Centrepoint team, although it was later transferred to Human Resources. There was to be a Service User and Carer Sub-Committee to the Board, but the various failed merger attempts plus the time taken to establish the new trust had led to fragmentation of existing groups of service users and carers and a general loss of confidence that anything new or better could ever emerge. Progress was slow.

Centrepoint

For this reason it was essential for the Centrepoint team to quickly establish an identity and a presence within the trust. An associate director was appointed to lead the team, giving a signal to the organisation that this was important enough to warrant senior leadership, one step down from the trust board.

The team initially comprised a patient information facilitator with an assistant whose job it was to provide sensible, accurate and up-to-the-minute information throughout the trust using a consistent house style. With three organisations shoe-horned into one and many teams replicating each other's practice, this was easier said than done. Sometimes there were as many different leaflets, some offering conflicting or dated information, as there were teams, even though each was providing the same service. The information facilitator also had a remit to work with the trust's information technology (IT) specialists to develop a desktop leaflet service so that all clinicians could access a single common source of information; this was also available to patients via the trust's own website.

An early requirement for the team was to get a PALS development worker in post, with an administrative assistant, and this was accomplished in time to meet the Department of Health deadline for the PALS service of March 2002. Service users were very closely involved in this appointment and a description of how it was achieved is included later when staff selection and recruitment is discussed.

Two service user and carer facilitators, one for the east side and one for the west side of the patch, were also appointed to the Centrepoint team. Theirs was a liaison and development role, staying in touch and supporting both staff and service users and carers through established network meetings as well as individual contacts. One of these facilitators had additional responsibilities as a volunteer coordinator and both contributed to the PALS service as points of contact and advice if staff in their area were unable to deal with a particular issue.

Several years later some of these posts have been amalgamated or revised, PALS has aligned itself with the Service Relations Department which deals with complaints and Centrepoint has been transformed into a PPI team. The name doesn't matter, what does is that the trust moved on and found new and better ways to develop and support its user involvement agenda, which will be described later.

Issues challenging a 'new' organisation and its approach to PPI

In these early stages there were a number of challenges, which will be familiar to anyone who has worked through a similar amalgamation of services. Some of these were resolved with the passage of time, others remain:

- As a result of the uncertainty generated by protracted merger discussions there had been a loss of momentum in each of the three organisations. Anyone who has worked in a large organisation during a major reconfiguration will have experienced the effects of uncertainty and anxieties about jobs and future prospects. There was a need to crank up the machine.
- There was also a need to identify examples of existing good practice and see that they were valued and sustained. What should we take and what should we leave behind?
- There was a need to establish 'common' ways of doing things – each organisation had thought of its way as *the* way – sometimes people had to relinquish what was known and familiar.
- Deadlines associated with the NHS Plan and its policy requirements still had to be met and the Commission for Health Improvement was lurking in the background, eager to inspect us. In the event, this inspection took place less than two

years after the 'new' trust first took breath, when systems were still in their pilot phases.

- Keeping everyone informed when communication systems and processes are underdeveloped or non-existing is time-consuming and frustrating. In spite of this the trust needed to get everyone on board, so ways of raising awareness of the PPI agenda across the trust had to be found.
- Although a PPI team was resourced right from the start, individual directorate budgets did not include a ring-fenced allocation to help them promote service user and carer involvement. There was little awareness that this would cost a great deal more than finding a few two-penny bus fares from petty cash every now and again.
- We tend towards a 'quick-fix' culture. Providing everything looks alright on the surface (and the box can be ticked) there isn't enough time to do the steady detailed work necessary to bring about real changes in people's thinking.
- 'Partners' were seen as other healthcare professionals or, at best, social service workers. There was little interest in working with the voluntary sector, PCTs, local government officers or universities, let alone service users and carers.
- Partnership working, which is fundamental to involving people in the PPI agenda, means that no one group owns or can determine the agenda or dictate the pace. This has to be jointly agreed – easier said than done when pressures vary between groups. In effect there is a loss of sovereignty and this takes maturity to accommodate, difficult within a new organisational structure. This applies as much to the involvement of patients as it does to different agencies.
- Reconciling ideological differences between agencies or even professions and agreeing core values also raises the sovereignty issue.
- There had only been limited success in the past in involving people and there was a need to stimulate those at the 'front end' of service delivery to recognise the importance of their immediate contact with service users and carers and make use of it. Board members also needed to be active participants in the process.
- In today's social climate people are reluctant to support community activities, so the chances of active engagement in healthcare issues were unlikely to be any different. Many voluntary sector organisations struggle to find volunteers and in local government the numbers of people prepared to stand as councillors appears to be dwindling. This is a cultural change requiring new approaches.

Getting going on PPI: trust and team priorities

The first thing the team had to do was promote itself, its availability and its purpose. We identified three main priorities, recognising that they would need to be addressed concurrently rather than ticked off one by one.

1 To meet the policy objectives, described in Chapter 3, the 'must do's'.
2 To work together to develop partnerships. This was to ensure that systems and networks were established throughout the trust and beyond. We needed to know what was going on, who was involved, where there were gaps and where there were areas of overlap. We needed to establish a 'joined-up' approach to patient and public involvement.

3 To change the organisational culture. Core values and an action plan were to be agreed with service users and carers and Centrepoint was to be a resource for both them and staff. It was to provide and receive information, support feedback, audit and monitor activity, undertake a development role and promote a 'do-as-you-would-be-done-by' approach among trust staff. This would also include close work with the Human Resources directorate.

Meeting the policy objectives with concrete and specific outcomes was the easy bit. The PALS person was appointed and, after consulting with service users and carers, established a model that required all members of staff to take responsibility for attending to worries that patients and their carers might have. This was followed by an extensive training programme.

Centrepoint also surveyed 245 of the people who had used the trust's services to find out whether their problem was less severe than it had been, whether they felt they had a better understanding of it and whether they were pleased with the services they had received. The results were on the whole positive, but it was the detail that gave us real insights into what mattered to those who used our services and what should therefore contribute to any subsequent strategy. People often steer clear of qualitative data, arguing that it may not be 'representative' and also it is much harder to analyse than quantitative data. However, we were able to learn that 'time' issues weren't just about waiting times for appointments or indeed being on waiting lists. They included concern about staff being late, chatting to each other, being hard to access or not showing up for appointments and appreciation of being 'given' time instead of feeling that everything was rushed. There were reactions to how far people had to travel for appointments or having a venue unexpectedly changed or being able to have a home visit rather than having to travel. Respite care was a particular issue as well as consideration of flexible approaches to carer support. Most touching were the many references to individual staff members by name, demonstrating an appreciation of caring staff attitudes. All of this was fed back to the trust board and individual directorates received details of their performance and were required to respond with an appropriate action plan.

Much harder than all of this, in those early days, was the expectation that we would produce a Service User and Carer Strategy which would be a blueprint for our future activity. There was a sense with this 'new' organisation that once we had strategies for everything, we would be defined, we would have a sense of direction and a guidebook to help us find our way. I was not so sure. Having asked various service user and carer groups that had survived the merger upheaval what they thought of creating a strategy together, their answer was clear. 'No, thank you,' they said. 'That sounds like a lot of rather boring work and who will read it when it's finished? We'd rather have some actions that show us you are serious about what we think, and we can also see whether you do what you say you are going to do. We'd rather have an action plan.' I took this to the trust board who accepted their reasoning and the Centrepoint team set about devising a process, working with service users and carers, to obtain the plan. This became 'Telling It Like It Is', which had we but known it was the trigger for changing the thinking about service user and carer involvement across the organisation. And the trigger for 'Telling It Like It Is', which will be described in the next chapter, was in fact a black bin bag.

Getting going: things to think about

Organisational climate: Is it a question of having to because the government says so, rather than wanting to because there is a genuine belief in real partnership working? Look for some champions and work with them on attitude change. What needs doing/thinking about differently? What can you do about it?

What's already being done? This isn't anything new so there are sure to be pockets of activity and good practice that can be shared. Do networks/opportunities exist for doing this? How might existing systems be adapted to improve this networking?

Resources: These are sure to be more than anyone wants to give you. Where are the resources to come from – a central 'pot' or individual service areas? How are they managed and is there a better way of doing it (e.g. groups of carers working out their own timetable for the use of respite beds)? Look for bidding opportunities and the skills to make use of them. What resources are you providing (e.g. advocacy service, PALS, interpreting service or signing for deaf people) and how are they publicised so that people know about them and how to access them? How much are they being used? If not much, is this because of limited need or poor publicity?

Staff selection and recruitment: Avoid our 'trial-by-sherry' experience by making sure that background preparation, briefing sessions and two-way de-briefing sessions have been thoroughly thought through so that the contribution of service users and carers is active and not tokenism. There is more about this in Chapter 11.

Developing a team identity: This is assuming you are not a one-person band. If you are, you need to think how to get help – it is simply impossible for one person to do everything if the job is to be done properly. Think about your aims and objectives and all the tasks associated with them. What are the skills that your team has to have, i.e. what needs doing and how will it be accomplished? How will team activity and availability be promoted? How will you define and measure your outcomes? Who needs to know?

References

1 Green S. Shaking our foundations, part 1: occupational therapy, its path to professionalisation. *Br J Occup Ther.* 1991; **54**: 1.
2 Green S. Shaking our foundations, part 2: into the future. *Br J Occup Ther.* 1991: **54**: 2.

6

'Telling It Like It Is'

Do as you would be done by

As part of the merger process, inevitably a lot of people came and went. Some found work elsewhere, some took early retirement. One of these was an unobtrusive man who had worked in one of the trust's accounts offices for 27 years. He had decided that he didn't want to cope with the upheaval of the merger and it was time to go. This he did during a holiday period when there weren't many people around to mark his departure, so he simply worked out his notice, shovelled all the personal possessions from his desk into a black bin bag and left. Those of us who knew him, as a quiet, unassuming, friendly individual who just got on with his job and was unfailingly helpful, felt saddened and sorry when we realised how he had gone. It seemed a shabby way for the organisation to have treated him, a shabby way for us to have behaved. Would we have wanted it that way for ourselves? No, of course not.

This principle of 'do as you would be done by', i.e. treat others as you would want to be treated yourself, became the touchstone for the work we embarked on. We wanted to find a way of identifying with both staff and patients exactly what their expectations would be if and when they were on the receiving end of the trust's services. As far as staff were concerned, was what they were doing good enough for themselves or those they cared about? We also had a hastily compiled vision and values statement based on the Kennedy Report which had been accepted by the board but had not been validated by our service users. Finally, it seemed like a good opportunity to publicise the existence of Centrepoint and the trust-wide support we were making available, so we billed our workshops as Centrepoint launch events.

Launching Centrepoint

We set up five workshops in different geographical areas across the trust's patch and we sent all members of clinical staff two invitations, one for themselves and one for a service user they had worked with. In the event, nearly twice as many service users attended as staff.

The idea was for everyone to share personal experiences of healthcare, both good and not so good, things that had happened to people that they felt comfortable talking about. We then wanted to see whether the good points reflected the values we had drafted and the bad points were things that needed attention in our own organisation. We wanted to learn from everyone's experience and to show that the trust was listening to its users and carers. In effect we were setting user-determined standards for user and carer involvement.

Valuing personal experience

Staff were not used to sharing their own experiences of healthcare with their patients, and yet as patients we are expected to talk about all manner of personal things to them. We certainly didn't want *anyone* to feel exposed or that they had to pour out the whole of their medical history. I showed some of my own family snapshots, pictures of my son on his beloved motorbike and the inevitable spills and frights he has given us as a result. My elder daughter is a young mother with two small children so her healthcare needs and those of her family are different. My youngest daughter has been diabetic from an early age so the whole family has grown up knowing of the health issues for her, as well as the necessary emotional adjustments for someone with a long-term medical condition. Between us we've had a lot of experience of the NHS.

Finally came a picture of my 93-year-old father and his carer, my sister, not long after he had had one of his hip joints replaced. Major surgery at that age is not without risk and we had set out to deliver him to the hospital with some trepidation. The situation wasn't helped by father's deafness and he got more and more rattled as the quietly spoken doctor who clerked him in tried to obtain the necessary information as speedily as possible. The harder father struggled to give the right answers, the more confused he got. In the end the doctor gave up and my sister and I sat apprehensively wondering how we could leave this intelligent, sensitive but frightened old man in this seemingly alien environment. Along came a nursing assistant. Putting a hand on his arm and going close enough to him so that he had no difficulty in hearing her, she asked him what was the matter and could she do anything to help. It was then that father spilled the beans. 'It's my waterworks,' he said. 'I've a bit of a problem and I'm really worried that I'm going to have an accident and you'll have to clear up the mess.' Poor father. Neither my sister nor I had any idea that this was what was worrying him but the nurse's reassurances worked miracles. He relaxed, settled and underwent his surgery without further difficulty. For him, the experience with the doctor had been inhibiting, the experience with the nurse enabling.

With this as an example, people went into small groups to share some of their own experiences. Together we looked at specific examples of what was good and what wasn't, making sure that a record was kept of everything for future feedback. Things that needed changing were listed and became our action plan and we also kept an eye on whether these actions fitted with the values that had already been identified from the Kennedy Report. It's no good talking in grandiose terms about improving 'communication' or 'changing the culture'. What we were after were particular examples of good and less good practice that could be shared across the trust. If communication needs to be improved, who is communicating what to whom and how is it being done: what's the problem? Cultural change: what exactly does that mean, what is the expectation and how will we know that it has changed? This gave us a massive list of actions to undertake but a key outcome was that service users and carers demanded a follow-up session in six months to find out what progress had been made. We could see that some actions would take longer than this to follow through, but we did not want to lose sight of the issues.

Figure 6.1   'Telling It Like It Is'. © Dave Follows Cartoons c/o Audrey Follows.

Identifying and working with themes

Afterwards, in order to get all the material into manageable chunks, the actions were sorted into four key themes: staff attitudes, time issues, information needs and partnerships. These were put together in a draft plan and circulated to the participants in the workshops to make sure that nothing had been missed, and also to the trust board. Each of the trust's directorates identified a lead user and carer representative to meet and agree how to work on the plan. The idea was to share good experience within the trust, consider difficulties and identify gaps. This might all sound very obvious but it is surprisingly difficult, within large organisations, to get good practice from one area transferred to another. People also need courage and confidence to talk about their difficulties outside their own directorate without feeling disloyal to their colleagues. The action planning group also needed to include finance people as many of the issues had cost implications; estates for those that dealt with the upkeep and maintenance of the fabric of the trust; human resources for those that had staff implications; the Quality Development team who could help with issues around the measurement of service quality and the Centrepoint team with their links with patient information, PALS and the service user and carer networks in the area. In other words, it needed to embrace the whole of the organisation.

Some examples from each of the four key areas show what the trust was doing at that time to try and make the vision and values a reality for the people using its services. For each of these themes, issues and required actions were listed and a suggestion made about who should be responsible for ensuring they were followed up and by when.

1. Staff attitudes

Increasing numbers of service users and carers were taking part in job interviews (*see* Chapter 11); for example, the mother of a 14-year-old boy with complicated healthcare needs had been invited to participate in the interview panel for the nurse who was to help her look after him at home.

A non-executive director had complained that she found the trust board papers difficult to understand so a number of volunteer 'Readers' Groups' were set up to give feedback on the 'reader friendliness' of the documents the trust produced.

A poster campaign ensured that in every waiting area there was information for people about how they could help the trust, with contact details and specific examples such as staff selection and recruitment, designing training for staff and designing and planning new services: the more specific, the better. People don't respond to generalised requests to 'help', they want to know exactly what it is they will have to do. A good way of doing this is to maintain a database of opportunities, but this will also require publicising among staff and coordinating to link it with people available. Alternatively, if there is a specific task that needs doing, why not advertise it in the area needing help? A few years ago there was a move to get people involved in clinical audit. What could sound more tedious and, in any case, what exactly is it? But ask the public if they would like to help with a survey to find out whether they think the local bus service to the hospital is adequate and they will jump at the chance. Figure 6.2 shows an example of audit made interesting and meaningful.

ORTHOTICS AUDIT -

what's that ?

- Over the next few months we would like to find out what you think about how we run this service and whether the shoes/splints you have received suit you.

- This will enable us to know whether you think we are doing it right and if not, what we should do about it.

- Please help us by filling in the questionnaire which the receptionist will give you - it shouldn't take long. She will tell you what to do with it when you have finished, but ask if there is anything you don't understand.

- In six months time, say in April 2004, we shall look at all the results and decide what we need to do to improve things.

- We shall also be telling you about the outcome so WATCH THIS SPACE !

Thank you for your help.

Figure 6.2 'Orthotics audit – what's that?'

The poster campaign to raise the interest of service users and carers was accompanied by a parallel one targeted at staff. They might well come across people who were willing to help during the course of their working day and could also identify areas of opportunity where they might be able to contribute. Again, this sounds obvious but many staff with regular contact with people and their families seemed unaware of this responsibility. The Centrepoint team maintained a confidential database of people who had come forward to help in this way.

One interesting move was to get managers 'back to the shop floor' by getting them to work a shift on a ward as part of their induction programme.

2. Time issues

This is a difficult area and one which the Patients' Survey, already described in Part 1, identified as tricky. Whilst being appreciative of the service they received, people were sensitive to the pressures on staff time and some felt guilty if they took 'too long'. In spite of the best efforts of healthcare staff, being under pressure shows and needs to be given attention. If it isn't, staff will become tired, demotivated and possibly leave their jobs or get sick. Patients will feel they are taken for granted, not listened to and are there under sufferance. Neither situation is healthy. In the 'Telling It Like It Is' discussions, patients were concerned about the long gaps between appointments but staff worried more about those in the queue who had not yet begun their treatment.

Suggestions ranged from ways of using time when appointments were missed to major service reviews to consider whether they were operating efficiently. It was seen as everyone's responsibility to try and make the best use of available time and this could mean taking time out to review a whole service, or individuals and teams looking at their own personal use of time.

3. Information

There were many ideas for different ways of getting information out to where it was needed. Some of the suggestions from the workshops were simple, many were heartfelt. Helplines such as NHS Direct were seen as useful ways of obtaining information, although not as a substitute for a proper consultation. Most of us like to feel that we are autonomous and making a phone-call or looking up a reputable website is much more immediate than waiting for an appointment if information is what we are after.

We heard about people's intense dislike of answer phones and preference for a real voice at the end of the line. The action plan led to a flurry of alternatives, including recruiting volunteers to man lines where people were often so busy that they switched on the answer phone just to get peace to complete a few vital tasks. To our surprise, the first place to engage a volunteer to do this was the finance department, resulting in them being teased about insulating themselves from demanding creditors!

Carers' needs for information were highlighted too, especially at the time of admission and discharge when it is often the patient who is the focus of attention. Carers' information packs were suggested, to be available in in-patient areas and out-patient clinics.

Directories of information seemed to be a popular solution where there was an information vacuum, but their accuracy, especially where they didn't cross-reference with each other, and the inadequacy of arrangements for them to be regularly updated, were challenged. The same applies to websites. Unless there is someone who is alert to new information and has responsibility for maintaining them, they quickly outlive their usefulness.

People wanted much more information about service changes, especially when the first they knew of a change to a service they used was when they read about it in the local newspaper. One action that resulted from this was to make the trust's in-house newsletter, originally meant for staff only, much more widely available.

Completing complicated forms was raised as a real problem for users of the trust's services, the main difficulty being that help was available from a variety of sources but not the information about how to access it.

4. Partnerships

Like time issues, partnerships could range from grand schemes, such as links between county-wide agencies, to interpersonal contacts such as two people talking together. The link between primary care and the mental health services was one which was particularly flagged up as needing attention. Just as important were small courtesies such as letting people know – whether they were staff or service users – about staff changes when people moved to new jobs.

There was appreciation of the wider picture with a request for the trust to do more about involving those who represented community interests outside the Health Service, such as local councillors and MPs who could be invited to patient and carer sessions to discuss concerns.

Outcomes

We have used the 'Telling It Like It Is' process countless times and it has never failed to startle and move the participants and, for many, to stimulate a refreshing identification with the service user experience. None of these examples of the many that were identified at the workshops is earth shattering. Some seemed too obvious to even need saying (like nurses telling patients that they were going to work elsewhere), but these seemingly insignificant examples mattered to the people who raised them. Collectively they would seem to suggest that important detail was being missed, a sort of inadvertent carelessness.

With a feedback deadline for the 'Telling It Like It Is' process six months later, there was no time to waste. Examples were shared across the action planning group so that directorates could learn from each other. More information poured in and gaps were identified. This amounted to an extensive trust-wide audit of all the PPI activity or lack of it, and told the group exactly what actions were needed to improve things. Perhaps the most important part of the cross-referencing process between directorates was that it passed the responsibility for following through the action plan, via their lead worker, back to them. They had the full support of the Centrepoint team if they needed help, but it meant that they were accountable for their own progress and this was what was to be fed back in six months' time. The next chapter describes what happened as a result.

'Telling It Like It Is': things to think about

Do as you would be done by: If you are an NHS worker, think about whether what you do would be good enough for yourself or your own nearest and dearest. If it isn't, what are the impediments? What can you do about them and who might be able to help?

Personal experiences: We've all had them: all been on the receiving end of services, all been to see our GP or accompanied someone else or had out- or in-patient hospital treatment. So how was it for you? What was good, bad or indifferent about it and what can you learn that you can use in your own field? Do you/can you talk about this experience to others and encourage them to think along these lines? What else might you be able to do to contribute this valuable experience to your organisation?

Recognising the value of personal experience: As well as the informal sharing of personal healthcare experiences that many people do over informal contacts and coffee breaks etc., this is about recognising its value in relation to our own working practice. How can we connect this personal experience with our work routines? How can we keep alert to the 'user experience' and sustain that attention and interest so that we don't take things for granted and forget what it feels like to be on the receiving end?

Raising awareness: If you are thinking of doing something similar to the sessions described in this chapter, a mix of service users and staff works very well but it can just as easily be done with staff alone. It is important to remember to use the 'we' language rather than service users being seen as 'they' or 'you'.

Running a 'Telling It' group: Emphasise the *listening* aspect – many of us have our hobby horses and need reminding about this. Bad experience creates an important learning opportunity. It shouldn't be brushed under the carpet but looked at constructively: how might things have been done differently?

Don't forget about payment for participants.

We chose to feed back the outcome to these sessions at a major event where the audit material was given to every participant and people were told about what would be happening next. The key to this is *involvement*. It doesn't matter how you do it, but people need to go away feeling curious about what is to happen next and that they might miss something if they aren't involved.

7

Getting on with the job

Feedback from 'Telling It Like It Is'

Most people won't have any particular reason for remembering 17 July 2002 even though it was a blisteringly hot day. Those of us who were at the feedback event which took place that day will probably never forget it. The aim was to give detailed feedback on progress with the action plans developed at the 'Telling It Like It Is' workshops, with no spin, no jargon, no frills. It was attended by 54 members of staff and 62 service users and carers, each of whom was given a report on the trust's recent patient survey and on each directorate's progress against the action plan. In addition, there were eight workshops where directorates presented examples of patient involvement they were particularly pleased about, with six of these being conducted by service users and carers. Examples included quality monitoring of forensic services, the use of advocacy for people with learning disabilities, selecting and recruiting staff with a service users' interview panel, patient participation in developing children's services and making a difference to black skin care. In addition there were plenary sessions by a local county councillor talking about the realities, i.e. difficulties, of engaging the community, how the trust had responded to the Better Hospital Food programme, and the reality of participation by mental health service users when consent to treatment issues were involved.

The real pin-dropping moment occurred when it came to the trust's chief executive's turn to speak. He told a story. It was about a young student who went to medical school and suffered a nervous breakdown. After two periods of in-patient treatment and lots of drugs and electro-convulsive therapy, he tried to go back to medical school but wasn't allowed to continue his studies. Not long after, he and his best friend were involved in a car crash and his friend was killed, leaving this man even worse off than he'd been before. With the help of a psychotherapist, he finally recovered and decided to do something else, eventually becoming the chief executive of an NHS trust. He was of course talking about himself and you can read more about his story in the final section of this book.

The impact of this information on the people who were there was palpable. At first there was silence and then a dawning awareness of the importance of what they had just been told, the courage it must have taken to tell it and its implications. What he went on to do was to promise to get a service user on to the trust board and it was this promise that led to the development of the Heart of the Trust Scheme and employment opportunities for service users and carers at the most senior organisational level.

At this point I was going to refer glibly to an increasing momentum within the trust to establish a working partnership with its service users and carers. The word 'partnership' carries that feelgood factor associated with sharing and understanding and respecting the knowledge that each partner can bring to the situation, but what does this mean in healthcare? Does it mean that those who provide the clinical services retain the superior status embodied in their hard-won medical education, but are a little more friendly when they have time? Does it mean that our board, from its elevated position, graciously invites one or two privileged service users to join it in its deliberations? Is the word partnership in fact a smokescreen to conceal genuine difficulty in knowing how to work together, as we don't seem to use it in relation to other people with expertise that we need – people like our solicitor who may steer us through a house purchase or a divorce, our car mechanic, or our accountant? With them, the nature of the relationship never seems to be in question.

The NHS isn't something we buy into according to the value we attach to the service, so consideration of the relationship we establish with those who provide the services, be they clinicians or managers, takes us into a murky world of slippery concepts like 'partnerships'. What is needed is recognition that the skills that we pay for through our taxes, which aim to support and heal us if we are sick, are of only limited value if the attitudes that underpin them do not include awareness and respect for the individual and their experience. As has already been identified, the importance of staff attitudes to patients recurs time and time again in responses to service user surveys.

Developing an honest partnership

What follows is a description of the growth of one particular partnership. 'Telling It Like It Is' and the Heart of the Trust Scheme were central to this growth, but there were many different aspects which influenced the thinking within the trust. It wasn't all plain sailing either, and in fact the voyage probably doesn't have an ending as the process is evolutionary, not finite. However, before embarking on a detailed description of the Heart of the Trust Scheme, it might be helpful to share some of the accumulated experience that influenced its design and contributed to this new thinking.

The traditional model of healthcare delivery has been one of skilled and knowledgeable clinicians, supported by a comprehensive management sub-structure, providing services for those who need them. The idea that these needy people might themselves have valuable and useful expertise as a result of their experience of ill health has only comparatively recently been recognised, for example in the Expert Patient Programme.[1] Alternatively, their expertise may have little to do with their healthcare experiences, but may be related to their ordinary life and work situation. This could be administrative, educational, clinical, financial, domestic, the sort of expertise that ordinary people acquire to earn their living, useful in any number of organisations. However, as a result of illness, particularly if it is associated with poor mental health, they may have found themselves discriminated against and unable to find employment. Clearly, there is no better way for an organisation that provides the services they have needed to help them recover to give them its own vote of confidence by taking them on to its staff.

South West London and St George's Mental Health NHS Trust

A well-developed project in South West London and St George's Mental Health NHS Trust, initiated in 1995, has resulted in many of that trust's staff being people who have used its services. To date, 126 people have been supported in to paid employment in the trust, 40% with a diagnosis of some form of psychosis and during 2004/05 a total of 15% of all new staff recruits had personal experience of mental health problems.

Three key components were identified which contributed to the project's success, the first being support for potential employees. This is currently being run as a 10-week work preparation course which includes seven weeks' experience in a work placement. This is long enough to gain skills, build confidence and get a reference. The course includes workshops on returning to work, gaining confidence and communication skills, and there is a weekly job club. This provides help with CVs, applications and interviews as well as acting as a support group. Welfare benefits advice is also available and work with staff groups is undertaken to address any concerns they might have about employing people with a health problem. Posts are carefully analysed so that potential applicants have a good idea of what will be required of them and detailed induction programmes include advice on how to make the transition from being a user of services to someone who works for the organisation that provides them. Particular difficulties have been to do with boundary issues and how much to tell work colleagues about health problems. Workplace mentors are available and ongoing support needs, both practical and emotional, are identified. Sometimes people need help with the disabling effects of symptoms at work or additional input during periods of difficulty. During its first four years, 71 people started the course, 53 of them completing the full 10 weeks. Of these, 21 are in paid employment, three in further education and six are doing voluntary work.

The second key component at this trust was a volunteer programme, used to provide people with experience and references in order to go on and apply for jobs in the open market. Although the programme has now been discontinued, it provided useful volunteer opportunities in both clinical and non-clinical areas, for example a buddy scheme to help particular clients, and administrative and reception posts as well as clinical support posts, for example in a clozapine clinic. Key elements were formal contracts for the volunteer posts, specifying what they entailed and the supervision available. There was also a carefully tailored matching process to ensure that there was a sufficient coincidence between the individual and the work they were required to do, to make the experience a realistic one, the idea very definitely being that it should be a stepping-stone to a real job. There were workplace supervisors, expense payments and active assistance in developing work skills and applying for jobs in open employment. It is all a far cry from the traditional volunteering opportunities of 20 years ago, associated with middle-class, retired people wheeling round trolleys of newspapers, soap and chocolate, and the symbiotic 'employment' of people in mental hospital utilities of years gone by.

The final component of their programme was to decrease employment discrimination throughout the trust, a key aspect of the 1995 Disability Discrimination Act. A charter was drawn up that specified the following:

- that mental health problems should not form a barrier to selection, providing the person fulfilled other requirements for the post
- that personal experience of mental health problems could make a positive contribution to the service offered by the organisation
- personal specifications for all clinical and client contact posts were to be modified to include 'personal experience of mental health problems' as desirable experience in addition to all other qualifications and qualities required for the post unless a specific case was made that a particular post should be exempt
- that the trust should monitor progress in recruiting people who have experienced mental health problems, via an addition to confidential equal opportunities monitoring, and working towards a target of 10% of the workforce being people who have experienced mental health difficulties
- that all trust job advertisements should carry an equal opportunities statement encouraging applications from people who have experienced mental health problems.

Guidelines from the Survivor Workers Conference 2002

These components are reflected in some useful good practice guidelines for employers that were drawn up by service users at a Survivor Workers Conference in 2002.[2] The conference was targeted at people who had used mental health services but the guidelines are just as relevant for users of any health services:

- there should be workload monitoring with appropriate structures to ensure that people can pace themselves realistically
- all employees should have equal access to training and career advice
- particular care should be taken to ensure that the harassment and bullying policy is closely observed
- employers should look and respond to the all-important question of whether their organisation was a 'safe' place in which to 'come out' about personal needs for support. People who 'come out' about these needs may feel isolated or patronised
- peer support systems are essential and time for this needs to be budgeted for and adjustments made to ensure that the support is available
- there needs to be an open and participative culture where information sharing is valued and comfortable and people do not make assumptions about each other's knowledge
- there needs to be a long-term strategy to integrate 'survivor worker' issues into human resource systems. This needs a supportive management style, not an oppressive one
- payment needs to be at the rate for the job.

The discrimination issue

Work is a key factor in sustaining good mental health and there is clear evidence[3] that employment schemes, such as the one already described, are beneficial to both staff and patients. Work contributes a sense of well-being and self-worth and can therefore be seen as a very positive influence on people's state of mind. Sadly, it can also be a contributory cause of mental health problems. Every day we read about longer and longer working hours in Great Britain and increases in stress-related problems. In a healthcare organisation employing 2400 people, 600 of them are likely to experience a mental health problem in one year alone. It is impossible to measure the extent of the social disruption and human misery this is likely to cause, but the loss of working hours is a more tangible consequence.

Public services appear to discriminate against people with mental health problems and yet it is an area where they ought to be leading the way. Healthcare organisations should be asking themselves whether they enable people with difficulties to work for them or whether they exclude them. Do they make it easy for us to acknowledge our problems and seek appropriate help or do they make us want to conceal it for fear of what others will say? It is interesting that the outcome to the chief executive divulging difficulties that he had overcome so effectively was to make it much 'safer' in the organisation for other people to do the same, contributing to the growth of a more open culture, which in turn reinforced anti-discriminatory attitudes that the Human Resources directorate was already promoting as a result of government policy.

So far we have emphasised mental health, but what about other healthcare areas? In the past, organisations over a certain size were supposed to have at least 3% of their employees 'registered disabled'. Those who were registered were then supposed to be grateful to have a job as a lift or car-park attendant. Fortunately times have changed and there is much more recognition that people don't have to be labelled as some sort of inadequate when they are perfectly capable of holding down a job. In fact, many of us who think of ourselves as able-bodied may not be 100% healthy, but that doesn't stop us from keeping a job and being a useful part of the workforce. All of which raises the perplexing question of what we mean by 'health'.

The easy answer to this is to fall back on the well-known but now dated definition contained in the World Health Organization's 1946 Constitution,[4] which states that 'Health is a state of complete physical, mental and social well-being, and not merely the absence of disease and infirmity'. Mercifully, the determinants of health now include references to the individual's social context and recognition that political and cultural circumstances over which they have no control can also be influential.[5] But the question remains of who decides whether we are healthy or not? Is it the doctor who tells us we are disease free or is it we ourselves who, knowing of conditions that could be defined as disease, say that we are happy with the lives we are able to lead in spite of this? There are many layers to this fascinating philosophical debate, far beyond the scope of this book. For a thoroughly stimulating and readable exploration of them, please read *Health: the foundations for achievement* by Professor David Seedhouse.[6]

The two ticks symbol

The 'positive about disabled' two ticks symbol means that any disabled job applicants who meet the minimum requirements for a vacancy *must* be interviewed and considered on their abilities. It requires disabled employees to have their needs discussed at least once a year and if someone becomes disabled whilst holding down a job, the organisation has a responsibility to sustain their employment. It also has to make sure that everyone knows about its 'two ticks' obligations. This is all very well but there's a problem in knowing who might need help. These days you don't have to register as disabled and lots of people manage residual disability without anyone knowing about it and would prefer to keep it that way. They certainly don't think 'disabled' even though they might be dyslexic or have a speech impairment, a learning disability, a back injury or a tendency to suffer with depression.

Others may have a bit of a struggle but worry about being labelled, when acknowledging the difficulty could lead to something being done about it. They need to feel that their contribution to their employers is valued and that the culture recognises limitations and will help to minimise them, but is more interested in strengths. Niall Dickson, Chief Executive of the King's Fund, when asked for his best piece of management advice, said 'Be positive and value your colleagues – they are your only real asset', so it works both ways. Divulging difficulties is of course a matter of personal choice but it doesn't have to mean suffering in silence. Stimulating a more open culture that recognises that while our capacity to do a decent job does not have to be impaired, things could be made easier for us, should result in a generally more responsive and supportive organisation.

Heart of the Trust Scheme: the idea

Creating job opportunities to show that we valued service users as equals, and putting ourselves in other people's shoes, were the key themes that influenced the development of South Staffs Healthcare NHS Trust's policy for Patient and Public Involvement. There was a feeling that the organisation needed to 'put its money where its mouth was' and show that it did not discriminate against people who had recovered from illness or who were disabled. The aim was to help people fulfil their potential through work. Not only was there evidence of benefits to both staff and patients, but there was also strong commitment within the trust. Three opportunity areas were apparent:

1 testing the water by providing opportunities to rehearse work-related skills in a supportive environment within the trust. This was to be achieved by establishing a database of voluntary jobs in which people could check out their potential and find out how ready they were to move into paid employment. As with the South West London and St George's scheme, there needed to be a good match between opportunities available and people who were volunteering to fill them

2 creating more employment opportunities within the trust. Anyone, including those who had received trust services, should be able to apply for jobs within the organisation, and provided they met the essential criteria for the job should have an equal chance of being appointed. To be more effective in achieving this, the trust needed to:
   – raise staff awareness and decrease disability discrimination

- work closely with Human Resources to ensure that policies and procedures were properly drawn up to reflect this approach – and make sure that everyone knew about them
- identify job opportunities within the organisation
- set up systems that would make it happen, e.g. making the trust staff vacancy list widely available
- ensure that people who were employed had the support networks they needed

3 appointing people with recent experience of trust services as associate directors on the trust board. The board agreed to appoint up to six associate directors, each available for the equivalent of four working days per month for a maximum of a two-year period. They were to be recruited and selected according to trust guidelines using the standard application form, followed by induction, regular appraisal and review. They were to be appointed as trust employees and paid at the same rate as non-executive directors, providing this did not jeopardise their benefit entitlement.

Opportunity areas

Creating opportunities within the trust for people to practise work-related skills, to have pre-employment training and then to get jobs was given a boost when European Social Funding (ESF) was obtained in March 2003. This enabled the trust to offer work trials, training and development for service users and people from disadvantaged backgrounds, and opportunities for real employment. It also engaged the local population and those using trust services in wider development, employment and social inclusion initiatives involving partnerships with the local community. Once the scheme had found its feet successes were quick in coming, and in less than six months it had found employment for 32 people with another 52 in work placements, some within the trust, some in external employment.

Eighteen-year-old 'Anna' is one example. With only one kidney and registered profoundly deaf and blind, the employment odds seemed to be stacked against her. She was referred to the scheme via her local job centre and within four weeks a placement had been found for her and funding was available for her transport costs, work clothes and help with training and support. She now works full-time for the trust as a ward hostess in a newly established eating disorders clinic.

Another, 'Andrew', had his life transformed when he got his job. Confined to a wheelchair, Andrew was rightly disgruntled that no one seemed to be able to find a use for his considerable IT skills. He looked and behaved like a surly loser. Then he found a job developing and maintaining the trust's database of 'members' when it applied for foundation trust status and he became a different man – smart, proud and confident.

Individual examples such as these are highly significant within an organisation because of their halo effect. People who work in healthcare are rarely isolated so positive experience and optimism as a result of being given this kind of opportunity will yield far more than the simple benefits of one person doing a job.

The final opportunity to get service users and carers onto the trust board was another employment opportunity, but it was tackled differently. The next chapter describes how.

Getting on with the job: things to think about

In an organisation: If you work in a healthcare environment, look at your organisation's own employment record and what it is doing to value workers' personal experiences of healthcare. Do all job advertisements encourage disabled applicants? Are job opportunities automatically passed through to job centres and their disability employment advisors (i.e. not just appearing in an internal job bulletin)? Does your organisation have the two ticks symbol? If not, why not?

Are we as an organisation enabling people with mental health problems to come and work with us or do we exclude them? How do people know that jobs are available?

If we have health problems: It may feel as though public services appear to discriminate against us. Do we feel taken seriously, believed? Are there problems in handling benefits? If we have difficulty at work because of a health-related problem, how comfortable is it to acknowledge it and seek appropriate help and do we feel supported in this process? Do those of us with some sort of disability conceal it for fear of what others in our workplace might say? Should we feel obliged to tell others?

Among work colleagues: Do teams know who is disabled? Should they? Should this include people with long-term chronic conditions such as asthma, diabetes and mental health problems as well as more obvious disabilities? If one of our colleagues is off sick long-term, do we feel supportive or cross because our own workload is increased?

References

1 Department of Health. *The Expert Patient: a new approach to chronic disease management for the 21st Century*. London: DoH; 2001.
2 Snow R. Stronger than ever: the report of the 1st National Conference of Survivor Workers UK. Stockport: Asylum; November 2002.
3 Simpson M, House A. Involving users in the delivery and evaluation of mental health services: a systematic review. *BMJ*. 2002; **325**: 1–5.
4 World Health Organization. Constitution. Basle, Switzerland: WHO; 1946.
5 Wass A. *Promoting Health: the primary healthcare approach*. Sydney: Harcourt Sanders; 2000.
6 Seedhouse D. *Health: the foundations for achievement*. Chichester: Wiley; 2001.

8

The Heart of the Trust Scheme

The scheme in outline

The aim of this scheme was to design a process for successfully recruiting and selecting not one but six co-opted associate directors to the trust board, who had experience of using trust services within the previous three years or were carers of people who had. They had to live in the area the trust served and they had to have at least one day a week available in time. They were to be paid at the same rate as non-executive directors which, pro rata at that time, worked out at £4155 per annum.

The trust wanted them to be the eyes and ears of the organisation and the voice of its service users and carers. This was to demonstrate to everyone – people providing services, those receiving them and the community at large – that partnership working was central to the organisation. That is, central enough for board members to share their authority with people who knew what it felt like to be on the receiving end of the decisions they made. In order to be able to do this job, the appointees would need to have a thorough knowledge of the organisation and its networks and they would need drive and enthusiasm to negotiate the steep learning curve that this would demand. The idea was that they should be able to hit the ground running, so induction was important as well as appropriate support to enable them to get on with the job. As a pilot scheme, there would need to be an evaluation to see whether it actually worked and justified the expense. If it did, then the intention would be to increase the number of associates to enhance their impact across the organisation.

People said it couldn't be done. They gave two main reasons. The first was that board appointments had to be made via the Office of Public Appointments. This wasn't strictly true. Providing a board is in agreement, it can co-opt whoever it wants to join it. This meant that the first key task was to make a good enough case to get the board to agree to the idea. The other reason why they thought it couldn't be done was because of the benefits situation, and to a certain extent they were right. A fixed-term contract of 51 weeks had been deliberately designed, following advice that if for any reason people did not want to continue, their benefits could be reinstated providing they had been in employment for less than a full year. It is a wicked contradiction that our present benefits system inhibits rather than encourages people to seek employment, even when they very much want to do so, for fear that they will lose such financial support as they already have. Great care was taken to refer applicants with benefits issues to expert advisors to ensure that they got sound information, rather than the trust attempting to provide it. Even so, one of the associates had to reluctantly withdraw at the end of the 51-week period because the 'expert' advice she had received that she should be able to continue was incorrect. It is a minefield and one that does not encourage people to extricate themselves from the sad silo of unemployment. Even so, among the 38 applicants there were a great many other people who had used services, who were not in employment but who nevertheless managed to provide for themselves independently.

Having reviewed precedents from elsewhere, the trust found there were no real solutions to the problem of representativeness to ensure that its wide geographical area and range of services was covered. It is interesting that the argument sometimes used to undermine the credibility of a service user at a meeting, that they are not 'representative' of a larger constituency of users, never seems to be levelled at professionals who are clearly attending in a representative capacity. On the basis that several associates are likely to provide broader representation than a single one, a decision was made to appoint six associates to work as a team, but available for one day each a week on a flexible basis.

Advertisements for the posts in the local press were preceded by broadcast interviews on local radio by the chief executive and press releases. Three informal open evenings were held where people could come and find out more about the jobs and have their questions answered. Evidence of the board's commitment to the scheme was there right at the start with the open evenings being attended by the board chairman, the chief executive and various directors. This support has been sustained, with associates reporting unanimous encouragement and respect from board members and being given prominent roles at all high-profile trust events. Their presence and contribution has been seen to be valued at the most senior level of the organisation, an important signal to everyone who is a part of it.

It comes as something of a contradiction, given this level of support, to say that there was no budget available to pay for these posts, and there was concern that should non-recurrent funding be sought as a pump-primer, the lack of guarantee of continuity might deter some applicants. Faced with the dilemma of launching the scheme with uncertain sustainability or not launching it at all, the trust opted for the blind faith approach in the hope that if it proved successful, somehow money would be found to keep it going. It was initially supported by £30,000 of Modernisation Agency funding via the Strategic Health Authority's Workforce Development Directorate and designated a pilot scheme, subject to evaluation. This slightly wobbly position was made clear to all applicants as the trust didn't want to raise their expectations unrealistically.

Selection and recruitment

Every stage of the selection and recruitment process, including drafting of the job description, was checked with both Human Resources to ensure that we were not in breach of any NHS regulations and local service users (some of whom were already trust employees or members of voluntary sector organisations). Useful advice was given on the user-friendliness of the information packs and the application materials. Of particular concern were the short-listing criteria, as the trust has disability symbol listing and needed to ensure that the standards for this were upheld. This is the two ticks symbol that identifies employers who have agreed to meet five commitments regarding the employment, retention, training and career development of disabled employees. The most important of these commitments at this point in time was the guarantee to interview everyone who met the minimum criteria for the job. With over 80 requests for information packs, there were likely to be a large number of applicants, so it was essential that these criteria were clearly defined. As well as a more formal job description based on a standard one for non-executive directors, other information was included about 'who we need and what you will do'. This was to counteract the feeling of some board members that the formal job description might be rather off-putting and it also included details of the kind of support available to associate directors if appointed.

On the first page of this information were the 10 short-listing minimum criteria, and on the application form people were asked to give 10 practical examples to show the trust that they had each of these qualities. Even so, some apparently suitable applicants, for example people who had held senior positions in business and management, had to be excluded from the short list because they failed to do this. It was a question of achieving a balance between making the application process as straightforward and unthreatening as possible whilst recognising that people were being invited to share in the responsibility for a very complex organisation with a multi-million pound budget. Dumbing down the appointments process was not an option.

Anyone who needed help with completing an application form or writing their CV was offered it and prior to submitting an application it was suggested that people should attend a trust board meeting. Public attendance at board meetings is rare but much to the board's surprise, nine people took up this offer. Each of the 14 people who were subsequently short-listed and interviewed was offered interview training and support, received a copy of the board papers for the following meeting and were invited for a buffet lunch beforehand. This was to enable board members to meet them informally before they were interviewed. At interview they were then invited to comment on how they had found the meeting, not as a test of memory but simply to see what their reaction had been.

After two full days of interviewing, the panel, consisting of the trust board chairman, a non-executive director (with a special interest in PPI), the Heart of the Trust Scheme manager and a service user representative from the regional office of the National Institute of Mental Health, England, appointed the first group of six associate directors. As it happened, they spanned a useful range of services, ages and geographical areas. All of these associates remained in post for the full 51-week duration of their contract. Two, because of not wanting to jeopardise their benefits, accepted contracts offering a reduced number of hours, the remaining four were employed for a single day's work each week. The contracts were fixed-term, trust contracts with the same safeguarding terms and conditions as applied to any other employees. Following evaluation, the trust board enthusiastically agreed to extend the contracts of those associate directors who wished to remain in post for another year, and increase the total number from six to nine. The selection and recruitment process was then successfully repeated to fill the gaps.

Interestingly, at post-interview feedback, three unsuccessful applicants commented on how the interview training and support had increased their confidence. None had expected to reach that stage and they had found it to be a great morale booster. Three others expressed interest in becoming PPI Forum members and were given information about this. Contact details for another who wished to develop involvement with a particular service were passed to that service and subsequently successfully followed up. Five people who weren't short-listed challenged the decision and in each case accepted the explanation given about the criteria. One man, at the end of this conversation, said, 'No, on that basis, I wouldn't have short-listed me either.'

Induction

During the eight-week induction period, it was agreed that all six associate directors would attend weekly on the same day. The detailed programme of individual introductions, visits to different service areas, team-building sessions, decisions about individual objectives and the planning of future team objectives, evaluation interviews, and meeting preparation including the reading and understanding of huge amounts of literature left everyone breathless. Initially it was quite tightly planned, but as the associates began to spread their wings they set their own agenda. All the associates at some point during this phase expressed concern about whether they would be able to do enough in the time available to make a difference, and in fact all contributed considerably more of their own time than they were contracted for. This wasn't ideal, but such was their enthusiasm it was hard to stop them.

Their views varied about induction. Of the six who were appointed first time round, three were familiar with the organisation because of previous involvement with trust service user networks. Whilst appearing to give them an initial advantage in terms of their confidence, because they knew their way around the organisation and who to approach for help, it also created differences in their perception of their role and influenced team development. Associates who already knew the organisation had acquired this knowledge through having some kind of responsibility for service user and carer involvement. They were keen to use their new role to get on with their individual pre-existing work. They tended to see the induction programme as an unnecessary interruption to things that were already in hand. What was missing here was recognition that as associate directors, their role, their responsibilities and their opportunities had changed. 'Knowing' the organisation as they already did was not necessarily an advantage and their initial confidence, although helpful to the others in finding their way around and making sense of the healthcare environment, also proved a little daunting to them.

There was an expectation from some associate directors that they would be 'told' what to do and that the job parameters would be very specifically defined. A decision had been made during the scheme's preparation to avoid this. It was felt that although the associates might feel initially insecure, a tight definition of their role could compromise the very authority that was inherent in their appointment to the board. It was therefore essential to achieve a balance between support and freedom to act on issues that were important to them rather than organisationally defined. Individual supervision and mentoring were essential at this stage to give them the courage of their convictions.

It is interesting here to make a comparison with the experience of foundation trust governors, those people elected from local communities to represent patients, staff and the public and give them a say in the running of their local foundation trust. Among them, there have been complaints of lack of role clarity, difficulty in establishing links between the organisation and the community, and doubts about the extent of their influence. Although the first group of associate directors started with a blank sheet as far as their role was concerned, resulting in some of them experiencing initial insecurities, they received regular and ongoing support and supervision as well as team-building opportunities. This, coupled with proactive involvement from the trust board, may well have contributed to a more effective association between themselves and the organisation.

By the time the second wave of associates had been appointed, a role 'culture' was beginning to emerge that helped to reduce these initial insecurities.

Getting on with the job and some outcomes

A pattern of activity emerged over time. With the induction period over, associates spent one day a month together, feeding back on what they had been doing and working on objectives. They made a regular monthly contribution to trust board papers and its in-house newsletter on their activities and things they had noticed around the organisation, and they have been conspicuous at its various high-profile events, giving presentations and acting as co-chairmen. They often invited staff to come and talk to them about their work and also had regular meetings with the trust's PPI Forum members. The rest of the time was theirs to organise as they thought most useful, but all too quickly it was consumed with requests for their participation, both individually and at a range of meetings.

The advantages of having a group are very apparent. Not only were they able to spread their involvement across all trust services and penetrate the organisation extensively, but they balanced each other's strengths and limitations and were mutually supportive as a team. This reflected care taken with the design of the scheme and the selection and recruitment process, but more importantly the extent to which they felt themselves to be valued by the trust and therefore they had the capacity to value each other.

Associates attended board meetings in pairs and in turn, but their views and those of the other directors about the value of spending time in this way were mixed. For all six to attend each meeting would have overloaded the board and been both time-consuming and inefficient. Not only were there pre- and post-meeting briefing sessions plus a half day for the meeting itself, but there were weighty board papers to be read and digested. Clearly their presence was making an important organisational statement, but the amount of time it took in relation to their availability was a concern. The truth of the matter is that most of the work of a trust board gets done outside the boardroom so that board meetings become largely a rubber-stamping formality. Although associates had equal opportunity alongside other board members to contribute to the agenda on issues of concern to them, with their very limited time their ambivalence about the meetings was understandable.

The commitment of the chief executive and the trust board was crucial in confirming the status of the associates and giving them authority. Initially, several of them expressed concern that they might lose their service user and carer focus and in effect go 'native' by identifying too strongly with the organisation and its workers. Charges of bias and 'being unrepresentative' are regularly paraded as weaknesses in the development of a service user and carer focus. What is generally overlooked by this argument is the variety of biases that we all carry within us, and as Brady and Hopkins[1] argue, if we exclude people on this basis then we should all be excluded, staff and service users and carers alike. As far as they could tell, the associate directors did not feel they were being unduly influenced by their close engagement with the trust. All reported increased confidence and authority and they appeared to earn wide respect and recognition, which was stimulating staff to draw in other service users and carers to help them.

Those associates are all over the place and into everything. Everyone seems to know about them.

Service Manager

When I have attended meetings outside the trust and informed other carers and professionals about the scheme, there have been two reactions. One is that people have been impressed with the trust for taking this step, followed by 'Isn't this a tick-box scheme?' My response is that it could have been but we simply aren't tick-box people.

Associate Director

No, I don't think I've gone native. I'm not as rough and challenging as I used to be, but that's because I've learned how to work the system in order to make things change. Before, I just used to put people's backs up.

Associate Director

The presence of the associate directors helped to increase the momentum of a major culture change across the organisation. Three board sub-committees (Human Resources and Organisational Development, Clinical Governance, and Service User and Carer) invited service users and/or carers to attend on a regular basis and directorates started to include service users and carers in their six-monthly performance management sessions. These were not token appearances as their feedback was entirely independent. Regular attendance also created the opportunity for the associates and other service users and carers to learn about the complexities of NHS organisations and understand the importance of objective setting and achievement. This means that they really can be the eyes, ears and voice of service users within the trust.

Early engagement with members of the trust's PPI Forum raised the question of the difference between their roles. Scrutiny from the patient's viewpoint was clearly a key issue, the difference being that the associate directors had an additional responsibility to see what they could do to bring about change when they identified a particular concern. To this end, they convened a bi-monthly Heart of the Trust Action Group (HotT Action Group), with a lead service user and carer staff representative from each directorate. This was a forum where problems could be aired, solutions sought and examples of good practice shared and it effectively closed the loop between senior representation and front-end service delivery. What is important here is that the associate directors were acting as facilitators. Rather than attempting the daunting task of trying to bring about change themselves within each directorate, they were passing the responsibility back to the staff groups working within it.

Another question raised has been about the relationship between the associates and the trust's non-executive directors. In some NHS organisations, non-executives are seen as service user and carer representatives by proxy, with the opportunity to penetrate the trust in much the same way as the South Staffs associate directors. So be it, but in this particular trust non-executives already had clearly defined lead responsibilities, for example chairing various committees, so the associates were seen as very usefully extending the board's remit in a different dimension.

The following outcomes are ones that the associate directors themselves have stimulated. Inevitably they relate to one particular organisation and the services it provides, but it gives an idea of the range and depth of their influence. One unquantifiable but significant outcome indicating cultural change is how much more open staff have become about acknowledging their own experience of services or that of their families. It has become acceptable to say 'Yes, I know what it feels like', and to recognise the value of that knowledge.

Specific outcomes achieved by the associate directors

- Following their induction the associates developed a team objective: 'to improve the opportunities for meaningful daytime occupation in the trust.' They had been struck by the regularity with which complaints about lack of anything to do recurred in patients' surveys and also the lack of consistency across the trust in provision of both activity and equipment. With the help of occupational therapists, they undertook a trawl of what activities were available and where. Not only did they then review resource and transferability issues to try and improve equity of provision across the trust, but they also conducted a survey to find out staff attitudes to being involved in patient activity and whether they saw this as part of their nursing role.

- Associates were invited by the chief executive to set him an objective to be launched at the trust's annual general meeting. They agreed he should ensure that 'Service user and carer involvement continues to be *real* and at the heart of this organisation'. To this end he supported an increase in the number of associate directors to be appointed when the scheme was reviewed by the trust board.

- One associate undertook a survey of volunteer involvement, distribution and support and this was presented to the trust board. It subsequently contributed to a review of the trust's use of volunteers, staff anxieties about involving them, useful suggestions about where they might contribute and the improvement of policies, contracts and training. A training pack was developed leading to clearer expectations for all parties and more efficient and effective use of volunteer time.

- Involvement of service users in staff selection and recruitment had been ad hoc. The trust's most recent Staff Selection and Recruitment policy now includes detailed advice on how to involve service users and carers at every stage of the process. This is as a result of associates having contributed to interviews and feeding back on their experience. This is described in more detail in Chapter 11.

- Partnerships with voluntary sector groups have been consolidated through the regular attendance of associates at joint meetings. Particularly useful have been the contacts with carers groups both for children and for those with a learning disability. The important thing here is not simply being there, but feeding back through the HotT Action Group so that there is a link for directorates with external support networks.

- Associates are highlighting what matters to service users and carers, e.g. waiting areas, quality of correspondence, admission experiences, etc. These are routine things which are so much part and parcel of ordinary daily activity that it is easy to overlook their impact on individuals, and for the organisation to give them a low priority. Unresolved issues that might have appeared insignificant to staff but which clearly matter to patients are given credibility, leading to change.

- Identifying and drawing attention to the resolution of an issue in one area has stimulated other centres to follow an example of good practice. This happened after a patient waiting area had been dramatically improved with better lighting, pictures on the walls, more information presented in a user-friendly form, optional music and up-to-date magazines. The brighter atmosphere has had a positive effect on both staff and patients using the area.
- A major issue identified by the associates was the scheduling of mental health consultants' ward reviews, many of which took place at the same time on the same day. This resulted in overstretched nursing staff having to service the reviews and therefore not being available to patients. Review timetables and procedures were themselves reviewed to resolve this situation. This sounds like a blindingly obvious need, but nothing had been done about it until the associates drew attention to it.
- Associates drew attention to a pre-existing Advocacy Service when they discovered that it was being underutilised because some staff were unaware of its existence and their responsibility to tell patients about it.
- Support for carers and parents of disabled children was a particular concern for the associate directors. As well as drafting a carers' strategy for the trust, they initiated new support groups using examples of good practice in one area to stimulate new developments in another. These included a 'school for parents' which gives them training in how to help their children with their disability. In one instance a serious crisis was averted by one of the associates when one of the children's centres was required to move to a new base. Insufficient attention had been paid to the anxiety this had generated for parents, but the intervention of the associate ensured that their concerns were recognised and dealt with appropriately.

Impact on the people doing the job

All of the associates commented on how much they had enjoyed working together and the camaraderie that developed, which they found very supportive. Their confidence increased and this enabled them to move around the organisation with ease and authority. Some enhanced their speaking and presentation skills and there was general enthusiasm for the status they were accorded and the sense of being valued. Initial concern that they might lose their independent view and have their voice either ignored or stifled would appear to be unfounded. This voice perhaps became less strident, but if anything gained in strength and purpose as they found more effective ways of working within the organisation to achieve their objectives. Of the first six appointees, four departed having completed their contracts. One needed to become a full-time carer for her mother, one left because had she remained she would have had to relinquish her benefits, one got a full-time job as a carer's support worker and one 'wanted a rest'. Later, because of starting a 'new life' elsewhere, another of the original appointees left, but the selection and recruitment process was repeated to ensure a full complement of associates.

In the early days of the scheme, it was suggested that appointments should be limited to a maximum of two years. This was to ensure that the essential user perspective did not lose its edge or become overwhelmed by professional attitudes. In the event, a process of natural attrition has evolved resulting in a regular injection of 'new blood'. This easily outweighs the disadvantages of losing culture carriers and the time and costs of repeating the selection and recruitment process.

The future

A successful application for foundation trust status, considerably enhanced by the presence of the associate directors, has meant yet another change for this organisation. In the future, it will be looking to its governor members to undertake more strategic monitoring, whilst associate directors continue with local promotion of the Service User and Carer agenda, based on their opportunities to be directly involved with the trust's different services. Valuable lessons have been learned, however, especially about the importance of induction and ongoing support, and it is anticipated that the associate directors' contribution to meeting these needs will be invaluable. Foundation trusts will require huge numbers of members, some of whom will be elected to become governor members (around 40 to 60 per trust) with specific legal responsibilities as well as the opportunity for providing service user feedback, mentoring, brokering community support and getting involved in specific work projects. The induction process for these governor members will be crucial in determining the extent to which they can make a real and active contribution to the trust's work and management. Indeed, a study at one of the first trusts to gain foundation status called for clearer national guidelines to define governors' powers and responsibilities following complaints from the governors that they had little influence and were uncertain about what was expected of them, undermining their role as 'community watchdogs'.

Key principles for bridging the divide between the community and the services it needs and active participation of its citizens are:

- respect for their values
- close attention to their level of knowledge about NHS matters and appropriately tailored development and team-building opportunities
- adequate mentoring and supervision
- clearly defined channels for information exchange
- participatory opportunities at every level of the organisation.

Heart of the Trust Scheme: recruitment materials

1. Job information

SERVICE USER AND CARER ASSOCIATE DIRECTOR

Who we need and what you will do

YOU SHOULD:

- have interest and enthusiasm for improving our services
- be comfortable talking and listening to what people have to say, both those who work with us and those who use our services
- be able to observe what we do and give us feedback on what needs changing

- be able to challenge us where this is needed and stand up for what is important for patients and carers
- respect and appreciate views different from your own
- be able to take responsibility and follow things through
- have high standards of personal behaviour and absolute integrity
- be able to work in a group
- be able to think about the future
- be able to think of different ways of doing things and add your own ideas.

YOU WILL NEED:

- experience of using or caring for someone who uses this trust's services within the last three years
- four days a month available on a flexible basis
- to live in the area served by this trust.

YOU WILL:

- work alongside other associates and the senior team contributing to the board
- help to ensure the best use of our resources to maximise the benefits to patients
- attend and contribute to trust board meetings and keep in touch with our patients, carers and staff
- report back to the trust board on what you have been doing
- be the eyes and ears of the organisation and the voice of our service users and carers.

HOW WE WILL HELP YOU:

- Before you start you will be offered a confidential 'Better Off in Work' interview to make sure you do not lose out if you are on benefits.
- Your pay will be £4155 a year. (This is taxable and subject to Class 1 National Insurance contributions. It is not pensionable.)
- You will be able to claim a staff travel allowance to help you move around the trust.
- In your first two months we will help you to settle in by showing you around the trust, introducing you to our workers and some of the meetings they go to.
- There will be a whole day during this time to work out how best you and the other associate directors can do your job.
- There will be regular briefings so that you know what to expect at board meetings and how you can contribute.
- Every three months we will discuss your progress and look at opportunities to increase your skills through training and staff development.
- We will give you regular support and supervision.

2. Job description

SERVICE USER AND CARER ASSOCIATE DIRECTOR OF THE TRUST

Objectives
1 To operate as a co-opted member of the trust board.
2 To provide independent scrutiny and constructive challenge within the board.
3 To ensure that the needs of patients, their carers and the interests of the local community are always at the forefront of the board's thinking.
4 To play a part in building constructive partnerships with the local community, groups and other organisations.
5 To safeguard the rights of service users by general scrutiny of services.
6 To ensure that the board is focused on service user and carer-related outcomes when formulating trust strategies and policies.
7 To support service user and carer involvement throughout the trust on behalf of the board.

Responsibilities and role

- As a user and carer associate director of the trust you will normally work alongside other associates and the senior team as equal contributors to the board. You will be expected to use your skills together with your personal experience of your community and the NHS to contribute to the work of the NHS trust.
- You will contribute to the strategic development of long-term plans for healthcare in your community.
- You will help to ensure the best use of financial and other resources in order to maximise benefits to patients.
- You may be asked to take part in the appointment of trust staff.
- You will have access to various meetings and board sub-committees and the associated papers.
- You will help to ensure that the NHS trust promotes equal opportunities for both its staff and its patients.
- You may be asked to attend official occasions where trust board representation is requested.
- You will help to ensure that the trust meets its commitment to patients and targets for treatment.
- You will be expected to exercise an involvement and concern which goes beyond your personal experience as a user and carer.
- You will contribute to building and maintaining a close relationship between all those in your community concerned with healthcare delivery, promotion and prevention.

Induction, appraisal and personal development opportunities

- As a trust associate director, you and your colleagues will receive two months' detailed induction programme to prepare you to take an active role in contributing to the board meetings. This will include visits to sites where trust services are delivered and training opportunities that enable you to increase your skills and understanding of the work of the board.

- Initial appraisal will take place after three months and then on a six-monthly basis. At each session, progress will be reviewed and training and development needs identified.
- You will receive regular supervision and support.

Time commitment

- We expect you to spend up to four days a month on board responsibilities. This may be during the working day or in the evening.

Duties

- Following your induction, there will be a whole-day action planning event to work out how best you can do your job.
- We would expect you to visit trust facilities, attend a range of meetings and provide a regular written report for the trust board meeting detailing activities throughout the preceding month. You may be invited to speak about this report at the meeting.
- In order that you will know what will happen at the board meeting and what you have to do afterwards, there will be regular briefing sessions to review the papers and agree actions.
- We would expect you to agree with your colleagues a monthly timetable to ensure that service users and carers are represented at key meetings. This will require appropriate preparation.
- Your task is to be the eyes and ears of the organisation and the voice of service users and carers.

Place of residence

- As the voice of people experiencing trust services and therefore of the local community, you will normally live in the area served by the NHS trust unless you represent a service drawing on a wider population.

Remuneration

- Trust associate directors will receive remuneration of £4155 per annum.
- Trust associates are eligible to claim allowances, at rates set centrally, for travel costs necessarily incurred on trust business.

Appointment and tenure of office

- Trust board associates will be appointed for an initial period of up to 51 weeks. Appointments may be renewable at the end of this period subject to satisfactory appraisal and scheme development. A degree of change is often sought on boards and there should therefore be no expectation of automatic reappointment.
- To ensure that public service values are maintained at the heart of the National Health Service, all directors of NHS boards are required on appointment to subscribe to the Codes of Conduct for NHS Managers 2002 (appendix 2). This will also apply to trust board associate directors.

3. Further information

ASSOCIATE DIRECTOR POST: TOP TEN QUESTIONS

1 What will I have to do in this job?

– We'd like you to be the eyes and ears of our organisation, telling us about the things that are important to service users and carers and making sure that their needs come first in our thinking and decision making. Learning what makes the Trust tick and what the back-up squad does to help clinicians get on with their jobs will also be important.

– This means that you will need to get out and about, meeting people who use our services as well as staff who provide them. You will also need to go to quite a few meetings, shared out between you and the other Associate Directors, where you can take part on behalf of our service users and carers.

– There is a lot we can all learn from each other so feeding back will be an important part of the job, both informally to the people you meet and also to the Trust Board.

2 Will taking one of these posts affect my benefits?

– Possibly, but we have purposely given them a fixed-term contract of 51 weeks so that all of your benefits are automatically reinstated if for any reason you choose not to continue. If you are successful with your application, you will have the chance of a confidential 'Better off in Work' interview where you can discuss your personal financial situation. You will also be able to talk to our Work–Life Balance Coordinator about this.

3 Where will I be based?

– At Trust headquarters where there is an Associates' office, but we will encourage people to contribute in a number of ways to suit their ability to move around and their interests. If you don't live locally to the Trust HQ and don't have your own transport, this need not stop you from applying for one of these posts.

4 Do I need a car?

– Not necessarily, but if you do have one it would be useful and you would receive an allowance to meet the cost of any driving required by your job. For non-car owners, we would expect to be able to help you plan your work in a way that enabled you to do the job.

5 Who can I turn to if I need help or there are things I don't understand?

– There are a lot of people who are keen to work with you both individually and as an associates group. For example, there will be regular briefing and feedback sessions every month so that you can play a useful part at board meetings and make sense of the papers that go with them. You will also have access to board members and the opportunity to observe services, talk to any members of staff and follow up issues. As well as this, every associate will have choice of a mentor and regular super-vision as well as support from the Patient and Public Involvement team.

6 Who will be my boss?

- – Your official link will be with our human resources director, but the chair of the board and our chief executive have both offered their personal support too.
- – On a day-to-day basis, a member of the Patient and Public Involvement team will be there to share in the work with you and there are already other associate directors in post who know the ropes and will be able to help you get started.

7 What happens if I get sick?

- – You would do the same as any other member of staff, which is to let us know and ask for messages to be forwarded if you are unable to keep appointments. People are very understanding. If you are sick for a longer period, then again the process would be the same as for all trust staff and you would be told what to do.

8 How can I find out more about the job?

- – Read all the information in this pack and if you still have unanswered questions, contact Kate in the trust's Patient and Public Involvement team and she will be pleased to help you.

9 How long is the job for?

- – Fifty-one weeks in the first instance. This is so that benefits can be reinstated if you do not want to continue. We would like you to stay long enough to be able to do something useful in the organisation, but on the other hand it's always good to have people taking a fresh look at things.

10 How will I know what is going on in the trust?

- – We have a regular briefing sheet called 'Trust Matters' (there's a copy in your information pack) that gives us all the trust news. There is also 'Express' that comes out after the monthly trust management board meetings and tells us what the board has been discussing and deciding. And, of course, we exchange information via our internal e-mailing system, which you would have access to.

Heart of the Trust Scheme: things to think about

Getting service users and carers onto a trust board: This may seem like a good idea, but putting it into practice throws up many questions. If your organisation has or is likely to become a foundation trust, some of these questions may be relevant to the role of governor members.

- How comfortable are existing board members with the idea and what do you need to do to prepare them?
- What will your service user/carer board members be called?
- Do you have a budget to pay a realistic wage?

- What will the job involve and who will service user/carer board members be accountable to?
- Who will define the job description, check it, etc.?
- How will you organise the selection and recruitment process?
- How many will be employed, for how long and under what terms and conditions?
- Have you considered having a two-way probationary period in case of unanticipated difficulties?
- Do you have suitable office accommodation, appropriate facilities and equipment: an office, computers, admin support, etc.?
- Mentoring, supervision, support: who will give it and how?
- How will 'representativeness' be accommodated? For example, will appointees have a function beyond the boundaries of their own 'constituency'?
- What plans have you made for induction?
- How will you encourage involvement with the rest of the trust?
- Will they attend board meetings and what will happen in the 'private' session? Will they be excluded?
- What will be the position with board voting rights?
- What is the future of the organisation and is this a short-term scheme or is it sustainable?

Reference

1 Brady M, Hopkins H. Consumer and community participation in health research. *Aust Health Consumer*. 2001; 1 (Summer): 21–3.

9

'Singing from the same hymn sheet': developing a strategy, structures and systems

Why a strategy?

These days, given the frequent policy changes, system revisions and changes to healthcare organisations, trying to pin down a strategic approach can feel like trying to grasp a jelly; and even when you eventually feel you have managed it, you can discover that it is suddenly the wrong flavour. For example, in South Staffordshire, following the 'Telling It Like It Is' programme the trust had undertaken a detailed audit of service user and carer involvement and formulated an action plan to pick up on gaps and inadequacies, but this was not acceptable to the healthcare commissioners (CHI as it then was). In spite of explanations that service users and carers had dismissed the idea of developing a strategy as tedious and uninteresting when invited to participate, they insisted that one should be written. What they wanted was a clear plan of what the organisation had in place, what it felt had been achieved, what it was planning to do and how and when it would get there.

With hindsight they were right. From their point of view, they needed written evidence that there had been a process of systematic thought as to how the organisation was to deliver a particular aspect of government policy. This would be useful at both the macro and micro levels, contributing to a national response but also providing the organisation with its own plan and sense of direction. In general terms, the idea is to ensure that everyone is 'singing from the same hymn sheet'. Our mistake was in the language that we used. Instead of inviting people to participate in the development of a strategy, we should have asked them if they were interested in influencing the organisation and how it delivered its services – then the response might have been different. We tend to avoid things that sound abstract, too technical or theoretical. What we then lose sight of is their purpose. A strategy should not be constraining, it is after all a neutral term offering liberating opportunities to do what a representative group of people thinks should be done.

Another aspect of strategy development is that it recognises that there are different interests that have to be reconciled, and this is really important in attempting to bridge the gap between service users and professionals. It needs to be a rational plan for successful action and agreed outcomes for participants who may be interdependent but who nevertheless may also be in competition, for example for resources. In fact the *process* for developing a strategy may be far more important than the completed document. Consideration of how different vested interests can be reconciled may be an important part of working out a grand plan. This needs all participants to sit round the same table, to identify and prioritise the issues and discuss how they can be resolved. It does not mean that at this point in time solutions will necessarily be found, but objectives can be identified that will enable progress towards them.

In effect, a strategy should be a statement of an organisation's aims and objectives and how these are prioritised. It should describe the structures, systems and processes that already exist or will be required to support the objectives, and should identify how anticipated challenges will be met and opportunities created. It should also indicate how resulting achievements will be measured, consolidated and developed to meet future needs, insofar as it is possible to predict these. As far as service user and carer involvement is concerned, it should in effect be a blueprint for how the organisation is going to *do* it. It will therefore need to identify a starting point, i.e. where the organisation is at the moment, what it is hoping to achieve and how it will get there.

Practicalities also need to be considered. There are plenty of helpful 'recipes' for strategy writing (e.g. in *Involving Patients and the Public* by Chambers *et al.*[1]), but these don't always deal with obvious questions such as who is going to write it, who is going to implement it and how it will be monitored to see whether it is making a difference. We wanted to share in the development of a strategy with our service users and carers, but they turned the idea down. They wanted to know what the organisation was going to *do* to improve things in accord with their suggestions. In effect, the final result was a strategy written around those suggestions with a nod to the requirements of government policy.

Key areas

I once heard of a trust that had a four-word service user and carer strategy, and this was 'No more Mrs Moffatts'. As a result of her care or lack of it, this unfortunate lady had suffered a series of setbacks resulting in her eventual demise, which might have been avoided, and a damaging inquiry. Whether this strategy would have satisfied CHI is not known, but it successfully served to remind staff of the clinical governance principles that needed to be supported in order for them to provide a first-class, up-to-date, evidence-based service. It also speaks the language of service users and carers, rather than plunging everyone into the murky and unfathomable rhetoric of organisational and health service jargon. We need to be mindful of phrases like 'providing a seamless service' or even the 'whole systems approach' quoted in example 1 below. A 'seamless service' sounds good but actually fails to recognise the realities of different agencies working together. Yes, they may have a common objective such as improving patient care, but in order to do this they may have to reconcile many different aspects of their learning, understanding and cultures. Talking about a 'seamed' service, rather than a seamless one, recognises that work has had to be done in joining the two in order to create a strong seam. Seamlessness suggests that if you align two agencies they will automatically and effortlessly merge and blend – a very unreal and unlikely outcome.

A four-word strategy is perhaps a touch minimalist, but here are two examples of aims from two different organisations that have been very simply expressed.

Example 1

1 To improve patient and carer participation in all aspects of service delivery.
2 To improve existing partnerships to achieve a true 'whole systems' approach to patient and public participation.
3 To develop new ways of working that demonstrate our commitment to our partners.
4 To enjoy the confidence of our service users and those who care for them, that we will listen to them, learn from them and act responsibly upon what we hear.
5 To develop a shared learning culture, with patients and staff respecting and learning from each other's knowledge and experience.

Example 2

1 To promote service user involvement in their own healthcare as active partners with professionals.
2 To enable service users and carers to have information about their health and healthcare to make informed decisions about it if they wish.
3 To involve service users in improving and monitoring the quality of existing services.
4 To involve service users in service decision-making processes, including involvement in planning and the development of new services.

I have come across a number of different groups, intent on developing action plans, that have spent so much time trying to differentiate between an aim and an objective that they have run out of time for deciding what they will actually do. It shouldn't be difficult. Aims are what you are trying to achieve, objectives are how you will get there. Aims therefore tend to be the broad brush stuff, as in the above examples. Objectives are about the practical details of how these aims will be met.

Healthcare objectives can be divided into three key areas:

1. Those determined by policy

These would include, for example, the need to have an established PALS, patient surveying and how it would be undertaken, a defined relationship with the PPI Forum and details on how accountability would be strengthened according to the requirements of Section 11 of the Health and Social Care Act 2001. This stipulates that involvement and consultation should take place not only when a major change is proposed but also in the ongoing planning of services, not just when considering a proposal but also in developing it, and in any decisions that may affect the operation of services.

If we are seen to be meeting the government's policy requirements, if we can tick the appropriate boxes to satisfy external auditors such as the Healthcare Commission, and if we package this neatly into a strategy, is this enough? My answer to this question would be a spirited no. Change doesn't have to be driven by government policy alone, but by values and beliefs about what comprises sound healthcare. Of course there should be a coincidence between these beliefs and government policy, but NHS trusts have on occasions demonstrated flaccid indifference in their local interpretations that has clearly influenced policy effectiveness.

2. Aspects of working together and developing partnerships

This should include defined systems to ensure that service user and carer involvement is at the heart of all policy and planning decisions. Easily said, but how do you do it? How do you involve patients and the public in meaningful partnerships so that they feel they have an active say in things?

The key here is to have user involvement threaded right through the organisation with user and carer representation at every level. This was the big advantage of the Heart of the Trust Scheme already described. Not only did knowledge of the scheme raise awareness throughout the trust, but it had readily available a group of service users and carers who could participate in a confident, informed and responsible way in planning and decision-making processes. They could also draw in other service user and carer colleagues from voluntary sector groups they were in contact with. What started to happen was that instead of users and carers being invited in as an afterthought, like children being allowed to stay up late for a special grown-up occasion, their presence was actively sought as key contributors.

For some organisations, this is achieved through established user groups or voluntary sector contacts, but the important thing is that it should not be left to chance. It needs defined processes familiar to everyone throughout the organisation so that it is an integrated part of organisational thinking.

Working together and developing partnerships is also about using feedback to systematically improve services and to share good practice. The Department of Health's annual patients' survey generates national data, useful for benchmarking against other organisations and promoting national consistency of sound and safe services. However, 'patient stories' and discovery interviews that relate directly to individual experience can be important *local* markers of change. When people describe in detail a particular healthcare experience and identify positive or less positive aspects, what is done with that information and do they ever hear what has been the outcome to an issue if there is one? In the first place, is there a process for collecting the information, and secondly, is there a feedback process to ensure that where possible the issue is attended to with details collated onto an appropriate database? And are all staff aware of their responsibility to do this? And a further point, do they receive the good news accompanied by management appreciation, as well as the bad? We all like to have strokes.

Knowledge of how this process works should be an essential part of staff induction and should be followed right through from the individual response to a board-level report summarising issues and actions taken. The intention should be to 'close the loop' by providing evidence that users' and carers' views have been responded to and that results are being delivered. Feedback opportunities such as clinical audit, PALS issues, reviews of complaints and patients' survey findings can all be integrated into business planning and performance monitoring, and these will enable people with experience of services to contribute to directly shaping them. They should also increase staff awareness and responsiveness. But having the data is only half the story: the key aspect is to have the processes identified for feeding back and then, where necessary, implementing change.

It may be helpful in a strategy to identify specific aspects of care where improvements need to be made in particular partnerships as an ongoing process. Carers, for example, are entitled to their own assessment of need and are sometimes ignored in care planning and design. The strategy can also be a useful lever for change in the sometimes complex partnerships between agencies required as part of care coordination, or where the needs of diverse communities need to be recognised and met. In these instances, gaps in practice can be identified, relevant policies and procedures written and, most importantly, staff and service users made aware of them so that they know what they have to do and what to expect.

3. Changing the culture

There is an assumption inherent in objectives associated with this key area that all healthcare organisations *need* to change their culture to accommodate patient and public involvement. Clearly this may not be the case. Recent government policy has been influential in changing attitudes and, as has already been described, service user and carer involvement appears to have moved up the political agenda. Not all are convinced, however, that this has made enough difference to the way people think about patient and public involvement. David Gilbert, in the final part of this book, bemoans the demise of the Commission for Healthcare Improvement, says that Section 11 is not being routinely applied, questions the impact of PPI Forums and notes significant changes in government policy language which suggest that we have reverted to being passive recipients rather than active partners in service planning and delivery. His view is that neither the government nor trusts are taking any of it seriously and that progress has been disappointing.

One difficulty is in defining the 'right' culture. We talk of value bases and the need to treat people with dignity and respect. We talk of equal opportunities and the accommodation of individual diversity through effective communication and challenging our own prejudices, but how easy is it to *achieve* this and to know that it is happening?

We revert to the question: if we are ticking all the boxes required by the policy, shouldn't that be enough? Perhaps it could be, but there are other indicators such as patients' surveys, audits, PALS feedback and complaints issues, not to mention more subtle signals such as any correlation *between* staff and patient satisfaction survey results. Staff sickness and absentee rates are another useful indicator not just of physical health but of organisational health and morale, and where this is low there are likely to be unhappy patients as well as unhappy staff. I am reminded of a friend who once worked in a shoe shop, who said, 'If I was feeling good about my job, the customers went out smiling.' Interestingly, she didn't say 'The customers went out with a pair of shoes.' What she was referring to was the importance of her attitude to those customers, not her skill in selling, although I dare say there was a link between the two. Healthcare is the same. We have a professional responsibility to deliver a skilled, evidence-based, top-quality service, but the man or woman in the street is just as concerned about *how* we do it as *what* we do.

Sharing information and wisdom

It is helpful to remind ourselves of the imbalance between the knowledge of the professional and that which is acquired as a result of the experience of being a 'patient' and the frequently disruptive impact this has on the life of that person and those around them. Each has something to offer the other and although strenuous efforts have been made to extend professional knowledge (e.g. about treatments and medication) to people using services because it is known to influence outcomes positively, there has been less effort to make sense of the users' and carers' experiences and integrate them into the meaningful delivery of services. This suggests a need for actions within a strategy which are directed at sharing different types of wisdom.

A service users' and carers' strategy should:

- show how the organisation will listen to, understand and respond to the language of its service users and carers
- identify a recognised resource in the organisation to promote public and service user partnerships and support everyone in developing them
- define agreed core values with service users and the public
- promote training and development opportunities across the board for staff and those they engage with
- include shared learning initiatives with no discrimination between providers and recipients of services
- determine how appropriate and up-to-date information will be made readily available about services and how people can access them
- demonstrate how the expertise of people with long-term health problems will be recognised, valued and utilised
- include mechanisms for engaging service users and carers in monitoring and the evaluation of progress, and ensuring feedback both to the organisation and to the people who use its services.

Bridging the strategic/individual gap

Strategies are seen as grand plans and it may be hard to imagine how they connect with the individual person's experience of services. It is crucial that we learn from that experience and that it informs every aspect of our work, but there needs to be a bridge between the individual and the personal and what is organisational and strategic. Key areas of a strategy should be responses to things that matter to patients. These are not hard to identify, they emerge time and time again from patients' surveys. Information, staff attitudes and time issues are recurrent themes, but a strategy needs to identify planned actions to ensure improvement and how these actions will be implemented and monitored for progress. Key questions are what does it feel like to be a patient receiving services from this organisation and what are we doing to improve that experience? And as a follow-up resulting from the discussion in earlier chapters of this book, would I personally (or those I care about) like to be treated in this way, and if not, how can it be changed? Service improvements and the support of quality standards may appear to be valuable organisational tools, but if they make no difference to the individual service user's experience, their deployment is open to question.

Key elements of this particular approach to getting service users and carers 'inside' the NHS have been recognition of the value of staff and patients together acknowledging their need and use of healthcare services and, as a result of this, the appointment to the trust board of people with knowledge and experience of those services. We have considered how this might influence an organisational strategy, but we also need to think about the 'interstitial' systems and structures that need to be in place in support of the approach, in order that the loop can be closed.

Closing the loop: a whole organisation model

Our case study provides a possible example of how this can be achieved. Following the organisational audit that was undertaken in response to service users' and carers' demands to know how the organisation was promoting their interests, there was clearly a need to establish a trust-wide coordinating group. This was to comprise a service user and carer lead representative from each directorate who would act as a conduit, reporting in to the group on service user and carer activity in their directorate and reporting back examples of good practice that could be shared. Each lead representative was to be supported by a member of the Centrepoint team who would help them, from within the directorate, to stimulate interest and follow through actions suggested from the audit and from subsequent meetings of the group. Its remit, to see that directorates responded to service user and carer expectations, was entirely internal, and at this stage there were no service user participants. Their input came at a later stage when progress within each directorate was being monitored. Also present (as has been described in Chapter 6) were representatives from support directorates such as Finance, Quality Development including IT services and Human Resources who needed to consider the implications of the discussions. Accountability of this group was to both the directorates and the trust board via its Service User and Carer Sub-Committee.

Directorate leads varied in how they interpreted their brief. For example, the Mental Health directorate set to work to develop its own service users' forum (Service Users' Reference Forum) which it launched with considerable panache. Service users subsequently played a very active part in providing feedback and contributing to performance management sessions, objective setting and service development planning and decision making.

The Children's directorate took a different line. Feeling oppressed by clinical and policy demands, they initially had difficulty in finding anyone prepared to be their lead representative. 'We're too busy with all this clinical governance stuff,' they said, 'to have time to do service user and carer involvement!' Nevertheless, regular meetings with support workers from the Centrepoint team told a different story. Many of their teams were actively using a range of quality monitoring and patient feedback tools. The only problem was that these needed to be standardised in order to provide a consistent approach and outcome. Another issue that emerged was about making information available and ensuring consistent standards across the large number of clinics provided in the trust's geographical area. It emerged that some families had been given information about how they could access funds to enable them to attend clinic appointments. Some teams had well-oiled systems for this, often via petty cash, but this was not universal. A call went out for any payment policies in use or explanations given to parents who needed help with obtaining fares to get to appointments. The process was then standardised across teams, and discrimination and missed treatments because of people not having money for transport was avoided. Similarly, a call went out to all children's teams for information about support networks so that this could be compiled into a central directory. (A word of warning about directories: they are hugely time-consuming to compile but unless someone is appointed to maintain them, they quickly date. Support set-ups come and go, personnel, addresses and telephone numbers change, and they can become a source of frustration rather than help.)

These examples reinforce the value of cross-referencing throughout an organisation. The difficulty is that front-line clinicians are generally more preoccupied with individual client contacts or team performance than they are with identifying with organisational aspirations and may be reluctant to spend time on them.

Once the first group of associate directors had been appointed, they quickly recognised the importance of having trust-wide influence in order to bring about change and looked for ways of achieving this. This they did by transforming the unwieldy sounding Operational Solutions Group into the rather snappier Heart of the Trust Action Group (HotT Action Group) and chairing and managing it. The service user and carer lead person from each directorate was expected to attend and bring with them a report on progress. Associates also contributed their own work and observations from around the trust. A glance at their minutes is revealing. Feedback included:

- a report on the quality of information provided by the Specialist Service directorate, including its consistency and use
- feedback on the launch of the Mental Health directorate's Service Users' Reference Forum (which the learning disability lead representative was going to discuss with colleagues with a view to developing something similar)
- a review of the process whereby forensic service users were paid for their contributions to meetings
- consideration of how service users could be involved in the planning of a new forensic intensive care unit
- the story of a father whose daughter suffered from an eating disorder, who suffered from mental health problems himself and who then went on to become a volunteer worker and trainer for other parents in contact with the Child and Adolescent Mental Health team
- news of a befriending service involving volunteers for people with a learning disability
- feedback on the associates' progress with their objective to improve in-patient activities on the mental health wards
- an invitation to the person responsible for ensuring that there was compliance with the NHS Plan policy of copying letters between clinicians and patients to come and explain it to the next meeting.

Although the accountability of this revised group remained the same with minutes being picked up both by operational managers within directorates and the Service User and Carer Sub-Committee to the trust board, the process was strengthened over time through the increased authority of this sub-committee. It is difficult to say how this was achieved, but the most important feature appeared to be committed support and interest from the trust board, which resulted in good attendance from everyone else.

Top-level support

Most trust boards do a large proportion of their business outside the boardroom via sub-committees. South Staffs Healthcare, where much of the work described in this case study was undertaken, was no exception. It had five sub-committees to deal with human resource issues, clinical governance, risk management, service development and, inevitably, service users and carers. It was also supported by a management board where there was representation from each clinical directorate and four management directorates (*see* Figure 9.1).

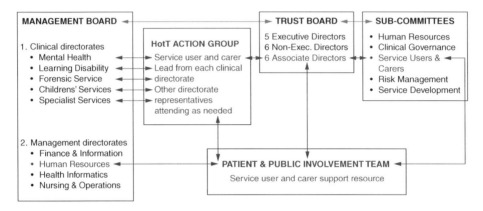

Figure 9.1 Closing the loop.

In the early days following the merger, the Service User and Carer Sub-Committee struggled to find its voice. Meetings were poorly attended and little progress was made in developing the Service User and Carer Involvement agenda; it felt as though we were wading through treacle. Change came with the appointment of a new non-executive director with specific responsibility for service user and carer involvement. An initial problem had been representation and who should be invited to participate in the meetings of the sub-committee. It was essential that service users and carers should be there, but how should they be supported? The model that was established was that every clinical directorate should have its own service user or carer representative attending the sub-committee meetings. Where they were lacking in confidence or needed help with reports or papers, they could be supported by each directorate's lead service user and carer representative, but the key attendees at the meetings were the service users themselves.

Within the time schedule for the meeting an initial half-hour was set aside for each service user representative to confer with their directorate support worker, but if they needed more help with understanding and contributing to the agenda, they were encouraged to arrange an additional briefing session in advance of the meeting. Although the sub-committee was chaired by the non-executive director, the opportunity was made available for the meeting to be co-chaired by any of the service user and carer representatives who might want to do the job. Other people invited to attend on a regular basis were a representative from PALS to provide regular reports on progress with issues identified by patients, a representative from the trust's PPI Forum, people from the trust's PPI team, and the director of human resources.

The first meeting of the sub-committee was held in the trust boardroom where the paraphernalia of power – individual blotters, heavy chairs widely spaced, and a long and imposing table – proved intimidating to some participants. Following a few meetings in the more relaxed and neutral environment of a local community hall with everyone sitting at smaller tables, arranged cabaret style, the sub-committee gained in confidence sufficiently to return to the boardroom. With the trust's chief executive taking a keen interest in this committee and its outcomes, and regularly attending its meetings, it soon became both lively and popular. Service users and carers had little time for formal meeting language and behaviour, but nevertheless agenda requirements needed to be followed through. With sensitive chairmanship, what evolved was a dynamic, progressive meeting, conducted efficiently, where it was possible to bring about change. Over time, there was a definite shift in emphasis from a meeting that was managed and dominated by staff to one where the majority of participants were service users and carers who had defined the agenda.

This case study of how one organisation developed its approach to patient and public involvement is nearly complete. Innovative approaches have been described as well as the framework that evolved to support the culture. However, organisations are neither 'approaches', 'frameworks', nor 'cultures', they are primarily individual people who are employed to do a job. In order to complete the picture we need to take a look at how their individual activity is melded into a consistent corporate approach through the use of policies and procedures, how employment practices were influenced within the Human Resources directorate and to gather together some more examples of the innovative practice that evolved as the culture within the organisation changed.

Developing a strategy, structures and systems: things to think about

Nobody wants to spend too much time thinking about any of these, but thinking about them and working at them can be productive ways of creating recognisable pathways through an organisation, helping people to find their way around.

Service user and carer strategy: Where is it and is it actively used? Who has copies and what do they do with them? Think about the language of your strategy and whether it is practical, user-friendly and easily understood. Who wrote it? If this is unclear it might be interesting to find out. How do you know it includes things that matter to patients? The answer to the previous question might well give you a clue to this. Does it include the three key areas: policy 'must dos', partnership and working together opportunities, and things that the organisation might need to do to demonstrate a 'do as you would be done by' approach? How long is it: five words, five lines, five pages, 50 pages? And what about the quality of the content?

Structures and systems for user involvement: Do these 'close the loop', making sure that there is a clearly defined two-way track between the trust board and front-end service delivery? Do they involve the whole organisation and, if not, where are the gaps and how might they be plugged? Do the feedback and monitoring systems actually work, ensuring that outcomes are identified and acted upon? Are there opportunities for cross-referencing so that different parts of the organisation can learn from each other?

Reference

1 Chambers R, Drinkwater C, Boath E. *Involving Patients and the Public: how to do it better*. Oxford: Radcliffe Medical Press; 2003.

And on to policies, protocols, procedures and people

Few who pick up this book and look at its Contents will turn to Part 2, Chapter 10 with immediate enthusiasm. Strategies, structures and processes may have been hard enough to swallow in the preceding chapter, but policies, protocols and procedures sound about as good as any sleeping pill. The emphasis throughout has been on rethinking how we approach service user and carer involvement and on how we can integrate our own healthcare experiences and professional practice. So what have policies, protocols and procedures got to do with that?

We could say that they are a tedious necessity, but they are much more. They are working tools, representing agreements and guidance at different levels as to how things should be done. Without them, no matter how skilled, knowledgeable and in tune we are with our experience of services, there are no guarantees for consistent standards and safe practice. Providing they are adhered to, they provide a safety net for us as individuals, whether we are providing services or receiving them. They also enable us to monitor the quality of what we do or what we receive according to defined standards. This has important implications for organisations and is in effect an aspect of 'closing the loop', making sure that the link between what the organisation does and what the individual receives is sound.

Complex clinical processes may be a matter for the experts, but how they are delivered, as well as what is being done, may make a considerable difference to the outcome. It's not that the 'what' doesn't matter – we depend on expert clinical knowledge and skills for that. Woven in to it, however, should be recognition that it is people interacting with other people. Going to the doctor or the hospital is definitely not like going to the garage to get a mechanic to see to your broken-down car, it is an interaction between people of the most subtle and complex variety. So as well as having the safeguard of clear instructions about how things should be done, it is also worth considering who is doing it and how we can ensure that we get the right people for the job. Later in this chapter, we shall be looking at recruitment and selection processes and how service users and carers can actively influence this.

Playing safe

The safety net of policies and procedures, linked with the complexity of our interpersonal contacts, is essential. It is all a question of risk. Where risk is an issue, there needs to be an agreement either between agencies or services or professionals or individuals, or any permutation of all four, as to how that risk should be identified and managed. There also needs to be written evidence to demonstrate what this agreement is and to define the issues and management processes. Then there needs to be written evidence that whatever process has been agreed has been followed. This may sound straightforward but we may forget that risk is not objective. If we ask different people about what is risky, we will get different responses according to the different cultural and social contexts that they are considering. This makes risk very hard to define and to make rules for.

Risk in healthcare is usually associated with the potential for loss, injury or some other adverse circumstance, but in considering risk we should also remember the possibility of beneficial outcomes and growth as a result of tolerating risk, as well as the dangerous aspects. For example, the risk that someone receiving post-operative care following hip replacement surgery will fall the first time they get out of bed is counterbalanced by the fact that this first, most 'risky' expedition will reduce the likelihood of dangerous blood clots forming or of falls at a later stage as strength and mobility increases. Risk is a product of uncertainty which in turn is inevitable with any contact between people, so there is very little chance of avoiding risky actions. Providing there is a clearly defined procedure (which in this particular example would describe in detail the course of action to be taken when getting someone out of bed post-operatively for the first time) and this procedure is followed, the main risk, i.e. chances of a fall, should be minimised.

Why differentiate? Why define?

Most of us struggle to provide separate definitions for policies, protocols and procedures and may well find ourselves asking why there is any need to differentiate between them at all. Shouldn't straightforward 'guidance' be enough? Well perhaps, but once we start to look at their meanings we realise that they are indeed different, even though the reason for their existence is broadly the same.

Policies

Having described at length in earlier chapters, the emergence of the government's Patient and Public Involvement policy and the evolution of the integrated approach to service user and carer involvement that resulted, it is clear that policies are about the grand scheme of things. They are about what governments or organisations are telling us to do because they think it is a good idea. Wanting to see things done in a particular way is likely to be influenced by their own ideological stance, public opinion, expert advice, financial constraints, past precedents and future expectations. Whatever the reason, the policy will be a statement of intent that is likely to involve a range of different agencies in its interpretation. Prudent conduct and skill come in to this. Policies are created to define what will be done in the least risky way in order that the desired outcome may be achieved.

We have already looked in detail at the PPI policy. Here is a more local example that demonstrates not only the possibilities but also some of the pitfalls of policy preparation.

An NHS trust had recognised that it needed to clarify how it reimbursed service users and carers for their contributions to service planning, monitoring, training and development activities. This had previously been done on an ad hoc basis dependent on different departments' budgets and what those who had control over them thought was reasonable – clearly no guarantee of consistency and equity across the organisation. Rates of payment were agreed and draft guidance and documentation prepared. By chance it was discovered that these rates would undercut those agreed by the local Social Services department. Service users who were contributing to joint health and social service events could therefore find that they were being paid different amounts according to which agency had invited them. Following discussion, the health workers discovered that social services had already spent more than a year devising their own policy for involving service users and carers in developing their services and were approaching the final hurdle in getting everyone within the agency to sign up to it. They were in no mood for last minute revisions even though they might be a useful indicator of collaborative working. They agreed that minor additions might be made to their policy, but nothing taken away. Buried deep within it was a protocol defining rates of payment for service user and carer contributions and how they should be made. This was adjusted to make it the same for both health and social services, the rest of the policy was reviewed to ensure that it was workable and the final document agreed by both agencies.

However, there's many a slip. Some time later, on following up a service user's complaint that there had been huge delay in meeting their expenses claim, we discovered that although the policy had been passed to the director of finance, the clerk who actually reimbursed people was unaware of the priority given to service user and carer issues. Her excuse was that she had been 'too busy doing other, more urgent things' and was unaware of the implications of the payment delay for people on a low budget. Such a policy is not worth the paper it is written on if the principles it embodies are not translated into a meaningful response at every level of the organisation. This is why personal identification with the patient experience, the 'do as you would be done by' approach promoted throughout this book, is so important. It needs to be an integral part of the thinking of everyone in the organisation.

Protocols

An early definition of a protocol, that it was 'the original draft of a diplomatic document, especially terms of treaty agreed in conference and signed by all parties', is ponderous but gives a useful clue about its meaning. This is that it requires agreement by a range of people who are involved but who may not all be associated with a single organisation. A more modern definition is 'a statement of rational procedures, recommendations or guidelines which all those involved agree with and are signed up to'. This suggests that a protocol is more practical than a policy, which may determine the 'what' whereas a protocol is about the 'how'. This links with our clarification of aims and objectives. Policies are like aims in stating broad intentions, what is going to happen, whereas protocols are more like objectives in determining how this will be achieved. The main difference is in the strength of the intention, with policies and protocols being more proscriptive than aims and objectives.

Whilst agreement between agencies is a key element of both policies and protocols, this can be the aspect most likely to be overlooked unless everyone who needs to be involved is engaged in their preparation from the start. For example, psychiatrists in a mental health trust may have a prescribing protocol that they have all agreed to conform to. That in itself may be an achievement! The protocol may relate to known risks and side-effects of some preparations or a particular range of less expensive drugs recommended by a government anxious to contain costs. However, once patients are discharged from in-patient care and need to obtain their prescriptions from their local GP, the rationale for prescribing decisions may be lost from view. Without engaging GPs in the protocol development, it could become a source of friction between the two groups as the following comment from a GP demonstrates:

> *Psychiatrists are not always prescribing in the way we'd feel was most appropriate. We don't have a feel for the rationale behind their prescribing protocol. There may be one but it's not being communicated and we're not necessarily in agreement with it.*

And while psychiatrists and GPs are squabbling over what should be prescribed and why, it is the patient who becomes the victim of their differences.

Protocols can facilitate communication but they may also be useful in protecting people from inappropriate intrusion or breaches of confidentiality. For example, a clear protocol about exchanges of clinical information over the phone should always include a check for the identity of the caller and the validity of their request and the need to log all calls. Checks should also include any known risk indicators that could influence the approach of the caller if they are likely to be in immediate contact with someone with, for example, mental health problems or where there are child protection issues.

When PPI Forums were first introduced, many set to work on protocols that determined how they would work with the NHS trusts and primary care trusts they were overseeing. It was essential that their members, many of whom had little or no knowledge of healthcare organisations or how to approach them, had worked out in agreement with the trusts how their visits should be organised and conducted, how to obtain information and how to liaise with different agencies. These would include the trust's Patient Advice and Liaison Service, the local Oversight and Scrutiny Committee, as well as communication with members of the community, reference groups, strategic partnerships and the local press.

Procedures

Procedures are more straightforward than policies and protocols. If we return to our original example of minimising the risks in relation to post-operative care, it is the physiotherapists who would have a defined procedure for getting people out of bed following their surgery. This would include a detailed breakdown of all the actions required to ensure that the process was followed through safely and comfortably for the patient. So a procedure is a particular course of action or a set of instructions for performing a specific task to which all the people who have to undertake that task are signed up.

That part is easy. What is more troubling is the extent to which all of this apparently tedious detail should be shared with service users and carers. Do people need to know that there is all this tightly defined guidance to ensure their proper care, comfort and safety? Do they need to know that the agencies they are involved with have jointly agreed policies and procedures to ensure that they do not fall through the net of care? At the risk of sounding like a fence-sitter, the answer to this is both yes and no. In the interests of transparency, there is very little that cannot be made available to patients and the public, should they wish to know. Against this have to be set the charges of 'needless bureaucracy' and 'too many trees', which are frequently heard when they are confronted by the piles of evidence that everything is being done properly. Mostly, we want recovery and good health, where that is possible, or to manage our lives as well as we can in relation to our own health circumstances. Do we want all of this heavy detail? Probably not, but it should be there for the asking.

Policies, protocols and procedures, with an overarching strategy, provide an operational framework, but it is the 'operators' themselves who really matter. We therefore turn now to the processes that ensure that the right people get the jobs. I once heard a chief executive being asked at a conference how he would deal with members of staff who seemed unsympathetic or even obstructive to the idea of developing partnerships with service users and carers. His lofty reply was that there was no place for them in his organisation. That's all well and good but what do you do about the 'plodders', the people who may have been in the same job for years, delivering safe but uninspired services, who simply do not want to change their way of thinking? Whereas their employment rights need to be protected, their attitudes may need a radical shake-up. As well as employing the right people, we also need to reflect on how this can be positively achieved.

Getting the right people for the job

Getting the job done properly is dependent above all on the energies, skills, experience, values and beliefs of the people who do it, and it is in recruiting and selecting them that the involvement of service users and carers can make a huge contribution.

Or can they? Why should we involve people with experience of services in selecting and recruiting staff? Providing the applicants are suitably qualified and their knowledge and skills are appropriate for the job, why should service users and carers be involved? Time and again, what emerges from patient surveys as a key concern of those experiencing services is the attitude of the staff with whom they are in contact, and although interview panels may think they recognise a kindly, warm, sympathetic, knowledgeable person when they walk into the room for their interview, this is not always the case. I am reminded of some feedback I once gave a mental health team following a standard-setting exercise with some service users. They had said that their keyworker should:

- 'be somebody I can talk to
- be a good listener
- be sensitive to how I am feeling
- be responsive
- be able to keep confidences
- be reliable
- respect my views
- respect my intelligence
- have a sense of humour
- have the authority to make things happen for me;'

all, it would seem, perfectly reasonable attributes that any of us would have a right to expect from somebody who was there to help us.

This was followed by six more pages of detailed standards associated with care planning. Such was the indignation expressed by this particular team that they might be lacking in any of these qualities, especially their sense of humour, that we never progressed beyond page one. Sadly, following this experience, I could see exactly why service users had wanted to emphasise their importance. The point here is that we can neither assume nor take for granted that we have knowledge of another person's perspective.

Involving people in staff recruitment and selection

I was once invited to comment on a trust's revised draft recruitment and selection policy and procedure. Right at the front there was a separate section entitled 'Involving service users and carers in recruiting and selecting staff'. This dealt with the importance of recognising the possibility that they should be involved, but nothing more. It then rattled on with all of the usual requirements familiar to human resources staff up and down the country, without any further mention of user involvement. The thinking had been 'We'll put it at the front to show that it's important', but there the thinking had stopped. The point is that if the sort of partnership we have been referring to throughout this book exists within an organisation, if the thinking is there, this will be apparent in everything it does. So involving service users and carers in the recruitment and selection of staff will not be a bolt-on extra.

There is a tendency for healthcare professionals to think that in order to bring 'outsiders', i.e. service users and carers, inside, they must think and act like them. 'Be like us and do things our way, and then we shall all know the job is done properly' is the thinking here. So if staff are required to have undertaken recruitment, selection and interviewing training before they can be let loose on staff appointments, then so should service users and carers. There is indeed a lot of very useful learning to be obtained in relation to interviewing skills, anti-discriminatory practice and the need to recognise equality and diversity in the workplace. Having jumped through this particular hoop, service users and carers may then be encouraged to sit on an interviewing panel and participate in the same way that everyone else does, with a set agenda of questions. All too often, this means conforming to the procedure as defined by the professional team, each taking a particular area of questioning and contributing to the final discussion and decision-making process. This is a useful but traditional approach to interviewing which is often complicated by detailed rating systems to ensure that challenges to the fairness of the process can be defended. It is not necessarily the best way of enabling service users and carers to assess the suitability of potential employees from their particular perspective.

For example, a service user complained bitterly when she was 'given' a question to ask at a job interview by a senior member of staff, and then floundered when the response that came back to her meant nothing. She had felt unable to refuse to ask the question but would have been much happier devising her own and responding to the reply.

This example reminds us that staff who might normally conduct interviews may themselves need help in thinking through the differences it will make to their approach when service users and carers are involved. Inappropriate assumptions may be made or there may be expectations of them which they are not able to meet. An inexperienced service user interviewer might prefer not to participate in asking questions but would wish to contribute to a decision-making discussion. Alternatively, there may be service users and carers with more personnel experience than the staff interviewers; it cuts both ways. Once the principle of sharing staff recruitment and selection with service users and carers has been accepted, issues around how it should be undertaken can be dealt with during training. Underpinning this is another principle that, where appropriate, joint training should also be made available.

Even with the traditional approach there is a great deal more to recruitment and selection than interviewing, and service users and carers should have the opportunity to contribute at all stages. This needs anticipating as it can include everything from helping to design the job description and defining desirable and essential attributes to being involved in short-listing and the interview itself. As a principle, service users and carers should participate in any appointments to posts where there is immediate contact with patients, and this includes jobs for reception staff, domestics and people who work in other service areas. Some trusts have set themselves a 100% standard of service user and carer participation in staff recruitment and selection.

There are, of course, different ways of appointing staff, depending on the type of job and whether it is clinical or not. These create opportunities for flexibility both in the appointment process and in how service users and carers can contribute to it.

Senior appointments

Much earlier in this book (Part 2, Chapter 5), reference was made to the 'trial by sherry' where service users and carers were included among the people invited to 'chat' to applicants for senior positions at an informal reception. Without proper briefing and follow-up their contribution was marginalised, the gesture had been made but to no useful effect. However, it can work both ways. I once applied for a PPI job and turned up, armed with my PowerPoint presentation, to find that I was presenting to a group of five learning disability service users accompanied by their support workers, not a staff interview panel as I had been led to believe. As it happened, my presentation was more visual than that of my rivals and I got the job, but it was more by good luck than good judgement.

A better way of ensuring that service users and carers have the opportunity to contribute to senior appointments (which usually take place over several days) is to include a series of informal interviews where three or four people representing different areas of interest across an organisation have a chance to put their questions to each of the short-listed candidates. This requires careful scheduling and thought given to how responses will be rated, but it ensures that everyone has a chance to talk to them and that their views are represented when the final choice is made. As with any other sort of recruitment and selection process, proper initial planning and a process for feeding back views are essential.

Children's services

Discussion of service user involvement in children's services always raises the debate about whether parents are acting as proxy representatives for their children. This only needs to apply with the very young. Gateshead NHS Trust, for example, invited local schoolchildren to interview candidates for a new team that was to support the emotional needs of local children between the ages of four and 14. They had a separate children's interview panel that provided them with a very different insight from a typical adult-to-adult interview.

In a different example, staff from a children's community team were interviewing candidates for a support worker post to help a severely disabled little girl of six whose mother was determined to care for her at home. The mother was invited to participate in the interview and share in the selection of the support worker as the team recognised the importance of the two feeling comfortable with each other if the partnership was to work.

Forensic services

Forensic services are for people who experience mental ill health after they have been detained for breaking the law. There is no reason why people using this service should not participate in staff recruitment and selection. However, there is one particular area where caution needs to be exercised and this is in relation to confidentiality and the security of personal details. It is normal when short-listing to circulate copies of application forms containing names and addresses. Staff, rightly, have anxieties about personal details being shared with people who may, when they leave the unit, take advantage of this information. Care must be taken to ensure that whilst adequate information is provided for the right appointment to be made, it does not compromise the safety of those who get the job. Under these circumstances, without adequate safeguards staff are likely to resist the idea of involving users in staff selection.

One way around this is to invite users from another service to participate; for example, forensic units are generally part of a larger organisation providing mental health services. This would obviously exclude the specifically forensic perspective, which could defeat the object of the exercise. An alternative, which would counter this limitation, is to work in partnership with another forensic unit with patients swapping to participate in the appointment process. With a limited number of forensic units across the country, this could make transport difficult, but it is worth considering.

PALS appointments

Finding the right people to work for the Patient Advice and Liaison Service is no more important than finding the right people for any job. However, their front-line contact with service users and carers and the potential sensitivity of what they may be dealing with is not to be underestimated. Here is a model that worked well and took full advantage of the opinions of service users and carers about the different applicants. In this example, other service users were involved in the initial preparation of the job description and short-listing, but it could easily have been the same team.

1 A member of a voluntary sector group was invited to seek out a small group of service users who would be willing to help. Four people volunteered.
2 Five days before the interviews were scheduled to take place, an informal briefing session was held. (A longer interval might have generated uncomfortable anxiety.)
3 Each person was given a pack containing a job description and a prepared interview assessment sheet that listed the interviewees' names, as well as a page for writing rough notes on each candidate.
4 The interview process was explained as follows:
   – Candidates would in effect have two interviews, one with a formal panel at which they would be required to give a 10-minute presentation and a separate one with service users.
   – Each of the members of the service users panel was asked to think of a query that they might be likely to put to a PALS coordinator. One thought of a benefits issue, another wanted reassurance about a specific medical condition, a third had an issue relating to the attitude of a member of staff and the final one had been given insufficient information about their discharge from hospital.
   – They would in turn put their question to each interviewee, developing further questions if they thought them necessary. In effect it was a PALS role-play session.
   – When each had had their turn, the interview was over. No staff members were included in this group, it was entirely self-managed.
   – After each interview, the users individually ranked on a scale of 1 to 5 each interviewee according to how well they felt their questions had been answered, the quality of the responses, whether explanations were clear and information adequate, and how comfortable they felt with the person. From these individual rankings, a joint response was collated.
   – After all the candidates had been interviewed by both teams, one representative from the user group joined the main interview panel to contribute the users' responses to the discussion.

This process was highly successful and resulted in a unanimous choice, but what if it hadn't? The model was also used for the appointment of a drop-in centre manager, and on that occasion there was a difference of opinion between the staff interview panel and the service users. In the event, the staff panel deferred to the users of the drop-in centre and their preferred candidate was given the job. She subsequently proved to be an excellent choice. With the PALS appointment, one of the service users found the process stressful and was unsure if she would want to do it again, but the other three said that they had enjoyed it and would like to participate if further opportunities arose.

Getting to know the organisation

Once recruitment and selection is accomplished, it will be closely followed by induction when the fortunate appointee is introduced to the organisation and their new job. Most healthcare organisations run a standard mandatory induction programme, including introductions to key players, fire procedures, PALS, health and safety issues – all the general things that new staff need to know about the NHS and their new employer. This may be squeezed into a single day or, more likely, spread over two. Organisations have been keen to demonstrate their sympathy with the raised profile of service users and carers, the commonest way of doing this being to wheel in a token service user for a 10-minute slot early in the induction programme. Given the wealth of detailed information that has to be got through, it would be surprising if anyone had any recollection of this contact or its significance – but what is the alternative?

Recognising the limited value of this approach, one trust decided to reverse the process so instead of the mountain coming to Mohammed, Mohammed, i.e. the people on the induction programme, were required to go to the mountain and visit service users and carers on their home territory: at drop-in centres, clinics and voluntary sector bases. Logistically this was complicated. A trust employing two to three thousand people may have anything from 40 to 60 new staff members attending induction each month, so this regular demand on external resources was considerable. However, it ensured that all new staff, whether they had a clinical role or not, had contact with patients whose brief it was to communicate how they thought the trust should demonstrate its commitment to their involvement. This very early signal was clearly important.

In this chapter we have looked at the frameworks that need to be in place to support people working in organisations, and also how we ensure that those who are employed reflect values and beliefs appropriate to the Service User and Carer agenda. The next chapter will continue this theme, looking at further influences and examples of how we can demonstrate the importance of working in partnership with users of our services.

Policies, protocols and procedures: things to think about

Have you thought about involving service users and carers? Perhaps they can vet a document once it has been drafted or, better still, be involved in the working group? There may be areas or activities where it might be inappropriate to include them, but it is better to have made a conscious decision about this than not to have thought of it at all.

Staff selection and recruitment: Are service users and carers involved throughout the process in designing job descriptions, short-listing, etc.? Do you or should you have a standard for this? What proportion of staff appointments in *your* organisation include service users and/or carers? Is this monitored *and* fed back?

Do you have difficulty in finding service users and/or carers who are able to participate in staff selection and recruitment? If so, is there a system for identifying people and a contact database, perhaps maintained by your Human Resources department? How is the opportunity advertised and are all staff aware that they can help to identify likely participants?

If your organisation has the two ticks symbol, how are the requirements disseminated and how widely known and observed are they?

Is all the material put out by the trust (e.g. on its website) consistent with the principles of not discriminating against disabled applicants?

Does training for staff selection and recruitment, anti-discriminatory practice, etc. include service users and carers? Is there the opportunity for staff to reflect their expectations, concerns and anxieties about working with service users and carers when interviewing?

Are different/flexible models of selection and recruitment considered?

Induction: What do you remember about your own induction into your present organisation? Did service users and carers participate and what was their impact? Might it have been done differently? Ideas for this?

How do you introduce your beliefs about the involvement of service users and carers to colleagues or members of your team?

11

The *human* resource

Nothing is more important in healthcare than the people who are providing the service. Correction: the only thing more important than the people providing the service is that they never lose sight of who they are there for. This may sound like a truism, irritatingly obvious to people who give their all, working for the NHS. Sadly, the continuing witness of service users and carers belies this assumption.

However, if the people who are working in healthcare organisations need to be mindful of why they are there, organisations too need not to lose sight of the fact that they are people, with hearts and souls, private lives and problems, and joys and sometimes sadnesses. Having a job is ordinary, it's what most people do, it's normal and it's how organisations work. They are dependent on each of us heaving ourselves out of bed in the morning, sorting out children, partners, the washing, coping with the traffic, etc. It's ordinary. Underneath the surface of those routines and that ordinariness that ensures that somehow the organisation meets its targets, produces its business plan, gets its star ratings and delivers the goods, there are thousands of us, supposedly ordinary people, getting on with our jobs.

Well, I don't think our individual experience of each other within an organisation *is* so ordinary: we look after each other, some of us share our difficulties, some of us prefer to keep them private, and sometimes we make things special for each other such as when people retire or there's a special anniversary, a baby born or something else to celebrate. We are individuals with all sorts of different life experiences that shape us, and these are precious, even if they are not known. They make us what *we* are and actually are a part of what that organisation becomes and what it is able to achieve. I'm certain that this is because of the quality of each individual contribution, so selecting the right people in the first place is important but so is how they are subsequently nurtured within the organisation.[1-3] In this chapter we are going to look at some further examples of the support that we can give each other, whether we are service users, carers or providers.

Support for staff

Human Resources departments are the places that provide 'official' staff support and they have huge responsibilities. Across an organisation they have to make sure that its employment practices are legal, consistent and, above all, ensure that as nearly as possible the right people are in the right jobs. They then have to help us to understand our responsibilities as employees as well as helping us to get to know the organisation we are working for. After that they have to ensure that development opportunities are there and that regular individual performance review is undertaken. This is the more routine aspect of their work but initiatives, like 'Improving Working Lives' that required a comprehensive review of job descriptions and pay structures, are also part and parcel of what they do.

An immediate response to new initiatives or new government policy is to wheel in a training programme to ensure that the people who have to implement it know what they are doing. All too often, those on the receiving end are ignored or given minimal information. Training for service user and carer policy developments did not appear to be necessary for anyone. Information about the various components was circulated to organisations that were told what they had to have in place by when, but there was an assumption that everyone knew what was expected. This is a bit like parenting. Because everyone must have had a father and a mother, it is assumed that when they come to reproduce they will know how to parent. Many of us know how misleading that assumption can be. Because clinical healthcare staff are in touch with patients and have professional skills and training, can we safely assume that they understand the patient experience? No, of course we can't. Interestingly, there is evidence, certainly in the mental health field, to suggest that we as patients do not value 'professional' qualities but see the 'good' nurse, for example, as someone with interpersonal skills and the 'human' touch rather than specific therapeutic knowledge.[4] Healthcare staff are *not* experts in understanding what it feels like to be receiving services, unless of course they have already taken a step back from their professional role to remind themselves of their own experiences as a patient.

The value of reflective practice[5] which combines 'thinking' about the impact and implications of what one is 'doing' is now well recognised in healthcare education, as is customer care training, exemplified by high street chain stores. It may therefore be anticipated that people coming to work in the NHS will respond to a culture that recognises good service, enables freedom of thought and promotes debate. This should include discussing negative experiences, not as criticisms but because they create opportunities for learning. It is a pity that in the pressured, target-driven and ever-changing NHS, all too often staff are required to sing the company tune and be forever hastily positive about what they are doing, hyping up the 'good news' and finding ways of reinterpreting difficulties so that they appear to positive advantage. More time to explore these difficulties, understand where they have come from and how they might be resolved could generate important reflective learning opportunities.

Breaking the rules or falling between several stools

One tricky aspect of organisational culture, guaranteed to frustrate and inhibit initiative, is the requirement to observe seemingly bureaucratic and unnecessary regulations often related to health and safety issues. The rules work to protect the organisation, individual workers and the people receiving its services, but for the individual obliged to interpret these rules at a local level they can appear clumsy and insensitive to immediate need. Alternatively, they can sometimes be a useful excuse for inertia for those who want a quiet life.

Risk taking can be an expensive and litigious business for organisations and caution is of the essence, but a change in thinking from 'no that isn't possible because ...' to 'hmm, that may be tricky but let's see how we can make it possible' may be refreshing. For example, patients in a day hospital wanted to give their 'smoke room' (the size of a broom cupboard) a coat of paint in order to cheer it up and make it a more pleasant place in which to smoke. They were keen to do the work themselves but were denied the opportunity to do so, apparently because of health and safety regulations, the dangers of climbing ladders, inhaling noxious fumes, etc. Meanwhile, in another part of the same trust, patients *were* undertaking a similar task because higher staffing levels permitted the involvement of activity coordinators to share in this 'therapeutic' activity. This doesn't make sense. If people are attending a day hospital because they have progressed further down the road to recovery, then taking greater responsibility for themselves and their environment ought to be part of the therapeutic opportunity, of which 'positive' risk taking is an important aspect.

Then there are the issues that are seemingly nobody's business and therefore fall between not just two stools but several. On one ward a tumble drier remained idle for weeks because it contained fluff that no one, neither staff nor patients, was 'authorised' to remove. Earlier we had the example of the dirty windows in the forensic unit that no one appeared to have responsibility for. So is the quality of the environment something to be attended to by clinicians, by managers, by admin-istrators or by a now extinct and sadly missed species, the ward handyman? These seemingly trivial examples emphasise the idea that partnership working in an organisation and the 'do as you would be done by' approach means everyone, not just staff who have immediate clinical contact with patients. And this means noticing the in-between sort of jobs that don't seem to be anyone's responsibility but that nevertheless affect the quality of the patient's experience. Being aware of this, ensuring that systems are in place to bridge these gaps and appropriate learning opportunities are available for *all* staff to make sense of the PPI agenda is indeed a subtle organisational responsibility.

It's everyone's job

Saying that involving patients and public in healthcare is *everyone's* job may be a bit of a cop-out. It can mean that *no one* actually takes responsibility for ensuring that it happens or, for that matter, monitoring it. But it cuts both ways. Setting up a team with specific responsibility to support patient and public involvement (such as Centrepoint, already described in Chapter 5) or a PALS can leave everyone else thinking that it isn't their job. To counter this, some PALS departments have undertaken Herculean training programmes throughout their organisations to sensitise all their staff to the issues, concerns and niggling worries, no matter how irrational, that any of us may find it difficult to voice when receiving healthcare. The job of support teams is to ensure that they keep their ear to the ground in order to find out where people might need help. Here's a neat example:

A ward development programme

This programme was designed to empower staff, many of whom had worked in the same ward for a number of years and had become increasingly dis-empowered themselves through weak management. They were therefore poorly placed to help service users with their empowerment agenda which threatened their own wobbly autonomy. Although bi-monthly Patient Feed-back Groups had been running for several years as part of a hospital quality monitoring programme, these had become routine, fewer and fewer patients were participating, staff were indifferent and suggestions were either ignored or resulted in defensive responses.

The PPI team first got wind of this when patient advocates complained about the unhelpful responses they were getting from ward staff: 'Oh, we weren't expecting you, there isn't a room available.' In other words, the person with whom the arrangement to visit had been made hadn't passed the message on to anyone on the next shift.

Senior managers were approached and gave their wholehearted support to a development programme, designed by the trust's professional development unit. It aimed to improve the partnership between those using the service and those providing it by facilitating a ward 'talking shop' and helping to overcome the sense of learned helplessness experienced by staff in the face of repeated failure to introduce change.

As a result, both staff and patients found new ways of relating to each other and an atmosphere of acceptable compromise rather than confrontation evolved. This in turn influenced the atmosphere on the ward and it became a more comfortable environment for everyone.

Staying in touch

Whenever people get their heads together to talk about improvements in service, whether they are users of the service or workers within it or some of each, talking together, a guaranteed topic will be 'communication'. It is an easy win as there is always someone who hasn't known about something and who should have done if only 'communication' had been better. It's a catch-all word used to cover a multitude of problems. Over recent years healthcare organisations have been growing like Topsy, and this has meant increasing difficulties in staying in touch with what is going on within them. Of course we have electronic networking, which helps, but keeping up with endless reports and meetings can be impossibly time-consuming. There are numerous examples of the difficulty: a useful Employment Links Group with multi-agency representation, quietly getting on with the job of sorting out practical differences in interpretation of work assessments for the benefit of people seeking employment, finding itself duplicated two years on because there had been no cross-referencing between Human Resources and Therapies directorates; a Carers' Special Interest Group not knowing about closure of some drop-in centres because the decision had been made without reference to them, causing distress and anxiety to needy carers; examples of efficient and/or effective working not being communicated from one area to another and, most uncomfortable of all, the failure of some PCTs to notify trusts that are providing services to their patients of patients' deaths. The list is endless. These situations occur by default, not evil intention, but they shouldn't happen. Knowing this isn't enough. Many healthcare organisations are now too large for their own good. Economies of scale are all very well, but not if they result in everyone having to run so hard to keep up that they don't have time to think about what they are doing.

Support for service users

Money

There is no more obvious way for an organisation to demonstrate the importance that it attaches to supporting service user and carer participation than to provide a budget for it. As has been stated earlier, this isn't just a tuppence ha'penny job to pay for a few bus tickets and cups of coffee, but enough to support a director's salary, maybe a staff team and all the accompanying costs necessary for them to do a decent job. Service user and carer involvement doesn't come any cheaper than any of the other support facilities that are considered essential to NHS provision.

As for payments to service users and carers, until recently these have been ad hoc, and consideration of the need for expense allowances such as travel and subsistence or for the provision of a 'sitting' service to replace absent carers, haphazard. Different agencies had attempted to develop guidance but their distribution was patchy and there were no guarantees that it would be followed. A new White Paper should change this. 'Reward and Recognition: principles and practice of service user payment and reimbursement in health and social care' aims to support local health and social care organisations by providing a consistent approach. It is designed to ensure that service users are treated fairly and appropriately according to their circumstances and that they should be able to make informed choices about the arrangements concerning their involvement. This suggests that not only will health and social services have to give serious consideration to the implications for their budgets, but the involvement of service users may be influenced by the question, 'Is this going to be worth my while?'

A frequently occurring difficulty when making payments to service users and carers is having the money available on the day. This means not only having the budget, but ensuring that the processes for accessing it are straightforward and don't take forever to negotiate. Ideally, within an organisation there should be a universal standardised system and tariff that people know about and use, so that the payment of service users is a matter of routine rather than anxious scramble.

One small reminder. Not everyone either expects or wants to be paid for their contribution, as I discovered when a group of service users once replied when asked if they had claimed their expenses, 'No, thank you. We're here because we want to be.'

Training

Creating opportunities for service users and carers to share in joint training and development sessions for health and social care staff is an obvious way of sharing knowledge and understanding of the behind-the-scenes support necessary for clinical services to be delivered. Assuming that such training is not segregated to separate staff from patients, it also has the simple advantage of bringing people into contact with each other. It is now common for people from outside the NHS to participate in staff selection and recruitment training (with a view to their joining interview panels), in anti-discriminatory practice sessions, health and safety, meeting management and chairmanship, and so on. All too often, however, the reason for doing this has not been clearly thought through. There is a generalised feeling that if we are supposed to be working together more closely, then sharing learning must be 'a good thing'. This assumption is related to the premise referred to in an earlier chapter, that NHS staff see working in partnership with users as making them more like themselves. Undoubtedly, there are skills that service users and carers may not have had the opportunity to acquire which could help them to 'get inside' the NHS and be more effective service user and carer representatives. For this reason sharing training is important. It may also provide a helpful forum for cross-referencing of ideas and attitudes. However, there is no guarantee that people exposed to the same information will make the same sense of it on account of their widely disparate backgrounds and experiences.

Specific training programmes have also been written to help service users understand about planning, delivering, monitoring and evaluating services. Mental health services tend to be ahead of the game with this. For example, the West Midlands National Institute for Mental Health in England (NIMHE) branch has created a useful course (Effective Involvement Training for Mental Health Service Users) that includes among its core modules sessions on empowerment, understanding mental illness and mental health, stress management and relaxation, mental health policy, communication and meeting skills, and funding and commissioning processes.

Getting service users and carers to *contribute* their expertise to training sessions is another matter altogether. Increasingly, service users and carers are being invited to contribute their personal experience of illness to clinical teaching. For this, they should of course be paid at the same rate as any other external contributor to a training session. I have heard people who were HIV positive transform an otherwise rather routine clinical lesson by talking about their experiences of the condition and the care they received. They brought it to life, adding a vital additional dimension that is a far cry from the days when patients were wheeled into the medical school lecture theatre to be treated as malfunctioning specimens.

Recognition of expertise

It has taken the NHS a long time to recognise that people who live with long-term health problems get to know their condition, how it affects them and how to manage it better than anyone else. This realisation generated the Expert Patient Programme which was recognised by the Department of Health and launched in September 2001 with the publication of a report, 'The Expert Patient: a new approach to chronic disease management for the 21st century'.[6] This was based on work originally started in California in the 1970s by Kate Lorig.[7,8] The idea was that with specialised help, training and the support of healthcare staff, patients could learn to take responsibility for the management of chronic conditions. The benefits were demonstrable. People who had undertaken the programme reported reduced severity of symptoms, less pain, improved life control and increased confidence, activity and satisfaction with their lives.

Since then, an extensive programme promoting the approach has been undertaken in PCTs by lay tutors who are themselves 'experts' in managing their own long-term medical condition. Participants with a range of different chronic illnesses, including diabetes, arthritis, heart problems, asthma, depression, polio, liver disease and endometriosis, are recruited to enlist on generic courses following a specifically designed programme of learning over a number of weeks. Disease-specific add-on days are being encouraged as part of a follow-up support programme.

Initially recruitment was via GPs, but courses are now advertised widely in a number of broader social environments such as pharmacies and clubs with the additional benefit that they help people to increase their social networks. In Kent, work is going on to make the programme available to offenders with long-term conditions, information has also gone out to Learning Disability Partnerships, Mobility Focus Groups and voluntary sector forums, and the intention is to run courses for parents of children with a long-term condition.

As well as empowering individual patients, PCTs benefit through the acquisition of a pool of 'expert patients' whose opinions are readily accessible. However, there have been some difficulties. The lay tutors are only trained to deliver the course, not to teach. This was deliberate, the idea being that they should communicate experiential knowledge and not become professional 'teachers'. There is a feeling that this may have contributed to many participants dropping out as the course followed a very rigid programme and their individual needs were not considered. Lay tutors might also become ill and be unable to sustain a course programme and, inevitably, there has been concern about the cost of running the programme. Be that as it may, recognition of this kind of expertise is a step forward in the march for patient empowerment and is not confined solely to participants in the Expert Patient Programme. A number of voluntary sector organisations, including the Spinal Cord Injury Lifelong Learning (SCILL) training scheme and the Multiple Sclerosis Society, are jostling to develop their own courses using lay tutors. This has to be progress.

Individual ideas

Staff who feel themselves to be valued and well supported by an organisation are much more likely to show similar consideration for the people with whom they come into contact and to be thinking of ideas for improving their working partnerships. The following individual and team initiatives were all stimulated within this kind of environment.

- Executives and new human resources staff were required to spend time 'shadowing' service users and working alongside front-line staff on a ward shift. This brought them into contact with the operational end of the services they had strategic responsibility for.
- A mobile PALS unit was suggested for a community trust with over 70 different bases. Careful and well-publicised timetabling meant that two PALS workers could travel around the trust in a camping van which served as a mobile office, and be available to many more service users and carers than if they had to use normal office accommodation.
- A parents' support group was set up for parents of children with learning disabilities who were themselves disabled in the same way.
- A psychiatrist became an expert signer and lip-reader so that he could communicate with patients with hearing impairments.
- Another set up a drop-in service so that his patients could access his time without an appointment.
- The availability of calendars indicating significant festivals for different religious groups in an area with a high ethnic minority population meant that appointments were not made inappropriately and dietary needs could be recognised.

This particular team also acquired an Asian toy catalogue so that they could meet the needs of young Asian children in contact with their service.

- A database of service users and carers who were willing to contribute experience, knowledge and skills was established as well as a database of volunteers. Details of particular areas of interest (or concerns) were recorded as well as mentoring and supervision needs. Some of these users acted as 'readers', vetting trust documents (e.g. the Business Plan) for readability and interest value.
- Another database of information leaflets was collated with over 500 entries. This made it possible to ensure the provision of consistent, good quality information across a number of different bases. There is a 'house style' but different formats (e.g. large type) are available if required. It is anticipated that this database will become available electronically so that staff can print off relevant information during a consultation or patients can refer to it via the trust's website.
- A trust library, formerly only available to staff, had opened its doors to service users and had offered training to enable people to access reliable healthcare information on the internet.
- Negotiations with a local public library had resulted in offers of help from a group of voluntary 'buddies' who normally supported inexperienced members of the public using the library's free access to the internet. They were prepared to help hospital patients in the same way, either at the public library or by visiting the hospital wards.
- Another library initiative involved offering a service to voluntary sector support organisations. The library, working in partnership with the local public library and linking with other specialist libraries in the area, offered to make specialist healthcare information available to any voluntary sector support agencies that needed it.
- Learning disability staff showed a particular interest in the privacy and dignity aspects of the Essence of Care training. This is a patient-focused benchmarking process for healthcare practitioners which answers the question, 'How do we know we are doing everything we should to respect the privacy and dignity of the people we are caring for?' Staff from respite, residential and social care homes got together to work out a joint approach to the process.
- Two versions of the same letter:

    Dear Mrs Smith
    Due to unforeseen circumstances we have had to cancel your appointment with Dr Bloggs on .... We apologise for any inconvenience caused and will be sending you a new appointment as soon as possible.

    Dear Mrs Smith
    Very many apologies but I am afraid I have to cancel the appointment we made for you to attend the Outpatients Clinic with ... on .... I am sorry for any inconvenience this may have caused and I will be in touch in the near future to arrange a further appointment. I know this may cause you some concern so please feel free to contact me if you require further help, from 9 am to 5 pm, Monday to Thursday and 9 am to 4.30 pm on Fridays. My telephone number is ... ext. ....

- A job description for a ward representative for a User Involvement Group was drawn up, describing in detail what the person would have to do, how much of their time would be needed and what incentives there were for them to undertake the role.

Spreading the net

Helping people to 'get inside the NHS' does not only apply to direct contacts between service users and service providers. There are many community initiatives, sometimes associated with Public Health departments of PCTs, that serve the purpose of encouraging us to take a greater interest in our health and more responsibility for the state of our bodies and minds. As a result, we learn more about how to remain healthy, what can happen to us when things go wrong and how they can be put right.

For example, in Slough, Buckinghamshire, where there is a high rate of heart disease and a high Asian population with a known high risk of circulatory diseases, people from the local community are being trained as 'health activists'. Their job is to raise awareness and motivate their friends and colleagues to a healthier lifestyle and the avoidance of heart disease. One of the activists has pioneered a women-only swimming scheme for Muslim women where there are sessions at a local pool with guaranteed privacy and they can wear clothing that covers them more effectively than a swimming costume. Not only has this proved immensely popular, but it has improved stamina and reduced blood pressure levels. The project involves the PCT with the local council, Age Concern and local community groups and is a good example of partnership working.

The idea of health activists is spreading to other areas in the country with local community centres often becoming a focal point and magnet for the groups. By stimulating awareness of healthier choices, especially for groups that are sometimes hard to reach, health activists are playing their part in improving the health of local people and increasing access to services where it is necessary.

It is also useful for health service workers to recognise that they do not necessarily have to try and solve every problem. A Stroke Support Group had a number of concerns and asked to see a local Member of Parliament (MP). This generated considerable anxiety for the trust concerned. Were they going to complain at length when services had been doing their best to meet their needs? Would it end up as banner headlines in the local paper? Would heads roll? In the event, the meeting was highly productive and defused a potentially confrontational situation with both the service users and the MP having a much better understanding of the issues. Although he couldn't at that point in time put his hand in his pocket and draw out a wad of cash, the MP learned about the reality of the issues for those people who had experienced them and could therefore represent them accurately when the opportunity arose; and the stroke people learned about why it takes time for political processes to be followed through as well as the problems around resourcing and prioritisation. So 'support' for service users and carers can also mean being brave and trusting that openness and a direct approach will pay off.

And what about carers?

The first sign that carers' needs were at last being recognised came in 1995 with the Carers (Recognition and Services) Act which differentiated between the needs of patients and the needs of those who were caring for them by establishing the idea of separate assessment. This was followed in 1999 by 'Caring about Carers: a national strategy for carers'[9] which aimed to bring together existing initiatives within the statutory and independent sectors into an overall policy for services supporting carers.

Thank goodness their needs and the huge contribution that they make to supporting users of services are at last being recognised. Their statutory right to a Carer's Assessment applies even if the cared-for person does not engage with services, and they are also entitled to their own care plan. In addition, any number of carers' support organisations are in existence up and down the country, some related to specific conditions (e.g. Autism West Midlands and the National Schizophrenia Fellowship), some generic, supporting all carers in a particular geographical area. What they offer is important. The things that carers most need are information, advice, the opportunity to talk to other carers who understand the strains and stresses they are under, practical help such as a sitting service when they need a break and the opportunity for respite care when they can have time for themselves.

All of this may paint a deceptively rosy picture. There is no getting away from the relentless pressure experienced by carers, and the fact that apart from the policy directives the examples given so far are all provided by the voluntary sector raises the question of how and why this situation has arisen. The glib response is that carers are providing a service on the cheap, filling a huge gap that the cash-strapped NHS cannot afford. The truth of the matter is more complicated. Many of those who are cared for would, if they could, run a mile from the sort of institutional care that might be their only alternative. Many carers might feel insulted if it was suggested that they should be deprived of their role, looking after people they would do anything for because they love them. But they do need a great deal more help and support than is currently available to them. They also need to have the significance of their role recognised by service providers and not to be treated as though they are invisible. Just as service users need to have the validity of their experiential knowledge recognised, so do carers, but they need recognition that their experience is different from that of the service user.

Imagining that carers and those they care for are somehow joined at the hip can lead to inappropriate assumptions. For example, if carers are present during a consultation, it may be assumed that they are automatically acting in an advocacy capacity for the patient. Not so. They may have very different views about the situation that they might want to express independently and in private. Alternatively, they may be in urgent need of an advocate's support themselves because of finding the consultation situation intimidating or inhibiting.

Then there is the confidentiality issue. If a patient says to a member of staff 'don't talk to my family' but a carer asks for information, a stonewalling response may be ethically correct but fail to recognise the needs of the carer to understand what is going on or why decisions have been made. The Royal College of Psychiatrists has published useful guidance in relation to confidentiality issues as well as a checklist for carers of people with mental health problems of questions they might like to have answered. A more down-to-earth response has been produced for a resource pack by carers in Exeter and East Devon and staff of Devon Partnership Trust. They suggest that if carers approach them needing more information when their relative who is the patient has requested that it shouldn't be given, clinicians should ask exactly what people want to know and define the areas they can talk about and those that they can't. They might also suggest someone else whom a carer might be able to talk to, or that they can discuss general aspects without going into specific details about the patient. Carers themselves might recognise that they don't need to know about things that are confidential to the patient, but it would be helpful to have some advice on managing a situation so that it doesn't get worse. They could also be given facts, leaflets, books or helpline numbers and advice on how other people manage as carers in similar circumstances, or if there is anyone else they could talk to.

Carers' Support Groups are invaluable and the Carers' Association of South Staffordshire, which has over 2000 carers on its database, runs a group especially for young carers, organised by a funded young carers' support worker. Her job is to identify the many children who are carers and spend their time, in between going to school, looking after a disabled parent. As well as the support group, which is like a specialised youth club, outings are organised and opportunities for the young people to enjoy some fun and relaxation time away from their caring responsibilities.

Support and information sharing opportunities can be intermittent as well as ongoing. One trust organised a well-publicised Carers' Question Time every six months, to which were invited local 'experts' – someone from an advocacy organisation, nurses who had established a carers' training programme, someone with knowledge of the Carers' Assessment, someone from the Benefits Agency, the local MP. Carers were invited to submit questions in advance in case specialised information was required and to avoid duplication, but they also had the opportunity for one-to-one conversations if issues were too personal for an open forum. A sitting service was on offer as well as lunch, the idea being that precious time out needed to be enjoyable and relaxing as well as of practical use.

Recognising the value of a dialogue between carers and services, some trusts are now writing their own carers' strategies, spelling out crucial principles to guide the work of health and social care professionals, managers and policy makers in their relations with carers. As one such strategy from Birmingham and Solihull Mental Health Trust identifies, 'Carers represent an opportunity, not a problem. Properly supported, carers and families can reduce relapse, support individuals, promote recovery and even contribute positively to services. Unsupported, it is recognised that carers often develop mental and physical health needs of their own.'

Twenty years ago, at the age of three, my son Bob was diagnosed as being severely autistic. It was like an explosion in our family life. At that time the behavioural difficulties had not kicked in too much, it was just his lack of speech that we thought was causing him to be frustrated and difficult. However, it soon became apparent that our lives were to become more complicated than ever we could have imagined.

Things had to be done in a certain way to avoid tantrums, shops visited in a certain order, certain cereals eaten at breakfast, the whole family involved in routines that could not be broken. Autism was ruling our lives and simple changes, like going on holiday, became a nightmare.

Change really was our biggest problem, but gradually over the years things had to change – it simply couldn't be avoided. School came first, change of class, then a change of school, all causing turmoil and anguish. Then there was change associated with transferring from school to a post-16 residential life skills course, but not every change was negative.

Our son had a new key worker, David. He was a very fit young man in every sense. He was keen on all activities, jogging, sport, gym and fitness workouts. We spoke on the phone every week and also when I picked up my son on his alternate weekends home. David told me he was taking Bob and another young man on a course that included jogging, horse riding and timetabled sessions in the fitness room. Our son over the months started to look really well. He had always been overweight and had a tendency to be rather laid back where exercise was concerned, but after a few weeks on the course he was looking really great.

When Christmas time came and I went to collect him for the holiday, David asked if I would bring a camcorder ready for action and ring when I was at the gate at the top of the long drive to the centre. I leaned on the five-barred gate, wondering what to expect, when round the corner came a cyclist and in hot pursuit a short distance behind was David. Then I realised that the cyclist was my son and quickly (and weepily) started the camcorder to record this momentous event for the rest of the family.

For years we had tried to get him on a bike. Over and over we tried until he got too big for the bikes with stabilisers, so reluctantly we let it go – another 'not to be'. David had asked me at the start of the September term if I had any concerns with him teaching my son to ride a two-wheeled bike, and I'd said okay but never thought he would manage it with Bob, who by this time was six feet tall and weighed 13 stone.

Inevitably, David moved on and we were all really sad to see him go, but we shall always remember him for that special moment in all of our lives.

Thank you, David.

Jan Playford, Carers' Outreach Worker
(Former Associate Director, South Staffs Healthcare NHS Trust)

The human resource: things to think about

Staff supports: Think about the ordinary ways in which you and those you work with share personal things and look after each other.

In your set-up, do you take time to consider with each other how you can make use of situations that have been difficult or haven't worked to see what you can learn from them?

Are there examples of things you may not have been able to do because of 'rules'? Might there have been alternative approaches?

Are there things that need attention but don't seem to be anyone's job? Try making a list of them with your work colleagues and see who might be able to follow them up.

Support for service users and carers: Resources have already been mentioned. What about the processes for delivering them? Can you pay service users on the day of their contribution or do you have to anticipate it weeks in advance in order to be able to give them cash?

Does everyone who is likely to need the help of service users and carers know about these processes and how to access the right budget to meet the costs?

Are service users and carers given enough information about the things they are participating in and what are the feedback opportunities and the possibilities for briefing/debriefing sessions?

Are there widespread opportunities for service users and carers to both participate in and contribute to training?

References

1 Graham A, Steele J. *Optimising Value: the motivation of doctors and managers in the NHS*. London: Public Management Foundation; 2001.
2 Collins K, Jones M, McDonnell A *et al*. Do new roles contribute to job satisfaction and retention of staff in nursing and professions allied to medicine? *J Nursing Man.* 2000; **8**: 3–12.
3 Given A. Time machine. *Nursing Stand*. 1999; **12**: 12.
4 Forrest S, Masters H, Brown N. Mental health service user involvement in nurse education: exploring the issues. *J Psychiat Mental Health Nursing*. 2000; **7**: 51–7.
5 Schon D. *Educating the Reflective Practitioner*. Oxford: Jossey-Bass Publishers; 1987.
6 Department of Health. *The Expert Patient: a new approach to chronic disease management for the 21st century*. London: DoH; 2001.
7 Lorig K, Holman H. Long-term outcomes of an arthritis self-management study: effects of reinforcement efforts. *Soc Sci Med*. 1989; **29**(2): 221–4.
8 Lorig K, Mazonson P, Holman H. Evidence suggesting that health education for self-management in patients with chronic arthritis has sustained health benefits while reducing healthcare costs. *Arth Rheum*. 1993; **36**(4): 439–46.
9 Department of Health. *Caring about Carers: a national strategy for carers*. London: DoH; 1999.

Part 3

Bringing it together: the 'lived' experience

Introduction

> *But sometimes the knowledge of the scholar is a bit hard to understand because it doesn't seem to match up to our own experience of things. In other words, Knowledge and Experience do not necessarily speak the same language. But isn't the knowledge that comes from experience more valuable than the knowledge that doesn't? It seems fairly obvious to some of us that a lot of scholars need to go outside and sniff around – walk through the grass, talk to the animals. That sort of thing.*
>
> Benjamin Hoff, *The Tao of Pooh and the Te of Piglet*

The final part of this book has been written by people who have recognised the value of being an outsider, inside the NHS. From their different perspectives, each describes the effect that their 'outsider' experience has had on the jobs they have been doing.

When an organisation's chief executive openly acknowledges his own experience of mental health services, it makes it very hard indeed for anyone in that organisation to gainsay the importance of the service user and carer agenda. Mike Cooke is a passionate advocate of patient and public involvement and in Chapter 12 he tells us how this personal experience has influenced him and the trust. Mike's account demonstrates the contribution that greater openness in acknowledging our personal experiences can make to understanding how to get 'inside' the NHS.

As one of the original appointees for the Heart of the Trust Scheme, Donna Wedgbury's experience is as a carer for her young son who was born with cerebral palsy. She extends the description contained in Chapter 8 of the Heart of the Trust Scheme by telling us what it was like to be one of the associate directors. Donna describes this in detail in Chapter 13, and recounts some of the challenges she faced and what she feels were the benefits and the achievements.

David Gilbert and Lindsay Dyer are both campaigners at heart, but their campaigning zeal has taken them in different directions. Lindsay is the Director for Service User and Carer Involvement in Mersey Care NHS Trust. Like Mike Cooke, she has found her personal experience of using the NHS to be an asset rather than a disadvantage in the job that she has been doing. Following advice from service users and carers, she has been encouraging a focus on employing the right people in her trust. Her approach has quite a lot in common with that of South Staffs Healthcare NHS Trust, but readers will find the budget her trust has allocated for service user and carer involvement startling. This is described in Chapter 14.

David Gilbert has written two chapters. Chapter 15 is about his own journey from mental health service user to lay representative and then to being Head of Patient and Public Involvement for the Commission for Health Improvement. He describes what he learned from his attempts to influence things as an 'outsider' and then considers how this learning might be developed to help others become effective patient and community representatives.

In Chapter 16, David steps back from this personal experience to look at the political challenges that face lay representatives and the new learning that they might find helpful in their role. He suggests a programme of learning that could contribute to the programme of a new Department of Health resource centre, the National Centre for Involvement. This centre will identify the best and most appropriate training for PPI and its task will be to disseminate this nationally.

This recognition by the Department of Health that there needs to be a systematic approach as to how we understand our experience both as service users and providers can give us grounds for optimism about the future and is an appropriate place to conclude this book. Nevertheless, the final postscript that concludes Part 3 cannot resist drawing attention to some further issues and a few more questions to ponder!

12

Going the extra mile

Mike Cooke

A fundamentally important aspect of healthcare is the real and meaningful involvement of service users and carers in the design and development of services. Listening to their feedback, hearing them 'telling it like it is' and then trying to do something about it – promising to do something about it – is a tough road. This is the ticket I signed up to as chief executive with 15 years' board experience and, more importantly, 25 years' experience as a service user. Luckily, I am in recovery, allowing me to lead a part of the NHS of which I am very proud. This chapter describes how I tackled the balance between being a chief executive and a service user.

Leadership and being a chief executive

Senior and top leadership of a complex, huge business which matters to everyone, in an ever-changing environment, within a political spotlight locally and nationally is as challenging as it can be rewarding.

As a chief executive, my job is about leadership and this has three essential components. These are **Y**ou (yourself) and how you behave, what you say, what you think; **E**ffectiveness: what you achieve, the influences you have and what you get done; and **S**tyle: the way you do things, the culture and the tone set. **YES** is a very obvious acronym. The most important things I do are to think well, to talk and to listen, to put the right people in the right key jobs and to motivate them. I am in a high-profile position, well paid, luckily well thought of, but not complacent. And my diary tells another story.

Depression and being a service user

> *Depression, for me, is despair, lack of self-esteem, a crippling cocktail of high anxiety and low mood feelings. It is a frightening, lonely (despite the loved ones around you), self-destructive, extremely vulnerable and 'raw' place to be. It can bite you ... it is a 'black knuckle ride'. It is all-absorbing, very bruising and I guess extremely frightening to observe, particularly at a distance if you are not let in to the front seat of the roller-coaster to see what's really going on. And it's much worse inside, provoking at its lowest points the gravest thoughts of death, 'negative smog' and restricting any natural positive urge.*
>
> My diary 25 August 2003, Spain

That was written in a journal on holiday to help me reflect, diagnose and formulate my problems so that I could cope. It was also to help my family and best friends manage, so that I didn't have to fly home for treatment. I can be very lucid, very clear, but very manipulative when wrestling with such a phase of depression. Depression also scares people away: it is isolating and makes you want to have a low profile, be ignored and left alone. It is not well paid! Being a service user from my personal perspective is a much tougher place than being a chief executive.

Striking the right balance

I am sure I oversimplify the two perspectives of leader and service user, but there is a huge contrast, a huge amount of clear water between them. I am not unique in having these two perspectives, but unusual in that in the right place and with the right audience I am willing to talk about them both, despite the stigma still associated with mental health problems. I have learned that to use both perspectives, respecting each and being clear about them, has added a further dimension to my leadership, impact and personal influence. Striking the right balance between the two is the key. I am a chief executive because of my leadership achievements. I am a chief executive of a three-star mental health, learning disability and children's services foundation trust because of my service user background. It is a set of services I can really move forward and am more driven to contribute to.

Undoubtedly when you talk about being a service user when you are in a very senior position, some people think you are doing it for sympathy or effect. They may find it difficult to handle, but they may also be respectful of it. There is still a huge amount of mental health stigma around which is sometimes implicit, sometimes elusive to define or put your hand on. If I am in front of 100 people and I say 'I'm talking to you as a chief executive but also as a service user', my guess would be that a third might go with it, a third would be embarrassed about it but also respectful and a third would say 'I always knew that he was a bit bonkers!' It's about them as well as you.

Talking about very personal experiences can be quite indulgent in some people's eyes, and it can also be threatening for senior professionals who perhaps think that you are undermining the value of what they are trying try to do for service users. I am very willing to talk about it with service users because they know where I am coming from; but with professionals, I am respectful of their training and their unique and professional skills although I like to try and challenge that perspective a little. I believe that the power of service users and carers in patient and professional relationships does need to be increased. Good professionals can allow and encourage that to happen in the user–professional relationship, but it is a complex thing to understand and be respectful of. It is a risk too.

I don't want anybody making allowances for me because I happen to suffer from depression from time to time. I don't want anyone expecting me to be a lot better than my peers either because I've got mental health issues. I can control my own attitudes and what I say, but I can't influence what other people think about mental health issues that may be very real to them personally or very close to them.

One in four people get a serious mental health issue at some time in their life and sometimes people are not able to articulate the very difficult issues around that. I am able to, but only at this stage of my maturity and professional life. This is me as a person but also about me saying that I have an opportunity as a chief executive to talk about these things, hopefully in a way that engages and stimulates people but doesn't expect them all to react in the same way. You don't want to shock people but to inspire them and get them to think differently about their current practice.

The balance of power

In simple terms, power in organisational development is derived from two sources. The first is *positional* power: the title, the expected role, the formal authority (what you decide), the responsibility (the scope of what you do) and the accountability (whether you get it right and do it right).

The second, and I believe the most important, is the *personal* power: how you behave, whether people respect you and respond to your influence, what they say about you, your impact.

In positional terms, I am a chief executive of a successful organisation, accountable for targets, performance, systems reform and all that goes with that, with, it is said, an average shelf-life of one and a half years! I have been a chief executive now for seven years, five of them in this post. In personal power terms, I am a bloke, a cricket fan, a food and wine lover, a people person and a service user with considerable experience of different types of mental health services from different parts of the country.

You will already have read about 'Telling It Like It Is' and the Heart of the Trust Scheme that emerged as a consequence of that idea. Here are some different practical examples of how this balance of power between chief executive and service user can evoke a preferred style or changed style, depending upon what is going on and what will prove to be more effective.

Examples

1. Putting choices up front in mental health services

Based on the very serious bout of depression I have described, I came back from holiday needing to get myself sorted out as quickly as possible. For this I used my positional power as a chief executive to get exactly the right person to treat me in exactly the way that I knew would work for me. My personal insights made me reflect very carefully about the choices open to me because of my position. I was able to choose and book a service that suited me at a level of intensity that I required to keep me functioning as a chief executive at work. This made me think about choices we have in mental health services. I had heard a lot about choice of five hospitals, including a private sector option, time/place choice, the what/where of choice, and a certain service at a given time in a given hospital. Reflecting on my own experience made me realise that this wasn't the main driver for choice in mental health services. I felt that access was important but actually it was *who* I was going to trust with my mental health, *how* that would be undertaken and *why* I should engage with that service. I was able to make choices around all of those scenarios because of my knowledge of the services in my locality and the influence I was able to exert in getting in to those services. Why can't we encourage that for everybody? Why can't somebody who is not as articulate or as personally connected as me get exactly the same range of choice?

Based on that, I wrote a vision for a service user being offered choice in a non-patronising way in a non-stigmatised environment and we are now beginning to build services based on this vision, this model. So I *was* inside the NHS in a very powerful way and in a position to change the NHS front door based on my own illness. We are beginning to try it out in a new centre for young people because that's an area where we need to change the most and intuition tells me that other people will also like this style of service.

One of the things I had to do when I wasn't well was stand up and talk to 400 people, so I knew I needed some pretty important intervention to give me the confidence to manage it. It needed to be responsive but on my terms, in a way I could immediately engage with. Having the knowledge – the informed choice – to know how a service can respond in different situations is a very complex thing to navigate through. We need much better information, much more transparency of what services are where and how to access them, much more flexibility in the time services can be delivered – in evenings, weekends and twenty-four/seven availability for crisis issues.

There's no doubt I was trying to show a different form of leadership by writing the vision that resulted from my bout of depression. I talked about this at the trust's annual general meeting where it definitely resonated for the audience. Unbeknown to me, several members of staff went away and looked at their own service with that as a benchmark. There are three examples of services that have transformed themselves as a result of hearing about that vision and I'm proud of that. I was using my positional power as the chief executive at the AGM, a fairly symbolic occasion, to say this is what choice is really about and we want more of it. The three services – adult mental health, an offenders' diversion service and a young people's service – are taking a risk because they know that if they are much more accessible and more focused around service users' needs, they may be swamped by demand. What I have to do is make sure I back them with resources if that happens.

2. 'Mental Health Improvement Partnership'

We were one of four localities selected to host a national approach to improving mental health services across the system. Although I used my positional power as a chief executive to win the bid and get more money and support to work on mental health issues more progressively, it was my personal experience as a service user that shaped it. Once we had launched the approach locally, we were very clear that it would be service users and carers who would develop the agenda they wanted to explore in this partnership, although some staff took quite a lot of convincing as they had their own views about what should happen next. The issues the service users and carers selected were to improve the experience of in-patient services; to look at a values-based work force, i.e. 'what mind-set have you got before you (metaphorically) lay hands on me'; and thirdly, they wanted to look at transparent commissioning. Where does the money go in mental health, how is it allocated, how is it spent and how do we prioritise? What do we need to spend more and less on? Fourth was advocacy to support real choice, and fifth, information that is accessible. This was three years ago, but you could not have picked a more relevant agenda for future mental health services.

3. 'Learning Centre and Network'

One of the better ideas we've had as an organisation is to all learn together. I've observed some very eminent academics and leaders coming and talking to groups of professionals, who were no doubt interested and impressed but actually not always listening as intently as they might. Professionals listen hardest when they listen to patients and carers. I am quite sure that all learning together and empowering service users and carers as experts in their own field is the way professionals in the NHS, now and in the future, need to learn; and we have created an environment where this can happen: our Learning Centre and Network. I think there are some highly effective and creative ways of including, in a non-patronising, non-pressurising and non-threatening way, people who are very articulate about their own health. Key workers in the future need to listen to the need for personalised care, the need for advice that suits people when they want it, the need for advocacy when somebody asks for it. These are all crucial issues. Dignity, respect and involvement in treatment and care, including better access, have been very consistent messages from any poll in the last three years of people using the NHS. A Learning Centre and Network responds to this; it isn't just about developing doctors, nurses, psychologists, leaders or occupational therapists, it's about developing all of us together. Carers, too, play a massive role in supporting people at their most vulnerable times. We need to invest in them and help them learn and be experts in care and support and advice and information.

Funding the Centre, perhaps through the positional power and as chief executive, I was able to hang on to a grant we got for getting three stars. It was then a case of using my personal influence to make sure that we spent it in the right way and didn't produce yet another postgraduate medical educational or multidisciplinary learning centre. What we have is something very different.

4. Foundation trust

I'm very proud to be involved in developing the Foundation Trust movement so that it can accommodate mental health-style organisations. I think we have a lot to bring to the party on engagement and involvement of the public, in the hope that we can reduce mental health stigma, improve services and improve choices for people more quickly than we could do if we were just an NHS trust. There's no doubt that we've been inspired locally by the way people have responded to our approach to becoming a foundation trust, which is about 'going the extra mile'. Service users, carers and staff have all worked together with that discretionary effort that they will only give you if they feel valued, acknowledged and involved in an organisation or a system that's trying to improve things. There is no doubt that this extra endeavour that I see in my organisation, that I positionally support as chief executive and I personally am passionate about as a service user, is a legacy that will continue. Going the extra mile is a reciprocal thing. We do it as individuals but also, as an organisation, we want to do it for our patients to give them choices in future and sustain those choices to improve their lives and their abilities.

Conclusions

My overall conclusion about personal and positional power is that personal power is more important. If people respect you, your values, your integrity and maybe would know what you might think about an issue or would approach you for your opinion, that's likely to have a much more sustainable influence than just reminding people you are chief executive. Integrity is essential to sustain drive, deal with anxieties and deal with the pressures to deliver, and I am convinced that is the right way to lead in a mental health-style organisation. I am making some tough decisions, but can I hang on to my value base while I'm doing it? Yes, I think I can. What I have learned is that personal and positional power can be seen as the same thing. People might refer to me as 'the boss' or the 'chief exec.', but mostly they tend to say, 'What would Mike think?' We think about the values that we hold very closely here, and I think it is the personal influence on people that can set the tone of an organisation. I genuinely believe that to get the right services in the right style for service users, you have to co-produce the design of those services with service users to get them committed and motivated to want to use them and want to stay with them to get the most out of them.

13

Donna's story

Donna Wedgbury

I guess some people might say that I have already faced more challenges than most people face in a lifetime, and in a way these have prepared me for the challenge of caring for my six-year-old son, Harvey, who has cerebral palsy.

For a start, I had a tough childhood. My mum left home when I was five years old, leaving my dad to look after me and my three siblings. When my dad remarried some seven years later, it was fairly evident to me that I didn't fit into the new regime. Five years of turmoil followed, resulting in social services involvement and finally a foster placement for me in a kind and caring environment.

As a young adult, I had immersed myself into developing a career. By the time I became pregnant with Harvey, I was a senior branch manager for a well-known building society, a job which I like to think I excelled at and most certainly thoroughly enjoyed. However, I realised soon after Harvey's birth in 1999 that I would be unable to resume my career as I had to ensure that his needs were met – a difficult task requiring all the strengths and skills I'd previously invested in my personal and professional life.

From July 2000, Harvey and I went to a local Children's Development Centre where we soon got to know his paediatrician, Dr Patel, very well. It was apparent to us at our first meeting with Dr Patel that the way in which services were delivered in this locality was very much centred around the needs of the child and family and real parent/child participation.

A multi-agency approach had been adopted, with health, education and social services all being represented within the team of professionals helping our family 'manage' the situation we were faced with.

It wasn't long before Dr Patel and I were attending local conferences, giving presentations on service user and carer involvement and the benefits of multi-agency working. I became a parent representative for the Children's Development Centre, regularly attending team meetings alongside the professionals who worked there. I considered this a fantastic privilege and a great opportunity to be the 'voice' of parents using local health services. My professional background and my experience of receiving services for Harvey had given me the confidence and skills to become involved with clinicians on equal terms – something I considered a rarity in the NHS.

My involvement with the NHS trust strengthened and I delivered a presentation to users, carers and staff at the trust's 'Telling It Like It Is' conference in 2002, based upon our experiences. Feedback from this event was used to determine the trust's future action plan to further develop user and carer engagement. One of the outcomes was that a sub-committee to the NHS trust board was founded in 2003, at which I became a regular attendee.

Because of my family history and the fact that I had a disabled child, I became very interested in the welfare and well-being of vulnerable children and children with complex needs. I had seen and experienced the health system at close quarters and had benefited from being able to discuss things with all sorts of different people in similar situations to mine. This was both helpful and rewarding. The knowledge of users and carers and their expertise is unique. Being able to use this knowledge to influence the planning, development and delivery of local services seemed like a good idea, so when the opportunity to apply to become an associate director for the trust came up in December 2003, I decided to go for it.

Becoming an associate director

In order to qualify for the position, all candidates were required to live in the area served by the trust and must have been a service user of the trust or a carer of someone who had used services for the previous three years. A key part of the role was to attend board meetings and challenge professionals at all levels within the organisation.

As far as I could see, the trust was keen to encourage people who represented the diversity of local communities with a range of applicants that also spanned the trust's services. Everyone who was interviewed was offered the chance to have a 'dry run' with a local recruitment consultant several days before their interview, and this proved extremely helpful as many of us had not been in a real interview situation for several years. We were also required to attend a trust board meeting as observers and to meet the trust board team. We were then asked for feedback about this at our interviews.

Being an associate director

Six of us took up our new role in March 2004. There was a well-organised and detailed induction programme that involved visits all over the place, team-building activities that highlighted individual team members' strengths and specific areas of interest, and finally the development of personal objectives. We all had very different life experiences. This might have caused conflict within the team, but it was agreed early on during team building that each associate director would be able to carry out their role in their own way. It was evident that the trust wanted to oppose tradition and recognise individuality – a very unnerving experience for some associate directors as most of us were used to being governed by rules.

Although as a team we received guidance and support from other professionals, each associate director was allowed to find their own feet and involve themselves in their areas of interest. Training and support were offered on a team and individual basis, which were tailored to specific needs, and regular appraisal, reviews and supervision meetings were also provided.

It would be foolish of me to say that the whole process ran smoothly. The scheme required a steep learning curve both for us and the trust. However, I will say that as issues arose, solutions were quickly identified and implemented.

An evaluation of this phase of the Heart of the Trust Scheme captured useful and positive feedback, so the board agreed it should continue. Five new associate directors were appointed in May 2005, and I and another of the original associates agreed to continue in our roles. This has provided continuity, enabling the new team appointed in May 2005 to gel more effectively and establish team goals more easily. Areas identified as concerns during the first phase have been proactively managed. A good example of this is the way in which the induction programme was individualised for each of the phase two associate directors, dependent upon their previous involvement with the trust and their knowledge of the trust services.

Initially I was apprehensive about the responsibility I had with my role as an associate director. It could have been argued that these appointments were token-istic, as six individuals working for one day per week each could not influence service user and carer engagement on a grand scale. The reality is that the trust has demonstrated that patients and carers really are at the heart of everything they do. It has been a three-star trust for the past two years, there is a clear service user and carer strategy, and the way in which they engage with their users and carers is currently supporting their application to become a foundation trust.

A major concern of mine upon appointment was how staff working within local teams would receive me. As many of the staff were clearly used to engaging local users and carers, I found that rather than feeling threatened by my presence, they were more inquisitive about how I would carry out my new role. Also there was plenty of support from the chief executive and he communicated this to staff wherever he went.

Obviously my particular area of interest was with children's services, where I knew many of the staff from the contacts Harvey and I had already had with them. I had also been doing a fair bit of voluntary work there.

I was confident that I could develop a good working relationship with Harvey's paediatrician, who by this time had become the director of the service. In fact, I became in effect a critical friend to his directorate. Dr Patel clearly supported my appointment and initially communicated this to all of his team leaders. This level of support opened doors for me and enabled me to network easily, which resulted in my being invited to attend local team meetings to introduce myself.

Within weeks I was invited to attend numerous management meetings, working groups and strategy groups. This was a new experience for me as I was not there to represent my own viewpoint, but that of local users and carers. Initially it was very difficult to give feedback other than from my own perspective, but I got better at it as time went on. I often questioned myself after meetings as to the value I had added by being there. At times I had difficulty understanding the jargon used as I didn't have an NHS background and I often had no idea where a particular committee fitted in, what power it had, who listened to it and who would act on its recom-mendations. I often got the feeling that I had been invited along as the token parent or associate director, and I would say there are definitely some professionals who go through the motions of developing user engagement rather than really wanting it to happen. Challenging them in these situations has helped to overcome some of the barriers, resulting in a reassessment of the objective of the group or meeting. Others really genuinely want to know what service users and carers think. The problem is that professionals often lack experience in knowing how to involve them effectively.

As an associate director, I have promoted the importance of clinical teams working in partnership with local parent groups and support groups. As I have had personal involvement with many of these support groups it has enabled me to give invaluable feedback at all levels, so there has been a regular two-way dialogue. Many parents/carers become involved in local groups to support each other emotionally and because they believe in 'strength in numbers' and making a collective impact. Listening to what they say about services and being able to feed it back has meant real improvements, so they feel their voice is being heard.

Other partnerships have been trickier. It has taken a long time to develop a working relationship with the trust's Patient and Public Involvement Forum and I think the associates definitely benefited from having a good induction and support. It enabled us to hit the ground running whereas the PPI Forum members seemed to be a bit lost.

Now, two years into my job as an associate director, I feel that the idea has been successful. The teams with which I have worked have developed excellent links with local groups and service improvements have been made. New groups have been started and good partnerships established with the local health team.

The challenge is to turn good intentions into effective practice and to find ways of working with users and carers which make best use of their skills and knowledge. Successful partnerships depend upon the drive and commitment of individual workers. In my opinion, helping to facilitate strengthening these partnerships has been and will continue to be a key part of my role.

I have found the emotional pressure of being an associate director quite tough. Meeting local children and their families whose health needs are not being met can be emotionally challenging. As the mother of a disabled child, I can easily get drawn into these issues and become involved on a very personal level, so there is an art to being empathetic but remaining objective. I am not afraid to say that this has been a very difficult area to master. I have needed and asked for help with this from my mentors and supervisor, and I have also needed guidance to find my way through the horrendous layers of NHS bureaucracy which seem extremely complex and difficult to unravel.

How I can spread influence

Within weeks of my appointment it was clear to me that even if I did not set myself any objectives during my first 12 months, I could influence the way in which professionals would think and act simply by being visible at meetings, conferences and working groups. I am convinced that on some occasions service user and carer participation was high on the agenda because of my attendance, so subconsciously influencing staff in this way is in itself an achievement.

Six months into our role, the associate directors were asked to appear in a DVD to support the trust's application to become a foundation trust. We also attended public meetings and media events to stimulate local interest in encouraging service users and carers to become members of the trust. I would like to think that by sharing our experience in this way, we may have stimulated people's interest in how and where their healthcare should be delivered. The DVD focused on why it had appointed us and covered footage of a range of issues in which we had become involved. This became a valuable publicity tool. It has been useful in demonstrating to local communities, partner organisations and on a national level how users and carers can influence ways of working within an NHS organisation.

We also worked on a team objective within the organisation and this proved very successful, particularly as there was a group of us and we were able to support each other. Our team objective was to improve recreational activities in in-patient settings, and by pooling our experience and knowledge in this area we were able to challenge existing practices more confidently and improve the opportunities available to our patients.

By far the most difficult part of my role has been challenging and influencing the attitude and behaviour of some staff. Creating competition among teams, getting them to share experiences, offering support and guidance to teams, and training staff have been key areas that I have concentrated upon to try and influence how they were thinking about service user and carer involvement. I was able to do this as a result of my past experience with the building society, where I was involved in training and developing staff as well as managing teams.

Within the first three months of joining the NHS I attended a two-day induction course, which is compulsory for all new employees of the trust. Following this course, the associate director team worked with the trust's training manager to restructure the course and revise the content to include customer care training and specific service user/carer training. I have delivered this training on a monthly basis to all new employees since November 2004. During the training all staff are given many examples of how they can involve users and carers in their own team and they are encouraged to set themselves a personal objective around user engagement. This is a very important message from the organisation, right at the start of people's working association with it, that service users and carers really matter.

Two days into my role as an associate director, I co-chaired the trust's Annual Clinical Governance Conference with my chief executive – a very daunting but rewarding experience as it was attended by more than 300 staff and partners. During this conference I also gave a presentation about Harvey's and my experience of using local health services. I co-chaired this conference again in 2005 with the trust chairman and one of my associate director colleagues, when interestingly the number of service users giving presentations had doubled from the previous year.

Another major area in which I have been involved is the 'Going the Extra Mile' leadership programme. Staff in management positions have attended this five-day compulsory course, of which one of the days concentrates on user and carer engagement. Staff are able to observe an interview between the human resources director and myself, with me giving an honest account of my experiences as a carer and as an associate director. This element of the course always stimulates a lot of questions.

Being available to deliver training to teams and individuals has been a very rewarding and successful part of my job. There are many examples I could use to substantiate individual training, but I think it would suffice to say that all have resulted in the trainees looking at their practices and behaviour from a different perspective. You may at this point be wondering how this is all done within a one-day-per-week contract: the reality is I have been motivated to work for an average of two days per week for the trust since I started this role.

Training and development opportunities have not been exclusively for employees of the trust. Service users and carers have had access to various forms of training in order to become more confident and have the skills to contribute in a more effective way. For example, I have become involved in training users to play an effective part in trust business meetings and upskilling individuals to assert themselves during consultations with clinicians.

Motivating other users and carers to become actively involved with planning and developing local health services will remain one of my key objectives. I am very aware that many local people using health services feel that they are unable to contribute effectively. Helping them to feel empowered, supported and valued will help to give them confidence to make their voices heard.

More examples of sharing good practice at team, directorate and national level include:

- speaking at national conferences with the trust's human resources director has given me the opportunity to talk about the trust's strategy and expand on my perceptions
- being involved in a service user and carer celebration day, with more than 150 staff and service users celebrating their achievements and ideas, was so successful in October 2005 that it will now become an annual event hosted by the trust
- having the opportunity to contribute in directorates' performance management review meetings has ensured that successful practices have been shared with other directorates
- the associate director team write a column entitled 'We notice that ...' in the trust's monthly in-house publication. We highlight areas of good performance and practice as well as concerns. This newsletter is circulated to all 2500 staff employed by the trust.

With the transformation of the organisation into a foundation trust and the arrival of governor members, things are sure to change, but the impact of a team of service users and carers, operating at a senior level within a trust and with the full support of the board and appropriate supervision, is enormous.

14

A rights-based approach

Lindsey Dyer

My interest in rights must come from my father. He lived in the same rural village in Herefordshire all his life and generally saw farmers as malevolent beings, who, at any opportunity, would block footpaths and deny the public access to their land. As a small child I would regularly be dispatched to tramp for miles and report back on obstructions. Any infringement of my rights of passage would then be vigorously pursued.

My interest in mental health services came from his sister who, robbed of citizenship, lost years of her life in a mental institution. It comes, too, from the years of my own life lost in the prison of depression. From this heady mixture came a passion to protect and enhance the rights of people with experience of mental health problems. This led me in the 1980s to employment first as a development officer, and then as North West Regional Director for MIND, the National Association for Mental Health. Here I became a seasoned campaigner, working on some highly significant issues:

- forgotten children, which shamed authorities into stopping the admission of children with learning disabilities into long-stay institutions like Brockhall and Calderstones[1]
- the right to vote, which in 1998 showed that only 329 of 4345 people resident in North West psychiatric hospitals were registered to vote. The vast majority, including whole hospital populations, were effectively disenfranchised primarily because of senior staffs' attitudes to patients' rights[2]
- the right to work, which exposed the NHS in the North West as one of the worst offenders in discrimination in employment against former psychiatric patients and argued the case for the anti-discrimination legislation we now enjoy.[3]

The list of campaigns goes on. I mention my work at MIND because it shaped who I am and set the scene for my work with Mersey Care NHS Trust. Can someone who is a seasoned campaigner, despite the passage of the years, be transformed from a poacher into a gamekeeper? Can someone like me effectively 'campaign' from within a sprawling NHS organisation (over 30 sites, over 4500 full-time staff) for the right of service users and carers to be involved in decisions which affect their lives?

The start of a rights-based approach

There were some early signs for optimism. Service users and carers themselves made it clear at consultation events, when Mersey Care was being established, that bringing local mental health services together under one umbrella was pointless if all it meant was a change in management, a change in 'the label over the door'. They wanted to have a real say in decision making.

The chief executive and the newly formed trust board (April 2001) responded by investing in a board-level post of 'Director, Service Users and Carers'. This sent a clear message that service user and carer involvement was important and that cultural change would only come about with board support and board-level leadership. With a little encouragement from me, the board went further and became probably the only NHS trust in the country to adopt a rights-based approach.

The trust's strategy makes clear that:

> We must think about people's rights in everything that we do.[4]

This includes legal rights such as the right to life, carers' right to an assessment of their needs, the right of service users to aftercare, and social rights that are important to us all, like the right to be heard, the right to be free from poverty and the right to a meaningful life.

Critical to Mersey Care's rights-based approach is a board-level commitment to the right of service users and carers to be involved in decisions which affect their lives. People should be involved not because it is the policy flavour of the government of the day or because it will be good for them or good for the trust, but because service users and carers are *citizens* and have the *right* to be involved. Service user and carer involvement is the first of eight strategic objectives agreed by the Mersey Care Trust Board:

> ... to promote and develop the active participation of service users and carers in their own care, the monitoring of service delivery and the planning of service improvement.[4]

To its credit this objective is always uppermost in the board's mind. Whilst working with the board to set out the trust's stall, I established a policy on payments so that service users and carers who get involved in Mersey Care are valued and offered payment for their time (£10 an hour plus expenses). This was endorsed by the board who agreed an initial budget of £50,000 for these payments. This was followed by a series of 'road shows' where I could explain the rights-based approach and listen to what service users and carers said about how they wanted to be involved and what they wanted from me/a post like mine. Overwhelmingly they said they wanted a say about the staff who worked with them, the people who came into their homes and their lives when they were at their most vulnerable. It was with this action that the trust began.

Recruitment and selection of staff

We trained any service users and carers who wanted to contribute in every aspect of recruitment and selection of staff – the kinds of roles staff normally perform in a trust. They learned how to write an advert, a job description, a person specification, the legal requirements that have to be met, and how to go about short-listing, setting questions, interviewing and assessing candidates. Now over 80 service users and carers trained by other service users and carers (and better trained than most trust staff!) effect their right and take part as equals in the recruitment and selection of all Mersey Care staff – over 1000 appointments to date.

Involving service users and carers in the recruitment of trust staff is how we do things in Mersey Care, an important marker of a changing culture.

Research

A small group of service users and carers wanted to be involved in research and, as a result, the Service User Research and Evaluation (SURE) Group was formed. This was given trust support and has undertaken a range of projects of its own choosing, including the 2004 Patients' Survey, an audit of service user and carer involvement in recruitment and selection, a review of the in-patient detoxification unit in the drugs service and a cultural sensitivity audit in an adult mental health service. Others were concerned about the right to make informed decisions and choices and the quality of information provided by the trust, and so got involved in the development of the trust's website.

Moving out of the 'comfort zone'

Responding to what service users and carers wanted soon took the trust out of its 'comfort zone'. The Joint Forum, a Liverpool-based service user organisation had long advocated that service users should be involved in the review of serious incidents like homicides and suicides. This happens routinely now in Mersey Care, but required a new culture of openness to scrutiny when things go wrong.

Establishing organisational networks

As these initiatives were taking shape, I was working behind the scenes to set up a network of lead officers for service user and carer involvement in the trust. This needed someone to lead for adult mental health services, someone to lead for older people, someone to lead for learning disability, and so on. Some services agreed a full-time post, other directorates agreed to commit part of an individual's time. What was important was that service user and carer involvement was not something vested in me, but that I now had a network of people to work with and through. This reached into all of the corners of the organisation. There were people who would take responsibility for working with service users and carers in their neck of the woods, under the umbrella of the trust strategy for service user and carer involvement. This strategy, 'A Different Experience', was based on empowering service users and carers as people with knowledge and experience of mental health services, but also as *people* with a wide range of *life* skills, knowledge and experience.

Human resources involvement

The trust broke more new ground by appointing the first human resources manager in the country to work with service users and carers. It recognised that they are just as important a 'resource' as its staff. The role has grown over the years and the HR lead is now responsible for involving service users and carers in the recruitment and selection of staff, in the induction of staff, in the objective setting and appraisal of the chief executive and members of the senior management team, for an Access to Employment (ACE) scheme which supports at least 10 service users a year into the employment of their choice in the trust, and a 'Buddy' scheme providing extra support to staff with mental health needs.

And yes, you did just read that service users and carers are involved as equals in setting the objectives and assessing the performance of the chief executive and members of the senior management team! The further you climb the greasy pole in the NHS, the further away you get from the people who experience the services. They have the right to have a say about what priorities managers should pursue and how good they are at pursuing them.

Getting involved

So how does it work in practice? Service users and carers who want to get involved in Mersey Care are asked to register on a database that is kept confidential. Every month they then receive information about the current involvement opportunities available. This information can be made available on request in languages other than English and in other formats. Interested in getting involved in developing Crisis Resolution and Home Treatment teams? Interested in awarding a contract? Interested in becoming an Equality and Diversity lead? Interested in becoming part of PEAT (Patient Environment and Action Team) and inspecting trust premises and making recommendations? Interested in modernising trust services and how the trust will spend a whopping allocation of £171 million pounds for capital development, given that so few trust premises are fit for purpose? We have invited service user and carer participation in all of these activities.

The aim is to give service users and carers a continuous and growing range of meaningful choices about what to get involved in. These opportunities enable them to be involved as equals in all of the decisions made in a complex organisation that have an effect on people' lives. This involvement is in decisions that reflect their interests and enable the fulfilment of their ambitions.

The experience of the last four years shows that we can engage a wide range of service users and carers who reflect the population served by the trust, not just the same old faces. With an increase in the budget for payments to service users and carers (which now stands at £120,000), the trust supports about 150 service users and carers at any one time to effect their right to be involved in decision making in a meaningful way.

Some successes

The success of Mersey Care in involving service users and carers has been recognised in the recent Clinical Governance Review by the Healthcare Commission.[6] It described the level of service user and carer involvement in all aspects of the trust's work as 'exemplary' and 'impressive':

- the involvement of the Chair of the Service User and Carer Forum, for instance, as a co-opted member of the trust board includes attendance at private parts of board meetings: there are no secrets if service users and carers really have the right to be involved in decisions

- the involvement of Barnardo's young carers in the development of the first family room in the country in an adult mental health in-patient service. A room where children and young people visiting relatives in hospital can spend time with their mums and dads away from the wards in a homely environment.
- the development of the first service in the country for people with Asperger's syndrome
- the positive achievement awards given to service users, carers and partner organisations, as well as staff.

The aim has been to enable service users and carers to effect their right to be equal partners in decision making. Whilst the report of an independent body like the Healthcare Commission is pleasing and encouraging, at the end of the day the important test is what service users and carers say. So, in April 2005 the SURE Group agreed to carry out a survey of the views of service users and carers currently involved in the trust.

From the 93 service user/carer surveys returned, they found that service users and carers had been involved in 72 different decision-making activities in the trust.[7] The main reasons they gave for becoming involved were:

- to change and improve services
- to give something back
- to do something meaningful.

Comments received included:

> *I thought I could make a difference.*
> *To challenge staff attitudes and get them to think of the bigger picture.*
> *I am an ex-drug user but have been clean for 12 and a half years; with some training maybe I can give something back.*
> *If I can help one person then it will be worthwhile.*
> *To recover my confidence by meeting people.*

SURE asked when involved in trust activities whether service users and carers received:

- training they needed? 81% said 'always' or 'mostly'
- support they needed? 84% said 'always' or 'mostly'
- information they needed? 94% said 'always' or 'mostly'
- travel expenses on the day? 56% said 'always' or 'mostly'.

Of those who were asked, nearly 87% were involved in activities of some sort and more than half were involved in anything from three to 10 activities. Seventy-eight percent said it made 'some' or 'a lot of' difference to them (i.e. a positive difference), the most common reasons being that people felt valued, they had meaningful things to do, they learned new skills and they had more confidence. Only a small number (8.6%) said that it had made no difference to them.

Eighty-seven percent said Mersey Care had benefited from involving service users and carers, with just over 5% disagreeing and 5% being unsure. The main examples where improvements had been made were:

- information
- attitudes and clinical practice
- recruitment and selection
- family provision
- in-patient environment.

The conclusion? That a trust like Mersey Care isn't perfect. There is still a lot to do to make sure service users and carers are valued and receive expenses and payments on time. But we can begin to change peoples' experience of our services and their experience of mental distress by adopting a rights-based approach. There is always going to be a need for independent advocacy services, but mental health trusts can become organisations committed to *personal advocacy* and to enabling people with experience of using mental health services to speak for themselves and to articulate their rights, needs and concerns and to work individually and collectively for change.

The trust can also have a *public advocacy* role, speaking out about mental health issues, raising public awareness and persuading primary care trusts to invest in a new generation of mental health services.

We feel Mersey Care's main achievement so far has been in the field of exemplary advocacy, as a source of hope for disillusioned and demoralised people. This has demonstrated that things can change through a rights-based approach and by initiating and developing new and innovative ways of involving service users and carers and of providing services.

As Ron, a service user who has moved on to other things, said:

> *The time I spent working with the trust was a valuable part of my life. I gained a lot of self-respect, as well as receiving the respect of others, and I gained a tremendous amount of self-worth which I had not known for a long time.*

References

1   Brandon D. *Forgotten Children*. Preston: North West MIND; 1983.
2   Dyer L. Citizens' rights v voting wrongs. *Health Service J*. 1991; **101**(5265): 22–3.
3   Dyer L. Able and willing to work. *Open MIND*. 1990; **45**: June/July.
4   Mersey Care NHS. *Trust Business Plan 2004/2005*.
5   Mersey Care NHS. *Trust Clinical Governance Review (2005)*. Healthcare Commission; March 2005.
6   SURE. *Service User and Carer Involvement Survey*. Mersey Care NHS Trust; July 2005.

15

A change of heart

David Gilbert

'So, David, what do patients think?' Origins of a dilemma

After recovering from mental health problems, I wanted to improve things for others: to campaign for change, and support people through similar hardship. I joined my Community Health Council and local chapter of MIND and found myself on various local NHS committees, faced by a dozen powerful, well-paid, suited professionals. They would ignore me or enquire at odd moments, 'So, David, what do patients think?'

'What, *all* of them?' I thought. Since I was there to 'provide the user perspective', I told them about my experiences – both good and bad. Some thought, 'Great, here's someone telling it like it is at the coalface.' Others smiled benignly... or fell asleep. They wanted me to be 'representative' and go beyond my personal experience, but nobody could tell me what that meant.

So I forged relationships with service users, carers, members of the community and local groups. When I reported back their views, those who had previously seen me as credible, because I talked from experience, switched off. Those who had wanted me to be more representative had moved on to 'more important' matters: quality, risk and budgets.

In effect, I was used as free labour, marginalised as a quasi-operational lead for patient and public involvement, and exhausted myself (and other victims of consultation fatigue) in the process... and guess what? My report sat on the shelf and nothing changed. At the beginning I had been marginalised as 'not knowing enough' to contribute, but now I knew 'too much'.

So, what was my role? This chapter is about what I know now that I wish I had known then. I hope it will be useful for those who find themselves as 'lay representatives', that is, people who find themselves in the 'professional' arena representing those who have experience of services but are not 'professional' healthcare workers.

The outsider inside: the effective patient and community representative

'Experts' complain that not many people get engaged with public services and assert that this is due to apathy and disillusionment with the political process.[1] Others see public services being reformed and cry out for people's involvement in decision making.[2] What seems to escape both is that there are about 50,000 health-related voluntary sector organisations and half a million people involved in formal governing bodies.[3] Millions of people volunteer their time, take part in focus groups, fill in questionnaires, get consulted on local service changes, sit on interminable committees on cold February nights, and really care about health and health services.

One problem is the *numbers* of people coming through the ranks and the need to create further opportunities for those who give one-off views in surveys so they are able to sit at the decision-making tables and talk with the people in power. The other problem is *quality*: how to make sure that these people have the resources (money, skills, support, etc.) to take part.

In *Shrek 2*, the talkative donkey and Shrek are in a dungeon. Donkey rants that he has 'the right to remain silent ...' Shrek replies wearily, 'Donkey, you have the right, but do you have the *capacity*?' Likewise, with patient and public involvement there is now a statutory duty for all NHS bodies to involve people in decision making,[4] but few have the capacity to make it real and those who wish to make it real may also lack capacity.

What I always needed but never got was the support and training to make me an effective patient and community representative, clear in my role and confident in my abilities to change things. When I became Head of PPI at the former health inspectorate (the Commission for Health Improvement), we found that a lack of support for the lay voice was one factor that prevented PPI from becoming part of everyday practice in the NHS.[5] Many trusts wanted to support people but did not know how.[6] This inability and lack of experience is a huge obstacle to a 'patient-centred' NHS.

What I have learned is that patient or community (lay) representatives are 'outsiders inside' and must simultaneously play two roles:

- *community link* – externally facing, keeping in touch with local communities and bringing in wider perspectives
- *critical friend* – internally facing, flying the patient flag and offering strategic advice from a non-institutional perspective.

The Patient and Community Engagement (PACE) Team at the former NHSU (which was to have been the 'corporate university for the NHS') found that lay representatives:

- wanted clarity about their role, even though there was little consensus on what the role entailed or what was expected from them in terms of gathering views
- had to balance what they did outside the organisation (linking with communities) and what they did inside (as 'critical friends')
- needed to establish legitimacy to gain influence which depended on flexibility to respond to specific situations
- were motivated by personal experience, but needed to move beyond this and avoid doing work that paid staff were responsible for
- did different things to get patients' perspectives integrated into decision making
- had to strike a tricky balance between being supportive of decision makers and being independent and challenging, with little support or guidance on how to achieve this.

The effective outsider: the community link

The PACE Team also looked at the learning needs of representatives and identified two major areas within which their role needed to be explored:

1   what matters to patients, carers and the public
2   patient and public involvement.

What matters to patients, carers and the public: the dimensions of the 'patient's experience'

Ask any user of services what matters to them and they will have an opinion. Most people involved in trying to improve things for patients are motivated by experience; some grateful who want to give something back, others damaged who want to demand change. Without this passion and commitment the decision-making tables would be even more sterile places.

The downside is not that people 'have an axe to grind', but that their sight is partial. If my problem as a patient was not getting access to services, then it would be hard for me to fully understand that this is not the only thing that matters to patients and carers. If I have had poor treatment, how would I know that dissatisfaction is not the norm?

But you don't *have* to know everything! You only need to know broadly what the research evidence says matters to patients, and become conscious of your own experience and how these two aspects – experience and evidence – relate to each other.

On the whole, the things that matter to patients and carers are:

1   getting better, feeling better (outcomes of care)
2   getting the right care from the right people (clinical quality)
3   being treated as a human being (humanity of care), including respect, dignity, etc.
4   information, communication, having a say (involvement), including receiving information, clear explanations and being able to participate actively in decisions about treatment options
5   being supported – practical and emotional support, including access to statutory and voluntary sector services
6   support for carers and relatives
7   a safe, clean, comfortable place to be (environment of care), including privacy, hygiene, food
8   right treatment at the right *time* (access 1), including prompt response to an emergency, timely access to car, short waits, etc.
9   right treatment in the right *place* (access 2) – convenient locations, transport, parking, etc.
10 not being passed from pillar to post (continuity) – a smooth 'journey' through primary to/from secondary care, etc.
11 continuous care – 'after care', support in the community, etc.

Numbers 2 to 7 should be there at each stage of our care. Numbers 8 to 11 are about receiving *continuous* care. These things are important for all of us, regardless of circumstance or health problem. On top of this, there are particular needs for specific groups or particular barriers that people from different parts of society face when trying to get the things they need. Therefore, diversity and equality issues are central to all 11 dimensions.

Reframing my own experience

So how do these dimensions relate to my own experience? And how should I bring both personal experience and what matters to others to the table?

The temptation has been to exaggerate the drama of aspects of my own poor clinical care or to think I have nothing to say. One of my blind spots is a legacy of feeling vulnerable because of my illness and imagining that doctors must be heroes who know everything and should cure me. When I was ill I did not want choice, only for the pain to go away. I was a child wanting daddy or mummy doctor to magic me better. I think the paternalistic medical model survives in a modern uncertain world mostly because of a primitive desire to be looked after.

So I took my pills compliantly and prayed they would work. The collusion was complete: doctors and nurses did not need to give me information and were absolved of the need to chart the difficult waters of shared decisions. I complied with my own need to stay ignorant. I did not dare to challenge this conspiracy of power and dependence.

It is all too easy to concentrate on the non-clinical aspects of care that I 'know about': the environment of care and patient information. This ignores the fact that many patients know more about treatment than professionals, for instance those with HIV, people with learning disabilities or those with long-term conditions. However, the 11 patient experience dimensions help us to take a broader view.

Maybe I should gag myself and not tell my personal story at the decision-making table? Not at all, the *judicious* use of story telling – the use of narrative – can be very powerful. Health professionals deride the 'anecdote', but actually use them more frequently than lay representatives! Story-tellers and poets know that they can illustrate a wider truth and reframe issues in useful ways. The secret is in when and how to use them. Here is an example.

I was sitting on my bed in a psychiatric unit after lunch with the afternoon to fill. A doctor appeared, one of six junior doctors I was to see over the next couple of months. He gave me a perfunctory hello and then pulled gingerly on the curtain rail around my bed. 'What are you doing?' I asked, thinking his behaviour even odder than mine. 'Just testing whether you're going to do something stupid,' he said. Then he walked out, leaving me contemplating a suddenly increased set of treatment options.

A few days later, after a spate of in-patients trying to throw themselves through reinforced windows with disturbing results, and a flurry of late-night disappearances from the wards (one with fatal consequences), staff enforced a crack-down on patient behaviour to make the wards 'safer'. They locked the doors at 8 pm, making night-times longer and even more insufferably claustrophobic for patients. The chaplain who usually came round at 9 pm to chat to me could not do so. It felt as though the outbreaks of violence and self-harm were increasing as caged souls became more desperate.

Meanwhile, staff spent much of their time behind a set of observation windows looking out on to the TV room. Few mixed with us in the room where frustrations arose over arguments about TV channels, negotiations on cigarette trading and disagreements on people's favourite chairs.

How many incidents might have been avoided if *we* had been asked, 'How can things be made safer?' Instead, I imagine interminable risk management meetings were held that failed to fathom why things were getting worse. Getting user views requires a leap of faith and a longer-term outlook. What if the doctor had stayed for a chat instead of testing the curtain rails? What if there had been more to do on the wards? What if the chaplain had still been able to visit? What if they had removed that wretched observation window? PPI is not soft and fluffy: I still believe that people died needlessly because they did not ask us for our views.

Ten years later, I read about government targets to reduce psychiatric in-patient suicides, by reducing to zero the number of non-collapsible curtain rails! It would seem that risk management committees are still ticking the boxes and missing the point.

This story usually makes people sit up and listen. It makes several useful points, but has to be used with care. It can be shocking, but story telling is not about beating up professionals or emotionally blackmailing people into changing practice. Instead, stories should serve to reframe debates about what matters and illustrate that service users can have valuable insights.

Returning to my original dilemma from my first NHS committee meeting when asked 'what do patients think?', I respond by referring to the evidence and my experience. But a second type of response is equally crucial. This relates to how the representative catalyses wider engagement.

The lay representative and PPI

When it comes to what patients think, health professionals often mistake a decision-making forum for a focus group. One cause for this lies in terminology. The term 'lay representative' implies that such individuals should be a conduit for patient views or, more dangerously, the *only* conduit for them, or more dangerously still, the one who goes out to *get* those views. I believe the lay representatives should not be, or do, any of these things. He or she should be a PPI *strategic advisor,* able to question and/or advise on ways that the organisation engages more widely.

The point here is not to outline what it takes to mainstream involvement – this is covered elsewhere – but to think about a representative's relationship to PPI. This can be done by charting the sort of journey a representative takes, looking at how their role shifts and what sort of support is needed on the way.

A patient, service user, member of the general public or voluntary sector representative may become first a 'lay representative' on a project. A mental health service user might be recruited to join a group looking at patient information; a cardiac patient might join a panel on access issues. The starting point of their journey into the world of corporate decision making is usually closely related to their own experience. However, the NHS sometimes makes the mistake of putting someone straight into a corporate-wide role. Without a way of creating successive exciting, relevant, non-threatening and worthwhile opportunities, representatives will walk away.

 From this focused, locally based, client- or topic-specific project, the representative may get invited to do more, such as serving on advisory groups, on improvement initiatives or in areas where they have no particular experience. Then they might become part of 'direct' influencing mechanisms such as a governor member on a foundation trust, or non-executive director (NED) on a trust board.

Here are some consequences of this 'career pathway'.

From 'doer' to 'advisor'

In shifting the type of work they do, the representative will need to move from 'doing' engagement work to 'advising' others how to do it. Lay representatives may feel more comfortable going off and running discussion groups; it's in their blood to find out 'what the community wants' and may keep them going after boring committee meetings (even though others may fall into the opposite trap – sitting on never-ending meetings and becoming divorced from the community reality). In this way they can maintain an 'operational' role which lets others off the hook. But this risks confusing their role with that of staff, as Section 11 of the Health and Social Care Act 2001 places a statutory duty on all NHS organisations to consult and involve the public.

From 'PPI methods' advisor to 'organisational PPI' advisor

While shifting from doer to advisor, the representative should note that times have changed. The NHS is getting better at capturing the views of its patients, but still is not good at doing anything about them. The lay representative needs to shift from advising on the *techniques* of engagement (i.e. what sort of methods should be used to document peoples' views) to advising on the *systems and processes* to 'mainstream' involvement and act upon findings from focus group discussions.

In the early stages, this may mean merely asking simple questions: 'We found out what patients thought but have we done anything about it?' Later it might be about identifying the way that reports from engagement feed into decision making: who is accountable for this? How is PPI built into performance management and monitoring?

From 'PPI specialist' to 'strategic thinker'

The lay representative has to be more 'strategic' in their thinking generally (not just about PPI) and contribute to an overview of the organisation's efforts. This reflects another NHS problem: parts of the NHS do a good job at engaging patients and the public and some initiatives yield change. Why is a project on involving patients with cancer not shared with other directorates and/or sustained? This is the sort of question the representatives and others should address.

At CHI we had trained lay reviewers and worked as equals with them in inspection teams. Inspections looked at different trust systems and processes to ensure good quality care, including clinical effectiveness, risk management, staff support and human resources. But we also looked at things from a patient perspective and focused on how a trust involved patients and the public. Despite good intentions, there was often confusion about the lay reviewer's role. In the early days, the lay reviewer was sometimes – wrongly in my view – left to focus on PPI and the patient perspective rather than the 'hard' bits, such as risk management and clinical quality. This is a classic example of the PPI agenda being seen as a bolt-on extra rather than central to organisational thinking, as is described elsewhere in this book.

From 'outsider' to 'insider'

If someone becomes more of a corporate 'insider', for example as a non-executive director, the challenges above become exacerbated. The lay representative will need to sort out in both their head and heart how they feel about becoming less immediately attached to their community and more attached to the organisation's well-being. Coming from the community or voluntary sector, non-executive directors have in the past sometimes been asked to be the link to the community, or be the one who has board-level responsibility for PPI. A few have been marginalised from other roles and responsibilities in the process.

The NHS Appointment Commission's intention is that trust boards should have a *collective* duty to ensure that there are systems and processes in place to focus on what matters to patients and to take a strategic approach to PPI. The Langland's Commission on good governance in the public sector also emphasises that these things are a collective responsibility and should not be foisted onto one individual.[3]

From 'local' to 'national' player

It should be noted that there are similarities and differences between the lay representative role at local and at national level. Obviously, there is a major leap from working in a NHS trust to a role within, say, a Royal College or National Agency, or even the Department of Health. It is beyond the scope of this chapter to go into much detail about this, but I have found the general principles outlined in this chapter to be of use at both levels.

Applying the learning

Earlier I tried to show how the response to the question, 'So, David, what do patients think?' should begin with framing the evidence of what matters to patients, reflected through the filter of personal experience. This can be supplemented with a question back to the others around the table: 'So, what has this group done to find out?' It becomes a shared responsibility and the lay representative should not have to find out everything themselves. They can offer pointers, but when they respond in this way others are more likely to contribute. The lay representative may feel 'less special', but I have learned the hard way that this approach yields more action. And isn't that what it's all about?

The effective insider

The merits (and otherwise) of righteous anger

When I recovered from mental health problems and got involved in improving services, I was angry. I felt that I had been let down by the NHS and professionals and my relief about recovering was supplanted by a grumbling resentment towards 'the system'. I had been a campaigner against social injustice before my breakdown, so had particularly hard edges. This anger fuelled my motivation to be involved – without it I would be an accountant – but it has had its price.

Whenever I joined meetings, I played the angry consumer arguing for more of this and better that without having a clue about resource issues, let alone the constraints on professionals. Once I argued avidly for four community mental health teams to be available in our borough during a 'blue-sky thinking' exercise. Then the financial director said only one was affordable. Blue sky? More like red-faced at my naïvety!

On the 'other side of the fence' at CHI, I led the development of a PPI strategy. We conducted a huge national consultation exercise involving six road shows around the country with hundreds of voluntary and community organisations. Most people thought they were pretty good and would lead to change.

However, on one occasion a smattering of people from a national organisation hogged the floor with displays of righteous anger as to how damaged they had been by the system. They had a point but took over, preventing others getting their voices heard. They surrounded me afterwards and I suggested that, while their views were valid, I felt as a fellow sufferer that they were doing their cause more harm than good by the way they presented their case. Ten minutes later they returned to attack me for being patronising and formally complained about me to our chief executive. He stood by me. We never engaged with them again. Were their angry tactics justified? Possibly. Understandable, certainly; effective, not at all.

On another occasion I witnessed mental health service user representatives and professionals together planning a local project to work on a mutually agreed topic area. One service user suggested that we look at promoting the use of acupuncture in schizophrenia, because it had been 'brilliant' for him. The psychiatrists did not turn up for the next meeting and the project almost died. They all knew patients who had turned to acupuncture and been duped into paying large amounts of money for what they believed was ineffective treatment that led them away from seeking more formal care and treatment. The project leaders managed to broker a project about 'shared decision making about treatment', focusing on how information could be provided about choice of treatments, including complementary medicine. The point is that if user involvement is to work, both sides have to play the game, compromise and work on a mutually agreed agenda.

So what do these stories illustrate about the role of the lay representative in terms of being the effective insider? The following issues have also been raised during learning events on the learning and support needs of representatives.[7]

The effective insider: keeping it real

The central role of the effective insider is to keep discussions focused on what matters to patients. We have seen above that there are several ways in which a lay representative can avoid being seduced into wider operational matters. But when it comes to being at the decision-making table, more subtle skills are needed.

Asking the simple question 'What does that mean for patients?' is useful, but overdoing it may make you seem naïve. Challenging the flow of a discussion in a similar vein can be valuable: 'I'm not sure how much relevance this has to the patient-centred values we were talking about earlier?'

But what sort of other skills help?

Communication and presentation skills

Many representatives say they want to listen and communicate better, to work on their own 'attitudes' or 'confidence'. The over-riding issue is a need to build self-reflection into learning activities. People need to relate to different audiences and this requires flexibility of styles. Presenting your case in a committee setting requires different skills to speaking at a public event, to patient groups or the media.

Knowledge and understanding of healthcare

Lay representatives need to know enough about, but not become embroiled in, the systems and processes of healthcare. One major national patient organisation has invested a lot of effort in inducting its members into how the NHS works; but it did this, in my opinion, in too much detail and in a didactic fashion that made it overwhelming. It is common to hear lay representatives appeal that they want to know more about the NHS, but such learning needs to be relevant to the local circumstances and the role they are fulfilling. It is more important to know how to find the learning when you need it. A list of who to go to for different types of support and information at the beginning of a project or new role is invaluable.

Analytical skills

The representative is constantly faced with blizzards of facts, statistics and jargon. They need to understand information from the community (e.g. demographics, public health, analysing patient views), but also how to deal with data around healthcare providers. How do we critique information that comes from a different world? Again, the issue is not so much what sort of information should we be looking at, but 'where do we go to find someone to help us'.

'Critical friend' skills

The notion that patients and the public can be 'critical friends' is seductive. If I could have done this from the beginning, perhaps I could have asked challenging questions in a more charming way. The art of being a critical friend is as much to do with timing and awareness of situations as it is with bringing contradictory impulses together: your like and dislike of professionals; your desire to challenge and to support; your anger and your love.

The concept of critical friend is loosely defined despite creeping into regular Health Service discourse. I have never wanted my own friends to be critical. If they were, I doubt I would put up with them for long. However, lay representatives have to deal with professionals face to face, cope with feelings of vulnerability and know how to frame questions. Some will feel more comfortable with this than others. Being able to ask challenging questions in a non-threatening way is about more than just assertiveness training. But there will be times when asking the tough hard question is the right thing to do even if you are not appreciated for it, just as there will be times when it is the wrong thing to do.

Influencing skills

People also have to master some of the 'darker' arts of persuasion and behind-the-scenes influencing; all the things we learn by doing and the topics that are not valued in conventional learning programmes. People should learn how to use different influencing styles with different sorts of audiences, about negotiation skills and understanding where power lies.

It took me years to realise that I had to prioritise my efforts at those times when business decisions were made and with those who had the power to make them. It was often more productive to hang about management corridors as business plans were developed than to attend planning sub-committees.

Personal challenges

The following list is derived from my own botched attempts at being a lay representative at various levels: local, national and international. They are the things I found and still find most difficult.

1. Being professional

We have all heard professionals say that lay representatives should not become 'too professional'. In fact, lay representatives say it just as much. But those purporting to articulate the interests of patients and the public should be *more* professional. They should understand their role, be clear about what they are doing and how, be supported to do a good job, have clear shared agreements with others about how they conduct their business, take responsibility, feed back their views to the communities they serve and to the organisation, and behave responsibly. This is the essence of being professional.

We should not, however, conflate 'being professional' with 'going native'; that is, to confuse two meanings of 'professional', i.e. to do the job that should be done by health professionals and the need to 'behave professionally'.

Some might argue that patients and the public should not be expected to take on this onerous role; but this argument is usually invoked by clinicians who are used to dealing with individual patients and not lay representatives. However, I have sometimes heard ineffective lay representatives argue in the same vein, unwittingly colluding with the very people they want to challenge.

What brings most people to be involved are personal values. The danger in too much experience of involvement is the loss of passion, but this danger is overstated. It is not about 'leaving personal baggage behind', but being able to pack it in a smarter bag.

If people really care and are still linked to the world of patients through their own networks, the passion never goes away but is continually reframed in the light of experience. Good lay representatives are always seeking to sharpen their arguments and focus, always seeking the right point at which to make a crucial intervention. The second thing that happens is that professionals start to share the enthusiasm and passion of the lay representatives; the language spoken around the table becomes more animated. In fact, lay representatives can give permission to others to break free of their own restrictive debates, sterile and self-serving language. Not surprisingly, health professionals have their own tales of suffering to relate. We become more human by engaging in debate about what matters to patients.

2. Being representative

So, how can one person possibly 'represent' the views of an entire community? I have tackled that by proposing that the lay representative focuses broadly on what matters to patients and forges a link between the healthcare organisation and the community rather than do it all themselves. I suggest that lay representatives never have been, never will be able to be, never should be seen as, truly representative. It is an impossible dream.

I am not a political theorist, but I am pretty sure even a cursory glance at the role of the MP will put the lie to the possibility of someone being able to represent the total community's perspectives. Instead, what a good MP does to best serve the 'interests' of his or her community is to know what matters to them, know how to link with them and understand the priorities.

How can I argue that lay representatives go beyond the personal and do not need to run focus groups or link extensively with all communities in their patch as part of their role? Without these mechanisms surely they may become decoupled from their roots? How can I propose that lay representatives are not the sole conduit for patient views, but instead become some sort of catalyst or roving strategic PPI advisor? Perhaps anyone could do the job and lay representatives must be prevented from being representative, or that 'real' patients are not needed to do the job. No, being a patient or having had an experience of healthcare is necessary, *but not sufficient*.

In fact, I want to ban the phrase 'lay representative', despite having littered this chapter with it. First because the word 'lay' derives from the word 'laity' and refers to when the priesthood held sway. Secondly, because my argument is that the role should be 'advisory'. People should instead start thinking of themselves as patient and public advisors.

3. Mixed accountabilities

I often got into a mess as a lay representative. Should I be 'on the patient's side', always coming down on the outsider's side, always challenging and always reporting 'back' to the community? Or, once having been accepted by the powers that be, should I cleave myself down the middle and broker compromises; was I an advocate or mediator?

There is a subtle but important difference between having a role and responsibility and accountability. A lay representative needs to know early on whether the group of which they are a part has formal decision-making powers. If the group is part of a corporate entity, governance arrangements imply that the role of lay representative may be formally constituted (i.e. as a non-executive, or as a governor member on a foundation trust).

On a personal level, one has to resolve emotions about 'whose side are you on'. If you become involved as a non-executive director, for example, you may kiss goodbye to the community love you crave; you may become seen as the enemy. This is all part of the excitement, complexity and challenge of being an 'outsider inside'. I love it.

References

1 Lawson N, Leighton D. Blairism's agoraphobia: active citizenship and the public domain. *Renewal.* 2004; **12**(1). http://www.renewal.org.uk/
2 Lenaghan J. Shifting the Balance of Power: making it real across Birmingham and the Black Country. Unpublished paper. 2004.
3 Independent Commission on Good Governance in Public Services. *Good Governance Standard for Public Services.* 11 Jan 2005. http://www.opm.co.uk/ICGGPS/Langlands
4 Department of Health. Strengthening Accountability: Section 11 of the Health and Social Care Act 2001. London: Department of Health; 2001.
5 Gilbert D, King J. *i2i – Involvement to Improvement: sharing the learning about patient and public involvement from CHI's inspections.* Commission for Health Improvement; 2004. http://www.chi.nhs.uk/patients/ppi_report_0204.pdf
6 Pickin C, Popay J, Staley K *et al.* Developing a model to enhance the capacity of statutory organisations to engage with lay communities. *Journal of Health Services.* 2002; 7: 34–42. www.Kingsfund.org.uk/WhatsToStop.pdf
7 Gilbert D. *Working Well Together: what sort of learning and support do forums and others need to work well with the Healthcare Commission?* London: NHSU and Healthcare Commission; 2005.

16

Political challenges for the lay representative

David Gilbert

Patient and public involvement in the new NHS: the song remains the same

In the last chapter, we saw clearly that the role of the lay representative needs to change. Furthermore, the massive upheaval in English health and social care and changes to the way involvement will work mean that lay representatives, or what I would like to call patient and community engagement (PACE) advisors, will have to operate in a new environment.

A few years ago, PPI was on the up. In Wales, 'Signposts'[1] became the first national guidance on PPI. England followed by having a statutory duty for all NHS bodies to involve and consult patients and the public.[2] The Commission for Health Improvement was busy inspecting organisations for this, and its report, 'i2i – Involvement to Improvement'[3] triggered further feverish initiatives.

Senior managers took the cause more seriously when the National Primary and Care Trust Development Programme developed its competency framework for engagement[4] and strategic health authorities (SHAs) implemented performance management frameworks for PPI. We got our own 'czar', a National Director for Patients and the Public, and national agencies created directors of PPI and patient-centred units. Last but not least, the Commission for PPI in Health (CPPIH) was launched, with hundreds of PPI Forums to complement other involvement structures.

For the first time, champions of the work had strong backing. Even recalcitrant directors knew this pesky agenda would not go away. No longer could they simply get a junior colleague to run focus groups and leave the resulting report to gather dust.

Now, however, CHI has gone. The Healthcare Commission is committed to inspecting PPI via its Annual Health Check, but it is not yet clear how it will do this. Section 11 of the Health and Social Care Act 2001 is not being routinely applied. CPPIH will be abolished and there is continuing unsettled debate about the role and impact of PPI Forums.

More worryingly, government language has changed over the past two years. Department of Health pronouncements do not as often extol the virtues of services planned, designed and delivered *with* patients and communities. In the new world of choice and payment by results, delivery is the focus to ensure services are 'responsive' *to* patients and that reforms 'improve' services *for* patients. It is a world of choice rather than voice.

At a local level, chief executives, senior managers and clinicians are ambivalent about involving people in decision making on how services are planned and delivered. They have not seen convincing evidence that involvement makes a difference and anyway their minds are now on 'more pressing' matters: financial deficits, organisational changes and reform of the way that services are commissioned and delivered. Non-executive directors appointed by the Appointments Commission more often come from financial and business backgrounds now, rather than community and the voluntary sector.

Meanwhile, local work on PPI goes on, but much of it focuses on short-term projects in particular services, and too many reports remain on the shelf. Too few trusts take it seriously.

Some parts of the Department of Health, perhaps realising the possible vacuum in policy and practice, are beginning to resurrect the agenda. The new Health and Social Care White Paper[5] emphasises again 'voice' as well as 'choice'.

This is crunch time for PPI. If we don't get it right this time around there may be no next opportunity. The principles remain the same: patients, carers and the public should be central to planning, designing, delivering and evaluating services. But, in the (paraphrased) words of Doctor Spock: 'It's PPI, Jim, but not as we know it.'

PPI for a new world

An expert panel was recently convened to come up with recommendations to ensure that arrangements for future involvement and engagement are fit for purpose in a new health and social care system. There are four areas which advocate for PPI and the new breed of PACE advisors should take seriously:

- commissioning
- provision and quality
- accountability
- governance.

There is confusion about terminology regarding these different areas for involvement. Those commissioning and providing services both have to:

- *involve* people in planning, design and delivery of *internal* functions via:
  - involvement (capturing the patient and/or public perspective)
  - governance mechanisms (involving people in decision making)
- *prove* they do so to *external* agencies via:
  - accountability mechanisms
  - monitoring of quality and regulation.

Commissioning

Commissioning is the process by which the NHS decides how to spend the resources available to ensure equitable access to high-quality services that offer good value for money. The good news is that the government recognises that services commissioned must be based on a full understanding of the health needs of the entire population served by a primary care trust, achievable only through active, ongoing and systematic engagement of local people.

The initial phases require a 'public/citizen' take on needs, equalities, public health and gaps in services, for example. It will require particular 'techniques' (such as deliberative methods) where competing values come together or trade-offs need to be made. Later stages (e.g. designing service pathways and ensuring the quality of what has been commissioned) require involvement of patients/service users.

The bad news is that involvement in commissioning is underdeveloped. So far, there has been precious little involvement of patients and the public in developing guidance on commissioning and this will be a crucial test for the future of involvement, given current health reforms.

Ammunition for involvement comes from the catchily titled 'Technical Guidance for Practice-Based Commissioning' (PBC). It stresses the involvement of patients and the public in decisions over what services a practice commissions. This is 'to protect the integrity of the local health system and to check developing thinking against the views of patients and local communities'. The challenge is to make sure involvement has an impact on commissioning. A practice not following this approach will be in breach of Section 11 with the PCT responsible.[6] This is stern stuff that should reopen managerial minds.

Provision and regulation of quality

Some Health Service PPI champions complain of 'missing the boat' and not being involved in core corporate work. One told me she has become the 'lay rep pimp', continually being asked for tame lay representatives for committees. Others, though, are making sure their work 'fits' new agendas.

One PPI lead described his sterling work on choice, getting client groups involved in designing information for the 'choose and book' initiative. When asked whether patients were involved in transport issues, or the broader implementation of choice, he said that was not part of the remit. Without strategic 'nous' and senior support, patients stay part of reading panels, reviewing trust documents for 'user-friendliness' but little more, and PPI continues to remain at the margins.

There are several key challenges to involvement in provision in the new NHS:

- Advocates for involvement want stronger enforcement of the requirement to involve people, but providers want less 'cumbersome' statutory requirements so they can switch provision quickly in response to patient choices.
- Care and treatment will increasingly be delivered by different types of providers (NHS, private companies, social enterprises). How can involvement help ensure quality of provision in a mixed economy?
- As care becomes more individualised through choice, special focus is needed on the continuity of the patient 'pathway'. How can involvement tackle this?
- Ensuring the patient voice in monitoring services will fall mainly to the regulators: the Healthcare Commission and the CSCI who are due to merge in 2008. How well they do this will be crucial. Tough decisions will be required on the balance between regulation and support for improvement.

Overall, the balance between 'voice' and 'choice' in the new NHS will be keenly contested.

Accountability

'Accountability' is the new trendy word in involvement circles, but there is considerable confusion about its meaning. In simple terms it means 'being responsible for the effects of your actions and willing to explain or be criticised for them'. There are four key questions:

- Who is held accountable?
- For what?
- To whom?
- What are the consequences of failure?

There will be different answers to these questions according to the type of accountability. For example:

- *performance accountability*, demonstrated by specific outcomes
- *bureaucratic accountability*, demonstrated by compliance with rules and regulations, especially around funding and quality
- *professional accountability*, demonstrated by compliance with recognised professional practices
- *market accountability*, in terms of consumer choice
- *stakeholder accountability*, which applies to all the above.

Many argue that, given current trends, it is *commissioners* who should be accountable through a form of scrutiny that is *wider than just health*. It is possible that Overview and Scrutiny Committees will be granted an enhanced role in the new systems and structures for involvement. If this is the case, then OSCs will also need to have better patient/user input into this new 'accountability system' either through dedicated intermediaries responsible for gathering views or directly with 'networks' of patients and the public and local organisations. They will also have to use particular methods (such as citizens' panels) to engage with patients and the public.

Governance

Given that this is likely to be a hot topic for involvement, it is worrying that yet again there is widespread confusion about what the term 'governance' actually means. Health and education tend to use 'governance' in a formal sense when talking about boards of governors or public governors; the Home Office has a looser definition around 'ordinary people involved in decision making' that overlaps with 'involvement' more generally. In social care, user governance can mean user-*led* organisations.

As we have seen in Chapter 15, there is a difference between being 'involved' in ongoing initiatives (e.g. service user and carer panels), being a 'representative' with indirect influence over decision making (e.g. in improvement projects or advisory panels) and being a 'governor' with formal decision-making powers and accountabilities.

The Independent Commission on Good Governance in Public Services[7] highlights that boards should focus on what matters for service users and have a collective responsibility to listen and act upon user voices. The government and Monitor (the NHS foundation trust regulator) are likely to re-emphasise the importance of governance and how it relates to PPI. Some are beginning also to discuss whether PCTs might adopt the governance model of foundation trusts.

The work to be done is grooming potential governor members and non-executive directors from a widening pool of lay representatives. These future stars will have to move beyond personal agendas, understand their role and develop clear relationships with communities and directors – all things we have talked about generally in Chapter 15. More widely, the Home Office Active Citizenship agenda highlights a possible resurgence of activity to support 'citizen governors'.

PPI learning and development

The new role for the lay representative (or PACE advisor) is not going to be easy. People may find themselves in new organisational structures and/or helping to oversee new or refocused functions. And nothing can possibly change if people are not supported in this 'new' role. Learning and development is one part of the support that people need to fulfil their duties, alongside practical support such as secretariat and administrative back-up, help with accessing meetings, reimbursement, information and IT.

As yet, the NHS is not geared up to train and support patients and the public. This is not part of mainstream business. Some professionals know they need to provide lay representatives with induction training and the more enlightened stretch this to ongoing support, but few have considered or tried to finance learning and development opportunities.

Meanwhile the staff training and development agenda is taken more seriously. Though not perfect by any means, there is an annual NHS staff survey that covers issues of training and development, and there are national and local initiatives to ensure that professionals who wish to access learning opportunities can do so.

However, opportunities for staff to learn about PPI are few and far between; and for lay representatives, almost non-existent. The former PACE Team at the NHSU undertook work with the Department of Health and PPI leads in strategic health authorities to find out what learning people needed in order to ensure that PPI was part of mainstream business.

This sort of work has raised the idea of a 'core curriculum' for PPI for both staff and non-staff (see below). Unfortunately the work of the PACE Team was discontinued when the government decided to merge the NHSU's functions into the new National Institute for Innovation and Improvement. The NHSU was to have become the 'corporate university' for the NHS and in its strategic plan was committed to enable patients to be 'learners' as well as staff. Now, the idea of a core curriculum has been resurrected within proposals for a new National Centre for Involvement (NCI), first proposed as the National PPI Resource Centre (see below). This just goes to show that good ideas can sometimes outlast national fads for reorganising the NHS!

It may seem that my arguments thus far concern what people 'lack' in terms of being 'fit' for the job. If only those health professionals could teach us what it means to be a good patient representative! But here's the paradox: the sort of learning required builds on what we already know, value, love and live.

The 'deficit' model of training whereby we get others to fill our gaps in knowledge and understanding must be turned on its head. Clearly there are quite a few things we need to know about the NHS or its organisations in order to function properly; but mostly what I have brought to decision-making tables is common sense and a focus on what matters to patients. At the beginning this was derived a lot from my own experience as a patient, but this was complemented later on by common sense about what I could or should be doing. The learning I most needed was generic and holds true for many people on decision-making forums: *how can I make a difference?*

Some solutions

Health Action Skills (HAS)

When I started on my 'career' as a mental health service user, gradually becoming a community 'leader' or representative, I was struck by how little training and development I was offered along the way. The voluntary sector organisations I worked with were too poor, and the statutory services too unwilling or ignorant to boost my skills with formal learning opportunities.

The sort of learning needed depends on the stage of the journey. Little has been done to identify the 'steps' of what might be termed a 'user career pathway' across the public sector. And not much has been done on what sort of learning and support might go alongside this. In the NHS, the notion of a 'skills escalator' for staff has become fashionable, to offer opportunities for clinical and non-clinical staff to boost their career chances through creating learning opportunities, but until now no such idea has become fashionable for patients and the public. A patient and public version of the skills escalator is sorely needed.

I propose a strategy to promote 'Health Action Skills' for patients and the public. Patients and the public would have learning opportunities available at each level of their development as they move between different roles and functions in the health and social care system. If I am a patient, then I would be able to get learning and support to be an 'expert patient' able to manage my life and health condition better; but I would also be able to further my learning about community leadership and active citizenship and/or how to be a lay representative or governor member. At present, there are small pockets of good practice in terms of developing such programmes, but no overall national strategy to bring it all together.

This chapter has focused on the last leg of this journey, but I think it is time that those in the learning and development field recognised that the pool of future leaders and representatives lies in cultivating learning and support at an early stage of the 'user career' pathway. Just as staff recruitment and retention is dependent on people accessing training at an early stage of their career, so it is with people in the community. How might we develop this idea?

A core curriculum for PPI

It is clear that learning and development around PPI is crucial. There is a thirst for learning, but huge barriers to making sure that the right learning is available.

What is needed is a coherent approach to the planning, design and delivery of learning around PPI. Instead of focusing just on the needs of particular patient groups or PPI Forums, the focus should be on shared learning between staff and non-staff. Instead of focusing on developing individual modules, we should step back and consider the development of a 'core curriculum' or learning programme around PPI. In simple terms, what this means is defining what learning should be available for whom, and who might coordinate its delivery.

Table 16.1 is an attempt to think this through. It is purposely left blank to stimulate thoughts and ideas about the issues:

- the left-hand column lists the sorts of topics (or modules) that might be in such a programme
- the second column suggests whether this might be a core or specialist/optional module
- the third column indicates who might benefit from the module, possibly via shared learning across different groups
- the fourth column lists examples of the sorts of agencies that might wish to coordinate development of that module.

This framework and the list of topics builds on earlier work conducted by the PACE Team with the Healthcare Commission.[8] Learning opportunities might be made available to:

- PPI Forums
- patient and public interest groups (e.g. voluntary sector; OSCs)
- PPI champions in the NHS (e.g. PPI leads; NEDs; directors with PPI responsibilities; governor members)
- senior managers (e.g. without direct responsibility for PPI).

The list of topics is divided into four clusters:

- working with each other in our team
- working to develop ourselves
- working with the community
- working with healthcare organisations.

Themes three and four echo what I have been talking about in this chapter. What the framework does is to illustrate the possibility of making shared learning for PPI a real possibility. After all, the staff champion for PPI is in the same boat as the lay representative when it comes to arguing for the mainstreaming of PPI. They may need to go onto the same learning programme to find out how to influence decision making, and they will certainly find allies to their cause in so doing.

The table is only a draft framework for consideration. Stakeholders will need to work together to flesh out the detail. They will also have to work on the overall process of developing the curriculum. Given current turbulence in the PPI system, it will be necessary to identify roles and responsibilities in the following areas:

- *Funding*. It is unclear in the present climate who will fund further learning activities in this area. During times of organisational change, money earmarked for training can be a soft target for cuts. This should not be allowed to happen. Who will provide the money and resources to develop this framework and/or the individual elements?
- *Commissioning*. Who will commission delivery of learning in particular areas and to particular groups? One issue will be how to ensure that commissioning

Table 16.1 PPI learning programme: a draft framework for a core curriculum

Topic	Core or specialist module?	For whom?	Coordinated by?
THEME 1: Working with each other in our team Establishing good relationships (building the team)			
What are we here to do? (Role development)			
Strategic planning			
THEME 2: Working to develop ourselves Communication and presentation			
Leadership			
Project management			
Finance			
IT			
THEME 3: Working with the community (the effective outsider) Joint working			
Linking with communities			
Diversity and equality			
PPI and community engagement			
THEME 4: Working with healthcare organisations (the effective insider) Understanding healthcare			
Analytical skills (includes understanding evidence)			
Influencing skills (includes 'critical friend' skills; political skills)			

includes a commitment to shared learning. Will those commissioning learning for staff, for example, be open to inclusion of patient and public representatives on those programmes?

- *Delivery*. How will learning be delivered? It is beyond the capacity of one agency to deliver learning across this wide spectrum of topics; what sort of model will govern how learning programmes will be delivered? Signposting, accreditation and 'train the trainer programmes' are some of a range of possibilities.
- *Stakeholder involvement* in the above. It is crucial that patient and public interest groups have a say in how the above are taken forward.

The National Centre for Involvement

In mid 2006, a new independent national resource centre for PPI came into operation. Its vision is to develop and support PPI across health and social care to improve health. It aims to:

- promote the value of PPI
- create a one-stop shop for information and advice on PPI
- build the capacity of organisations, staff and patient/citizens for high-quality PPI
- develop and disseminate practical resources that aid PPI
- generate evidence-based models and examples of best practice
- identify and maximise learning opportunities at a national, regional and local level
- develop and facilitate networks and communities of interest
- become an exemplar of a responsive and inclusive organisation.

The Centre will work with networks of PPI advocates and champions from:

- PPI Forums
- forum support organisations
- health voluntary and community organisations (including faith-based and black and minority ethnic groups)
- strategic health authorities
- NHS organisations
- statutory authorities
- professional associations
- local authority Overview and Scrutiny Committees
- non-executive directors and governor members.

The Centre will work with these networks to ensure that it reaches diverse sectors of the community. So if you are from one of these networks, the Centre will provide a range of useful resources, such as:

- up-to-date information about PPI and PPI-relevant policy issues
- practical resources
- evidence about what works
- models of good practice
- peer support, discussion groups and other people to talk to
- information, advice and guidance about local learning opportunities
- opportunities to get involved with the Centre.

The National Centre for Involvement is a consortium of the University of Warwick, the Centre for Public Scrutiny (CfPS) and the Long-term Medical Conditions Alliance (LMCA), but will engage with a wider family of partners that has been involved in developing proposals.

The Centre will be able to help with any of the following:

- involving patients and the public more effectively
- involving people from communities that are traditionally excluded or marginalised
- making improvements based on involvement work to prevent focus group and survey reports sitting on the shelf

- sustaining and spreading good practice across other areas in your community
- making sure that PPI is part of mainstream business in your patch
- becoming more actively involved in the governance and management of local healthcare
- ensuring healthcare organisations are democratically accountable and responsive to local needs
- engaging more effectively with professionals supporting your own healthcare.

It is anticipated that the NCI will provide the tools to turn patient and public involvement into everyday practice.

References

1 Gilbert D, Lloyd P. *Signposts One: a practical guide to public and patient involvement in Wales.* Cardiff: Welsh Assembly Government and Office for Public Management; 2001.
2 Department of Health. Strengthening Accountability: Section 11 of the Health and Social Care Act. London: Department of Health; 2001.
3 Gilbert D, King J. *i2i – Involvement to Improvement: sharing the learning about patient and public involvement from CHI's inspections.* Commission for Health Improvement; 2004. http://www.chi.nhs.uk/patients/ppi_report_0204.pdf
4 National Primary and Care Trust Development Programme. Engaging Communities Learning Network. PCT Competencies Framework. 7. Community Patient and Public Involvement. (Updated March 2005.) http://www.natpact.nhs.uk/uploads/2005_Mar/ECLN_PCT_Competency_Framework.doc
5 Department of Health. *Our Health, Our Care, Our Say: a new direction for community services.* White Paper on the future of health and social care. London: DoH; 30 January 2006.
6 Department of Health. *Making Practice-based Commissioning a Reality: technical guidance.* London: DoH; 2005. http://www.dh.gov.uk/PublicationsAndStatistics/Publications/PublicationsPolicyAndGuidance/fs/en
7 Independent Commission on Good Governance in Public Services (11 January 2005). http://www.opm.co.uk/ICGGPS/ Good Governance Standard for Public Services.
8 Gilbert D. *Working Well Together: what sort of learning and support do Forums and others need to work well with the Healthcare Commission?* London: NHSU and Healthcare Commission; 2005.

Postscript

It may not have escaped your attention that this book poses more questions than it does answers. Indeed, you may feel disappointed that it isn't the all-singing, all-dancing answer to the difficulties you may have been experiencing, whether you are an 'outsider' trying to get 'in' to the NHS or someone on the 'inside' trying to open doors for those who are 'outside'. The problem is that there is no universal solution to these difficulties since they are as infinite as NHS organisations, and the individuals that comprise them. The parameter that we all have in common is government policy, but it is inevitable that we all find slightly different ways of responding to it, some more successful than others. The response of one organis-ation, described in this book, is not presented as an ideal way of doing things but as a stimulus to your own thinking, hence all the questions. If it is helpful to use it as a yardstick by which to measure your progress, or if it stimulates new ideas, then it has served a useful purpose.

One question, among many, that remains unanswered, is whose job is it to get 'inside' the NHS? This book has been about the attempts, indeed strenuous efforts, that those of us who think we *are* on the inside have been making, at the gov-ernment's insistence and because of positive evidence in its favour, to break down that impermeable membrane that has kept providers and recipients of services apart. Policy has been directed at the providers because it has been recognised that it is they who are keeping everyone else at arm's length, and as a group they are easy to target. However, we can turn this argument on its head and ask ourselves why it is that as members of communities with concerns for our health and that of our families, we remain remarkably passive. Until, that is, illness or accident befalls us and we have to personally engage with the system, by which time we are either weak or vulnerable and in no position to stand up for ourselves. We seem to have become cynical about our capacity to influence public services and are no longer confident about the possibility of being able to engage in an active and productive dialogue which will lead to real change.

Something else that we can turn on its head is this notion that it is NHS workers who are the ones on the inside. My view is that practically every one of us is already 'inside' the NHS by virtue of using services. Being inside means that we know what it feels like to be a patient – but it also suggests getting swallowed up by a system. It is that loss of individuality and depersonalisation which is so disempowering. It causes us as *patients* to feel that we are no longer in control of what happens to us, but us as *workers* to feel that we no longer have personal responsibility for what we do. This thinking needs to change.

A recurrent theme of this book has been to argue for recognition of our own subjective experience, connecting what we do as providers of services with what we know about from having needed healthcare ourselves. This can be worrying. It makes us more aware that we are both responsible and accountable for what we do, and this is particularly hard when we are up against service constraints over which we have no control. We also have to trust that the concepts of involvement, partnership and citizenship, embodied in policy, will be sustained by successive governments because it seems to take forever for change to become real.

Or does it? It is worth returning to the policy timeline in Chapter 1 to appreciate how much has changed in a relatively short period of time. And the new National Centre for Involvement, described by David Gilbert in the last chapter, is an exhilarating opportunity that could never have happened 10 years ago. In terms of a grand plan, things are definitely on the move, but this may be harder to appreciate at a local level.

When I was a child, I used to go skating on Saturday mornings at Richmond ice-rink. There were organised classes and one of the things we used to do was to join arms in two long lines, at right angles to each other, to make turning windmill sails. If you were at the outer end of the sails, you flew (or fell over!), but those in the middle hardly moved – much less fun. It is a bit like that with the service user and carer involvement policy. If you are at the heart of things, where change is supposed to be happening, it all seems to move at a snail's pace; but further out, where organisations and policy makers are making demands, it feels as though you are having to race to keep up.

The problem in the apparently slow-moving centre, whether it's a healthcare or voluntary sector organisation, a local self-help group or indeed individual service users and carers, is to sustain interest, energy, enthusiasm and belief that it really does matter. That is what this book has been about. The most useful responses are simple to summarise:

- **Keep your eye on the ball** – which in this case is to always take service users and carers as your point of reference. I have found in numerous knotty and 'political' management situations that seeing their needs as a priority never fails to give me a sense of direction.
- This one is a bit of a hoary chestnut but it cannot be ignored: **champions!** You need the support of the big cheeses whatever you are doing, so work out who they are and how you can get it.
- **Resources must be identified and pinned down.** They need to be recurring and it is better if they are devolved so that the people holding the budget know exactly what they are buying with it. Watch out for the 'now you see it, now you don't' syndrome which tends to occur after Christmas when belts are being tightened. People can see service user and carer involvement as a soft option – it isn't.
- **This is about whole organisation thinking, not just clinicians** – so make sure that *everyone* is involved and that the thinking is built into policies and procedures. As Lindsey Dyer said in her chapter, 'This is how we do it.'
- **Go for simple successes and publicise them.** Do you remember learning to use a computer – what an achievement it was to find the 'on' switch and for it not to blow up? Think how you use it now: e-mails, the internet, photos, flight and holiday reservations, information, etc. One simple success can lead to another, and before you know where you are you will have acquired know-how, experience and, most importantly, confidence. Oh, and courage!
- **Play the game.** I've been a bit of a rebel in my time but think that conciliatory approaches actually work better, but may take longer.
- **Fine words butter no parsnips** – it's actions that really matter.
- The fundamental question that applies in the name of anything that is concerned with service user and carer involvement: '**Would this be good enough for me, my family and those I care about?**'

Appendix

PPI: developing working partnerships within an organisation – trust timeline

2001

April	Merger of three existing Mental Health, Learning Disability and Community trusts to form South Staffs Healthcare NHS Trust. Trust board members and executive directors subsequently appointed.
September	Appointment of four associate directors, including one for service user and carer involvement.
October	Appointment of Centrepoint team to develop and support processes for service user and carer involvement.
December	'Telling It Like It Is' workshops planned and publicised.

2002

January	Four 'Telling It Like It Is' workshops held in different parts of the trust.
February	From February until July a major audit of all service user and carer activity across the new organisation undertaken with the help of representatives from each directorate. Formation of new group meeting every month, initially called Operational Solutions Group.
March	'Patient Advice and Liaison Manager' appointed – the first in Staffordshire – meeting the Department of Health deadline.
April	PALS focus groups undertaken. As a result, decision to train all trust staff to recognise and respond to users' issues and concerns.
May	Patients' Survey undertaken. Reported to board in July.
July	South Staffs. Healthcare Uncovered: feedback event for 'Telling It Like It Is'. Chief executive vows to get a service user onto the trust board.
August	Visit by Commission for Health Improvement. Dissatisfied because we have no Service User and Carer Strategy.
September	First meeting of revised Service User and Carer Sub-Committee to the board. Trust becomes more streamlined as most community nursing services are transferred to PCTs. Main services are now Mental Health, Learning Disability and Children's.
October	First Carers' Question Time held.
November	Employment Links Group convened. Bi-monthly meetings for social services, job centre disability advisors and community OTs to monitor practical aspects of work assessment process for people seeking employment following illness.

2003

February	Trust produces Service User and Carer Strategy.
March	Preparatory exploration of how the trust can get service users on to its board.
April	Second Carers' Question Time.
June	Proposal for Heart of the Trust Scheme submitted to board and agreed. Detailed proposal prepared for successful funding bid.
August	Selection and recruitment process for HotTS designed.
November	Associate director posts advertised.
December	Trust's PPI Forum convened following closure of Community Health Council.

2004

March	Six service user and carer associate directors start work. As part of month-long induction, meet with PPI Forum members. Internal evaluation of scheme begins.
May	Leadership of Operational Solutions Group taken over by Associates: rebadged HotTS Action Group.
September	Internal evaluation goes to trust board which agrees to further appointments for 2005: six. Associates present video about their work at trust AGM.
November	Associates make DVD as part of trust's initial expression of interest in moving to foundation trust status.

2005

January	New recruitment round for associate directors begins.
March	Five further associates appointed.
July	External evaluation undertaken.
September	Scheme wins national Human Resources award.

Index